IMAGES
of America

SOUTH AMBOY

IMAGES
of America

SOUTH AMBOY

George Francy

ARCADIA
PUBLISHING

ISBN 978-0-7385-3850-1

Published by Arcadia Publishing
Charleston, South Carolina

Printed in the United States of America

Library of Congress Control Number: 2005925447

For all general information, please contact Arcadia Publishing:
Telephone 843-853-2070
Fax 843-853-0044
E-mail sales@arcadiapublishing.com
For customer service and orders:
Toll-Free 1-888-313-2665

Visit us on the Internet at www.arcadiapublishing.com

This book is dedicated to my father, George B. Francy Sr., who had an enormous pride and love of South Amboy, and who, by example, started me on a life-long love of words and books.

Contents

ACKNOWLEDGMENTS

I didn't know what kind of response I would get when I started out on this project—I was not even sure if it would be possible. But out of pride and affection for South Amboy and sheer generosity, people loaned their photos and time, and I am humbled by their trust. If this book is in any way a success, it is a tribute to them. Perhaps the first to sign on was Phil Israel, director of the Sadie Pope Dowdell Library. Once I had his participation, with the loan of the library's extensive postcard collection, I knew there was a base to work from. Then the project simply grew. Anna Harris Friberg has probably the best collection of original photographs I have seen, and Ralph Mundy has the best collection of postcards of South Amboy. George Selover had some of the most unique photos, and information to match. Others who laid out their photo collections included Joyce and Ken Elyea, Bob Heiser, Claire and Gary Kuhn, Dennis Kelly, Barbara Russell, Betty and Charlie Stueber, Ruth Connors, John Durnye of the South Amboy Arena, Barbara Bixby, Anne Richmond, Betty Leveille, and the South Amboy First Aid and Safety Squad. No one was more enthusiastic about the project than Ed Szatkowski, who contacted the fire companies and called me back—not twice, but three times—to offer more photos. Tom Burkard supplied a few images and spread the word about this book in his newspaper, *The Sayreville-South Amboy Times*; Jim Gotti also spread the word in his paper, *The Citizen*. Ed Paczkowski supplied the cover photograph and photos of the parish he is so proud of—Sacred Heart. Similarly, Father Dennis Weezorak at St. Mary's and Debbie DeGregoria at Christ Episcopal Church responded promptly and generously. Fred Rose, a member of Christ Church, helped identify pictures and provided perhaps the only existing photo of the Stevens mansion. Pat Olexa, director of the senior center and head of the bicentennial celebration, and her parents, Madeline and Phil Purcell, were a constant source of help. Others who generously loaned photos include Ron Keegan, Police Chief James Holovacko, Rick and Judy O'Connor, my longtime employer, the *Home News Tribune*, Joanne Niestempski, Joanne Katko, Cathy McCarthy, Allie Clark, the Topps baseball card company, Don Rzepka, and Bob Holton. If there are any others I've forgotten, my deepest apologies and thanks. I shot the present-day photographs myself, with a camera and advice loaned by a great photographer, Seth Sloan. Joe Sumski was the first private resident to donate photos of his building on First Street. My sister, Linda Garnett, was a conduit of information and tips on more than a dozen occasions, as was my mother, Lorraine Francy. While I'm talking family, I'd better not forget my wife, Patti, and son Brendan, who were neglected enough in the long hours of this project. Mayor Jack O'Leary lent his endorsement and help early on. The first photo loaned (of many) was of Harold Hoffman, from Bill Marshall, South Amboy's "real" historian, my friend and mentor, who was endlessly generous with his knowledge, and in an earlier day would have done this book himself.

Introduction

From just about anywhere in South Amboy, several times each day, you can hear the train whistle. It is one of the distinctive things about South Amboy. And the way that sound reaches through the whole city is representative of how the railroad, and transportation in general, have been key to the city's existence. Although the train whistle somewhat melds into the background, the rail line brought the rest of the world to, or at least through, South Amboy. That is what makes it all the more impressive that this community of almost nine thousand retained its character through the years. Working-class families, mostly Irish and Polish, came, had children, stayed, and kept the town as their own.

South Amboy used to be much larger. It once extended southwest to where Cranbury is today, and south to the Monmouth County border, a sprawling township 18 miles long and 6 miles wide. Now it is one square mile. Monroe, Jamesburg Cranbury, Old Bridge, and Sayreville were all once part of South Amboy. Gradually those municipalities broke off in the mid-1800s, apparently with little objection from South Amboy's leaders. As South Amboy historian William Marshall tells it, it wasn't easy collecting taxes from those far-flung residents. And perhaps there was enough to worry about in the bustling city.

As with the rest of the country, the first inhabitants in the area were Native Americans. The name "Amboy" comes from a Native-American word, "Ampoge"; it also appears on deeds and maps as Emboyle and Amboyle, which eventually resulted in the name we have today.

South Amboy, too, grew out of another city. Perth Amboy, on the north side of the Raritan River, was a colonial port and the first capital of the territory called East Jersey, which would eventually merge with West Jersey to form the state as it exists today. The area to the south of the Raritan was called the South Ward of Perth Amboy, and its location is key, as South Amboy was on the way for travelers between New York and Philadelphia. But even before it was known as the South Ward of Perth Amboy, it was called Radford's Ferry, after a water transport that connected the Amboys. Legend has it that Ben Franklin passed through that way many times, and possibly John Adams as well.

It was a five-day journey by stagecoach to Bordentown, another resting point on the way to Philadelphia. To accommodate travelers, several hotels sprang up, with taverns for socializing, beginning South Amboy's long and prolific tradition of bars. The first is believed to be the Rattoon Tavern, located on Bordentown Avenue, which at the time extended to near the now-defunct Jersey Central Power and Light Company generating station.

John Rattoon appears to have been a loyalist to the English crown, although he entertained both English and Patriot travelers. He was reportedly a conduit for the letters in which Benedict Arnold offered to betray George Washington and the insurgent colonists.

Although the closest real fight was the Battle of Monmouth, near Freehold, New Jersey is known as the "crossroads of the revolution," and Washington and his army passed through and spent a lot of time in the state. South Amboy's connection may have been as a lookout point for ships on the bay, and there were reportedly raids for goods and skirmishes back and forth between the colonists and the British, who were anchored in or near the Raritan Bay. One of the important early residents was Major General James Morgan, who knew George Washington and who was put in charge of a militia for patrolling and protecting the area. The family name was applied to the Morgan section of Sayreville.

Unlike towns to the west and south, South Amboy did not have fertile soil, so its economy was based not on agriculture, but on shipping and manufacturing. Like several neighboring towns, there were good-quality clay deposits, which grew into a healthy industry of pottery and terra cotta, the cement-like material that is molded into the ornamental adornments on buildings locally and in major cities. There were once three terra cotta or pottery factories in South Amboy, centered on Swan Hill, at the south end of Broadway.

It was the railroad, however, that was the greatest contributing factor in building the city. The Stevens family owned land in Perth Amboy and South Amboy, and would later go on to settle in Hoboken, where they founded the Stevens Institute of Technology. Colonel John Stevens brought the first steam engine, the "John Bull," made in England, to New Jersey. His sons founded the Camden & Amboy Rail Road in 1831; here again, South Amboy's location on the route between the Amboys and Philadelphia was the reason, as the rail line basically followed the old stagecoach route.

While the Camden & Amboy was the first, it was only one of several railroads that passed through the city, including the New York and Long Branch. There was also the Raritan River Rail Road, which traveled west to New Brunswick and eventually became part of Conrail.

Many of those trains were headed for the water and the shipping that it provided. Pennsylvania coal was the primary material transported on box boats, or barges, to New York City, but there were also dozens of other types of goods shipped, including military explosives, which led to two of the most disastrous events in the city's history.

The first of these disasters was in 1918 at a World War I munitions packing plant that was reportedly the largest of its kind in the world. Although the plant was in the Morgan section of Sayreville, South Amboy was the closest settlement of any consequence, and it took the brunt of the damage. The blast started on October 4, and was felt as far away as Manhattan. A series of fires and explosions continued for three days, killing some 70 people.

The second, and more direct blast, occurred on May 19, 1950, at the "T" docks. Explosives were being loaded onto a barge when something went wrong, and 31 workers, called "powder monkeys" for the gunpowder they handled, were killed. Debris was blown to the streets near the waterfront, and reportedly every window in the city was blown out.

The Raritan Bay, which on some early maps appears as "Amboy Bay," once came much further inland than we see today. As some of the pictures that follow will show, the water lapped up near where the railroad line passes today. South Amboy residents in the 1800s and 1900s called this the Minnie ditch, for the minnows that could be caught in this shallow water and used for fishing. In 1953, the Army Corps of Engineers started depositing material outward into the bay, and in a reversal from the 1800s, South Amboy grew for once, by 66 acres.

This land is now key to South Amboy's future. Although talk started at least as early as 1962 about what use the land would be put to, it is only now, as the city reaches its bicentennial in 1998, that a plan has been formed under Mayor John T. O'Leary. There is already a new school, library, and waterfront county park. Housing for the elderly and detached homes are part of the mix, maybe followed by shops and a restaurant. In the downtown area, a government/business program is well underway to renovate storefronts to a "turn-of-the-century" look.

And, as always, the rail line is key. Although now solely a line for commuters to New York City, the train is the centerpiece of an envisioned transportation hub that would also incorporate buses and maybe a ferry, truly coming full circle to South Amboy's beginnings.

One

A City on the Bay

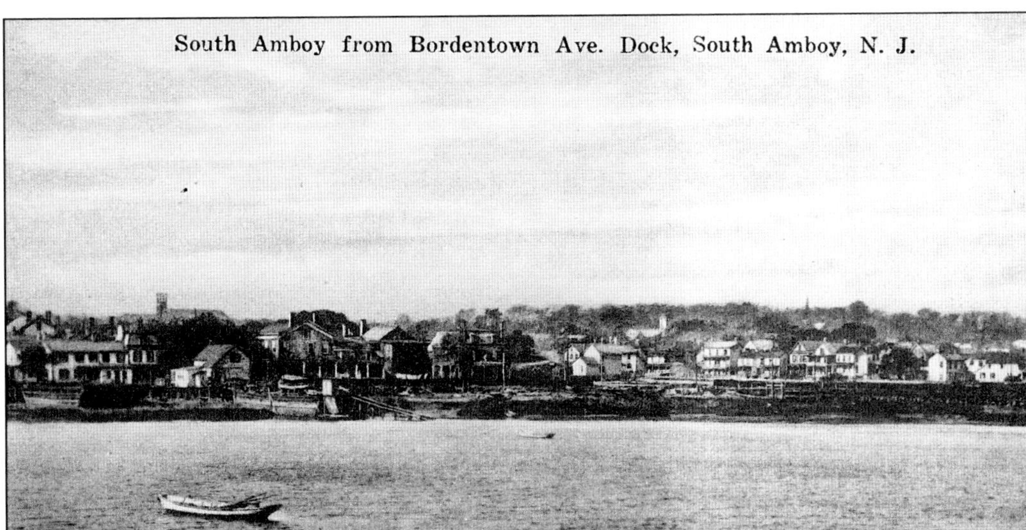

This chapter is a tour around South Amboy, featuring mostly street scenes and some of the bayfront. This photo, for instance, looks at South Amboy from the dock that used to be at the foot of Bordentown Avenue. The dock is long gone, and this view of Rosewell Street would no longer be possible due to new construction on the bayside.

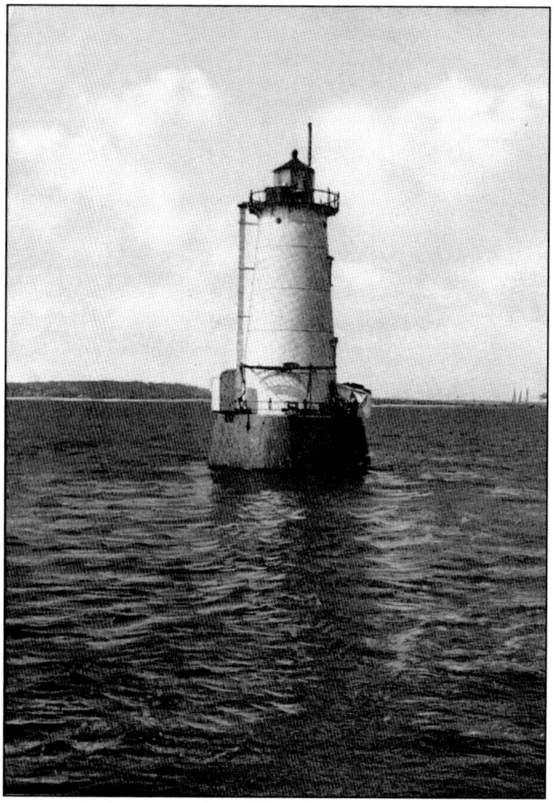

The Great Beds Light House, built about 1890, is just offshore in the Raritan Bay. It was adopted as part of the city's logo on police cars in 1996-1997.

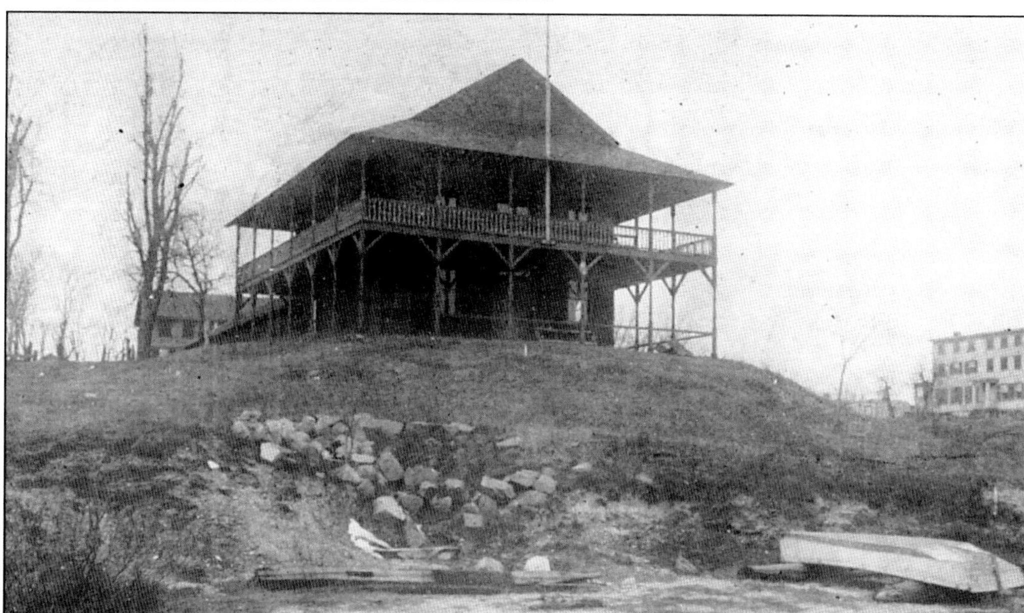

The Yacht Club was also near the foot of Bordentown Avenue, and may have been connected to the Stevens family, which, probably more than any single family, helped establish South Amboy by running the railroad through the city. John Stevens was an avid sailor, with entries in the America's Cup race, and he is said to have kept a sailboat off the city's shore.

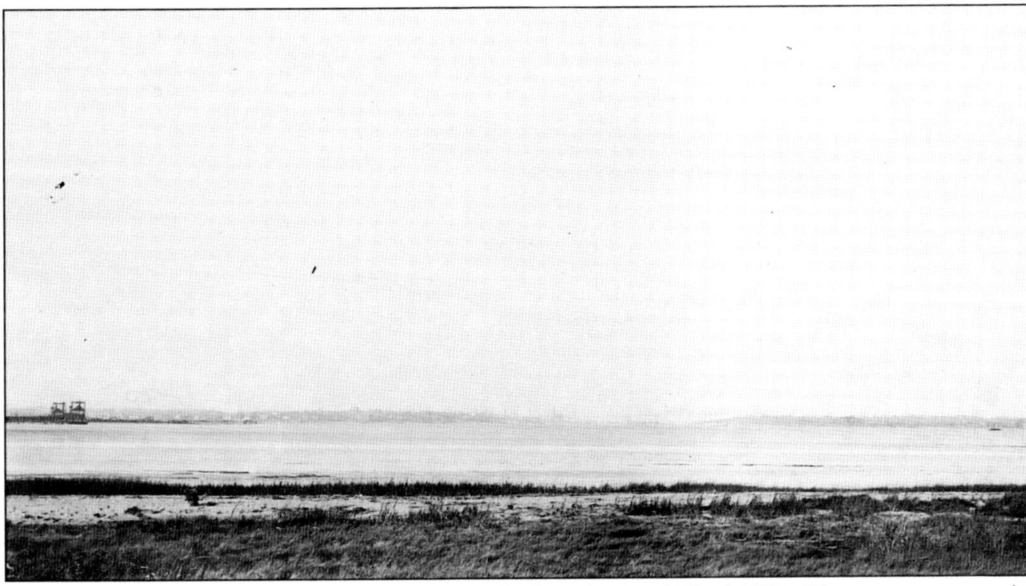

This is the bayfront called the Minnie ditch, before the landfill of 1953. The structures on the far left are the coal dumpers that loaded Pennsylvania coal into barges for shipment to New York City.

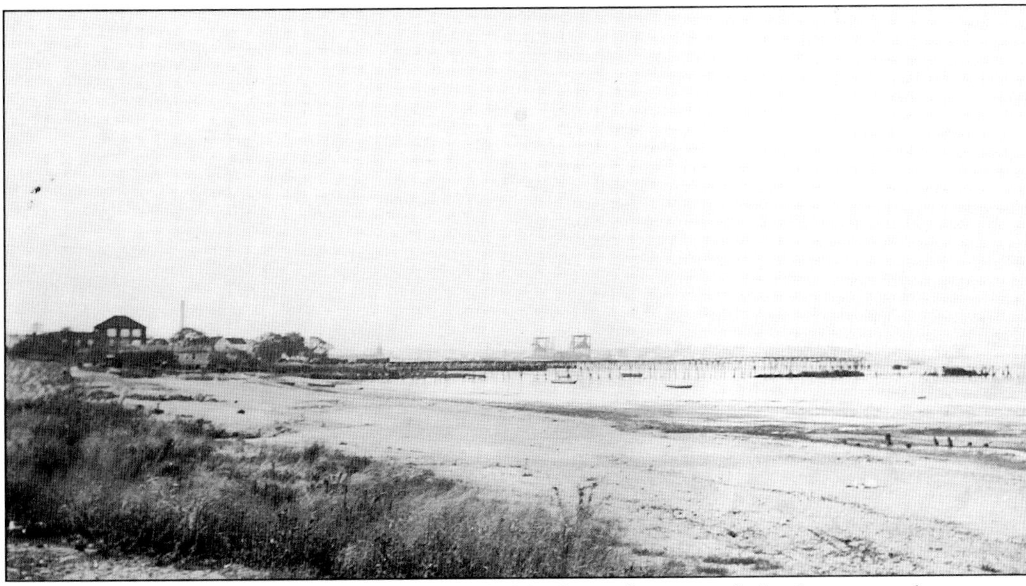

Here is another view of the shoreline, probably from the around the location where a new county park was built in the mid-1990s. While the landfill project added some 66 acres to the city, it reportedly also flooded some basements because natural springs that previously flowed into the bay had to find a new place to go.

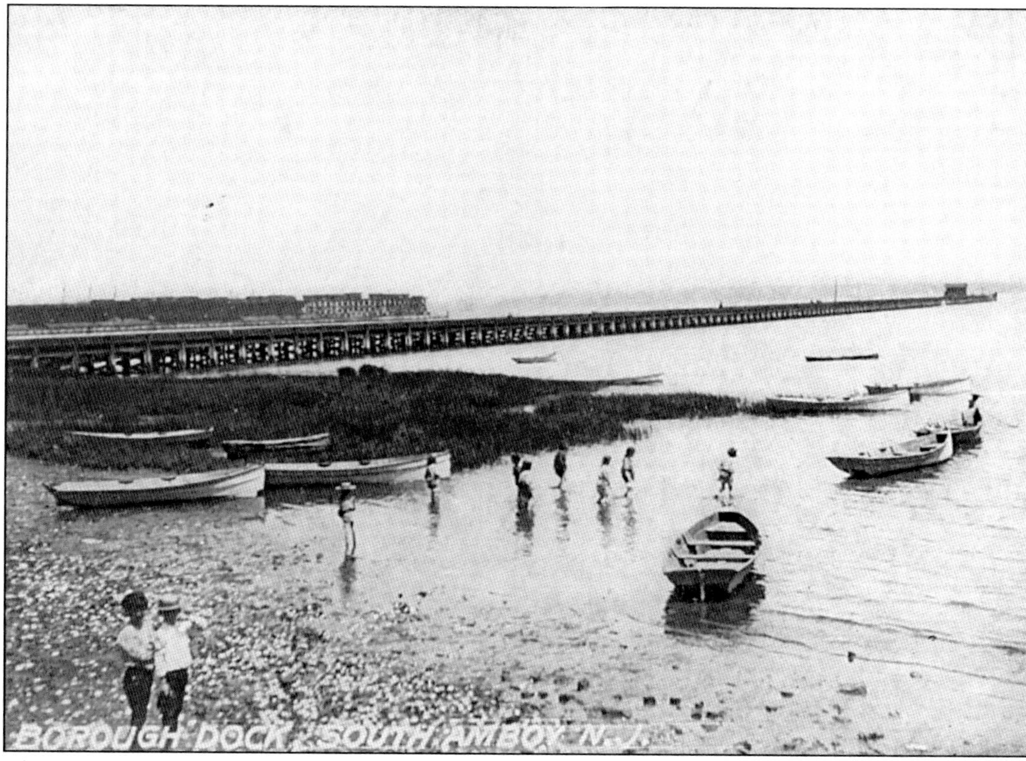

This is the dock at the foot of Bordentown Avenue. In addition to fishing, there were clams and oysters plentiful in the bay years ago, so much so that city residents were sometimes called clam diggers.

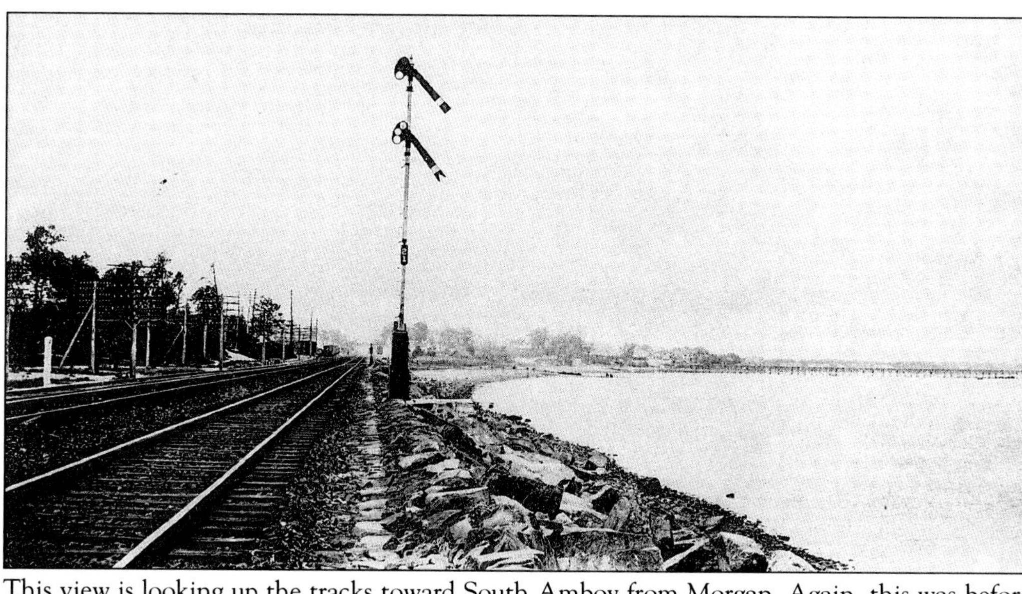

This view is looking up the tracks toward South Amboy from Morgan. Again, this was before the landfill, as evidenced by how close the water is to the tracks.

The "beach" in South Amboy is pictured here, looking from a spot near the South Amboy Boat Club. Not known for sunbathing or swimming, this area is still a great draw for fishermen or those who simply want to look out on the water.

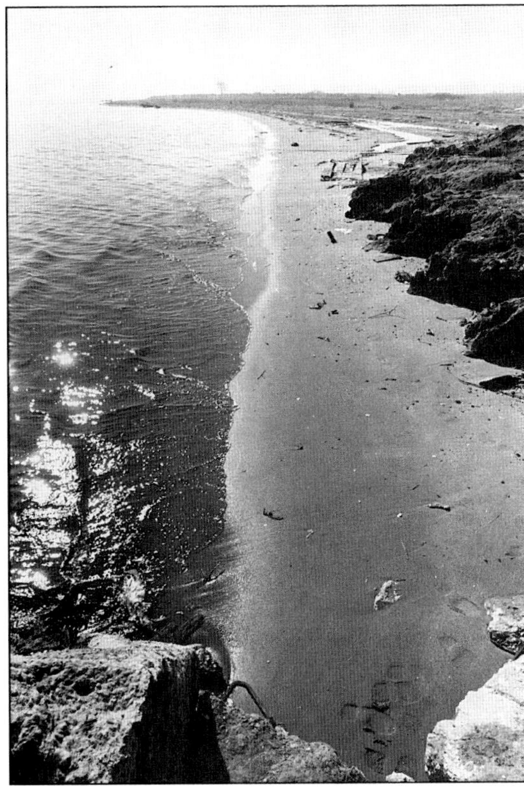

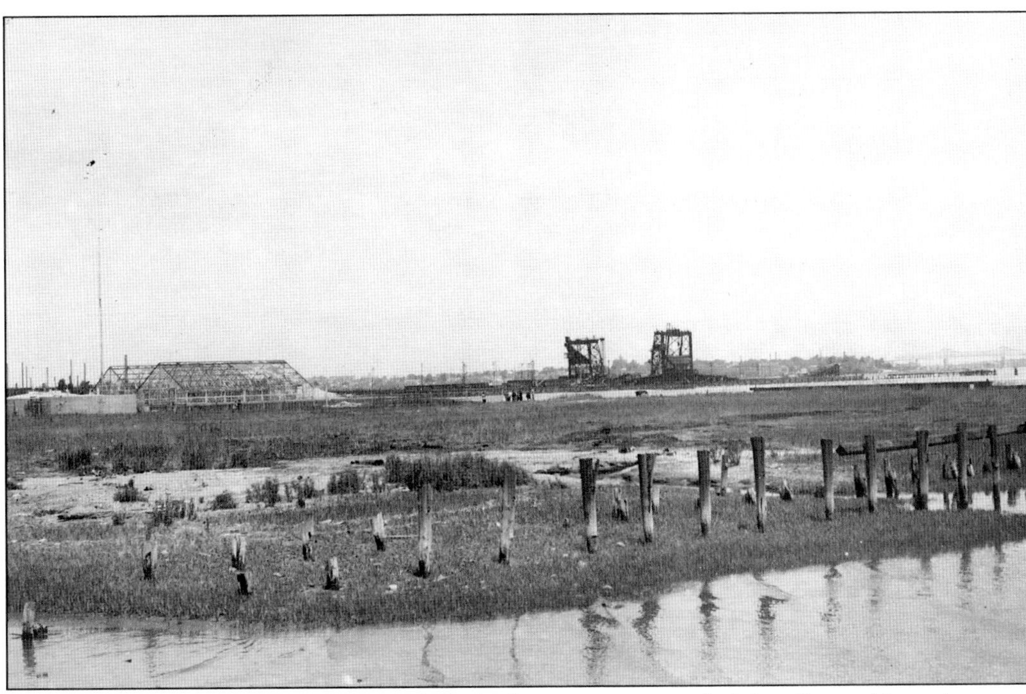

Here is a view looking out to the coal docks from approximately John Street. Note the sewer plant houses on the left and pilings from a dock in the foreground.

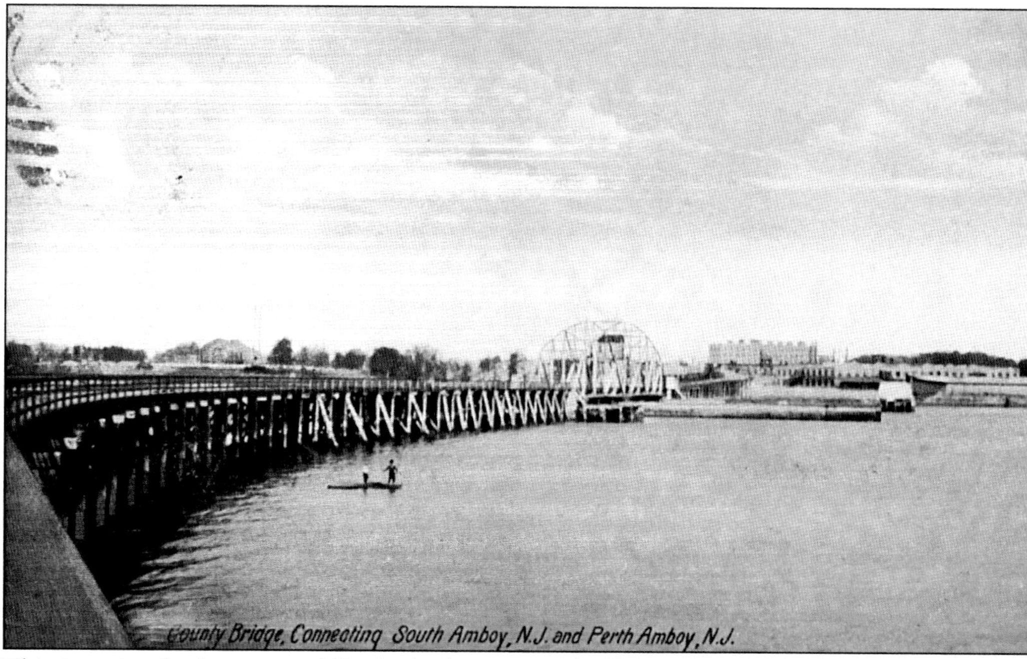

This is a view looking toward Perth Amboy across the Raritan Bay along a bridge that was at the foot of Scott Avenue in Sayreville. It gave the city a link with the larger Perth Amboy. It is long gone, taken down when the Victory Bridge was built in 1927.

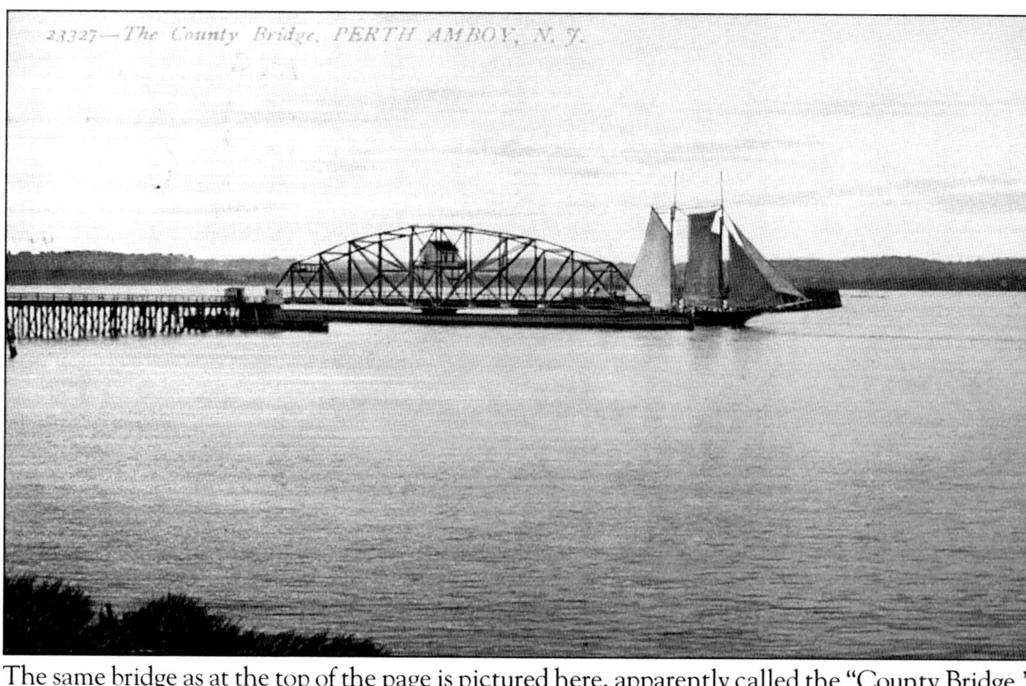

The same bridge as at the top of the page is pictured here, apparently called the "County Bridge," looking toward South Amboy from Perth Amboy. The bridge is open to admit a sailing ship.

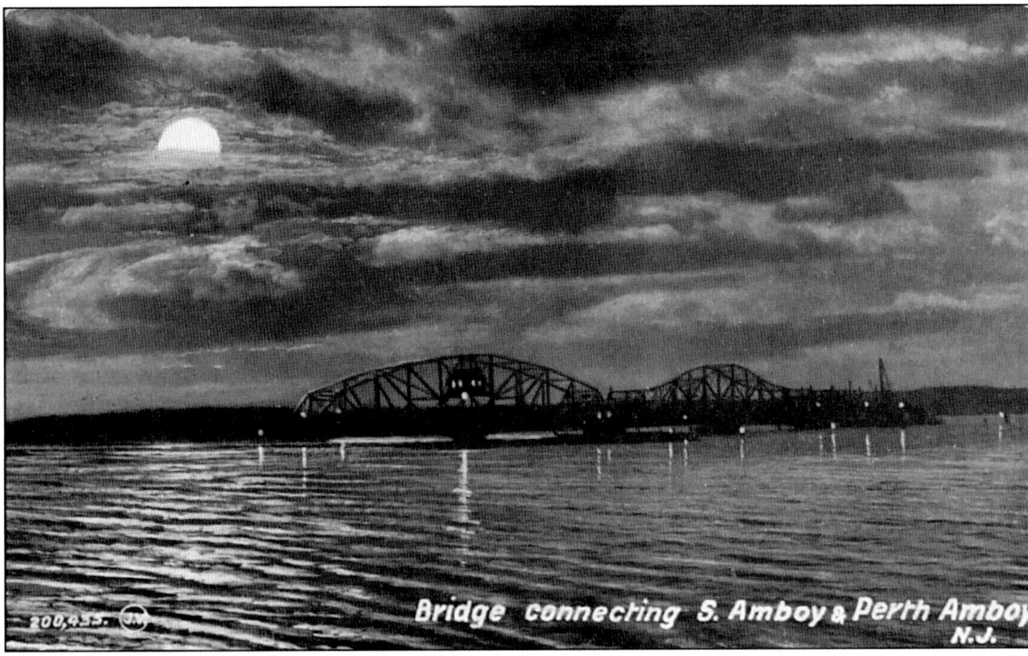

Moonlight washes over the bridge and bay in this postcard.

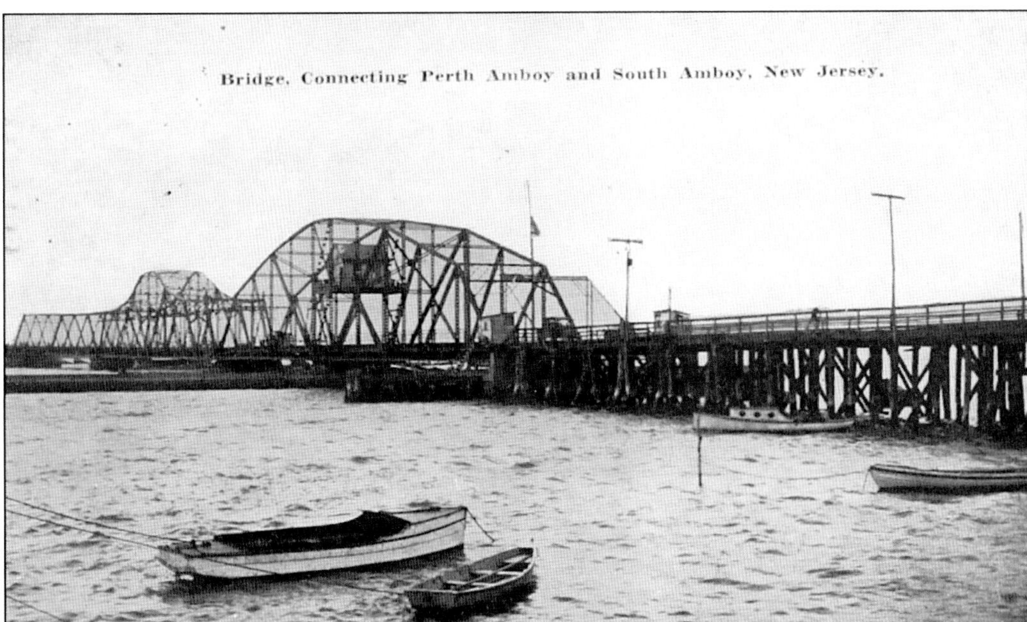

In this photo, the bridge's trestle has been extended.

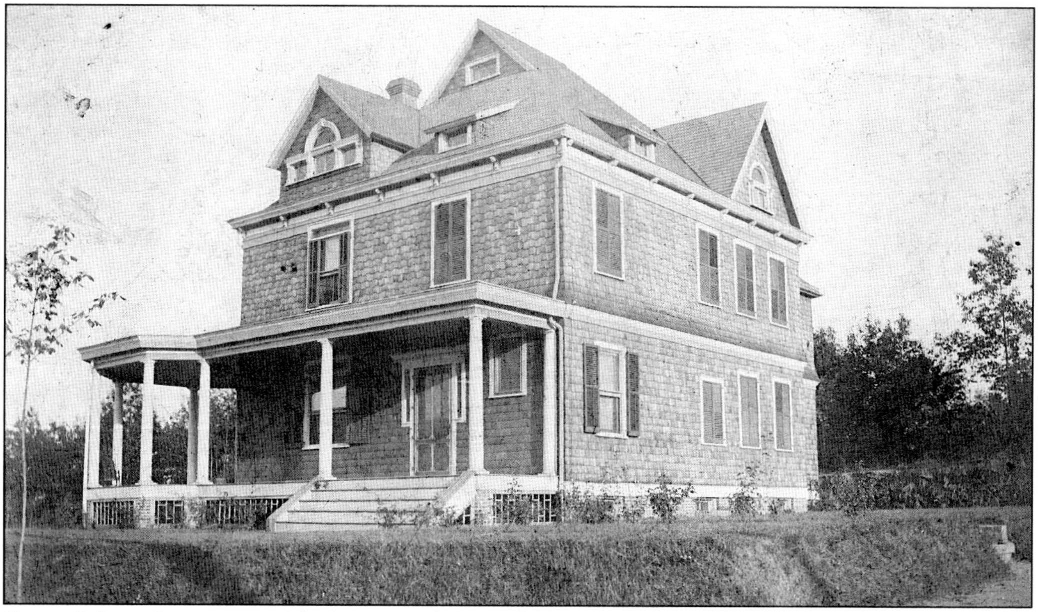

One of the advantages of living on a bay is the spectacular view. This is the home of Bill Marshall, the city's unofficial historian, at the top of Pine Avenue. Trees hem in the view today, and the house looks much different (this photo was taken from the Pine Avenue side, where the front door is located today).

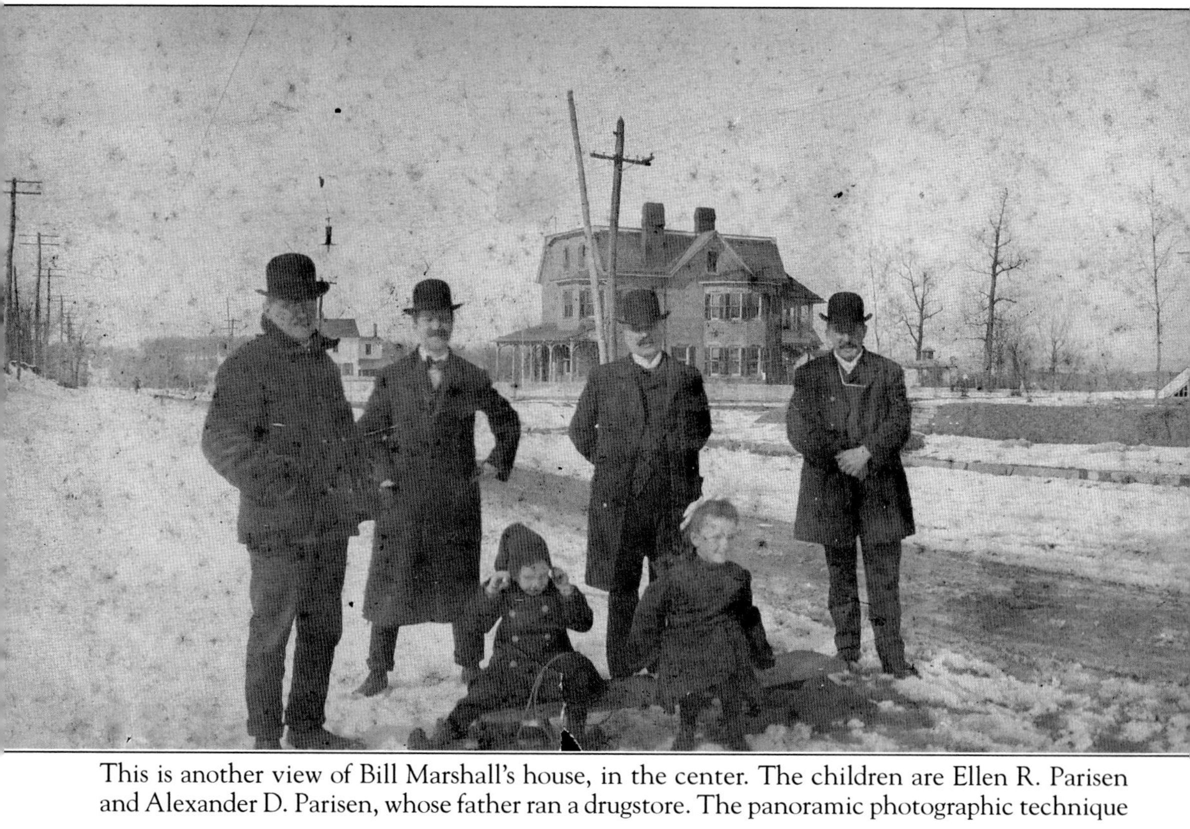

This is another view of Bill Marshall's house, in the center. The children are Ellen R. Parisen and Alexander D. Parisen, whose father ran a drugstore. The panoramic photographic technique

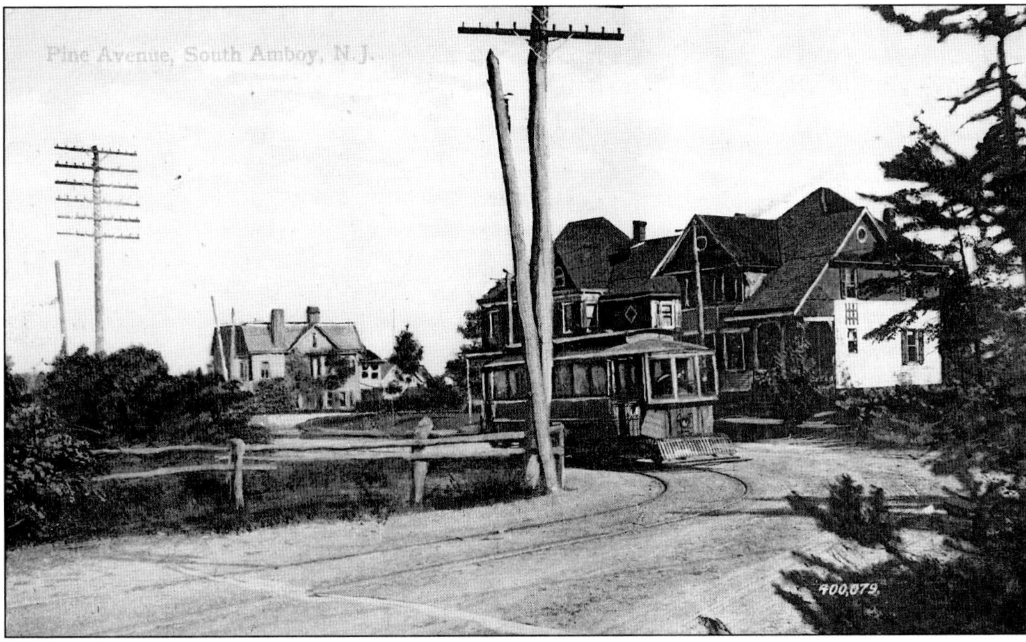

One of two trolleys that used to run through town is featured in this photograph. There was a turnaround at the top of Pine Avenue. Trolleys went south to Keyport and were in service until about 1930.

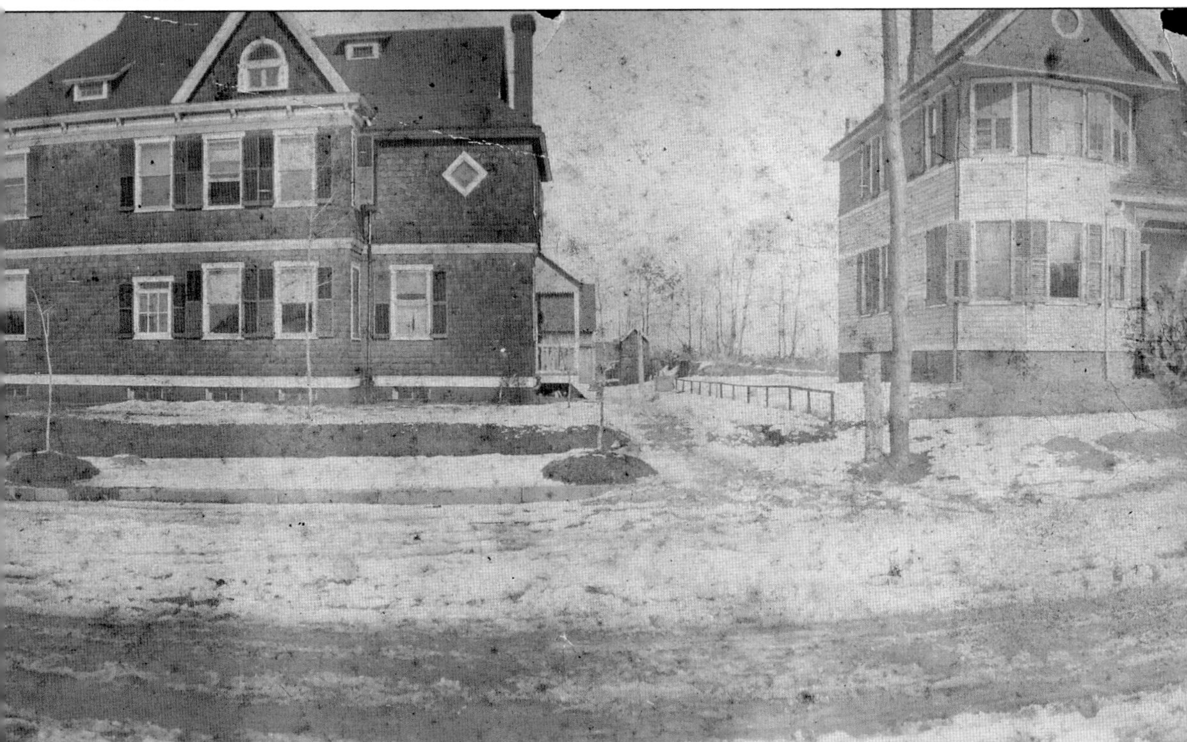

makes the homes look farther apart than they are. They are actually right next door to each other.

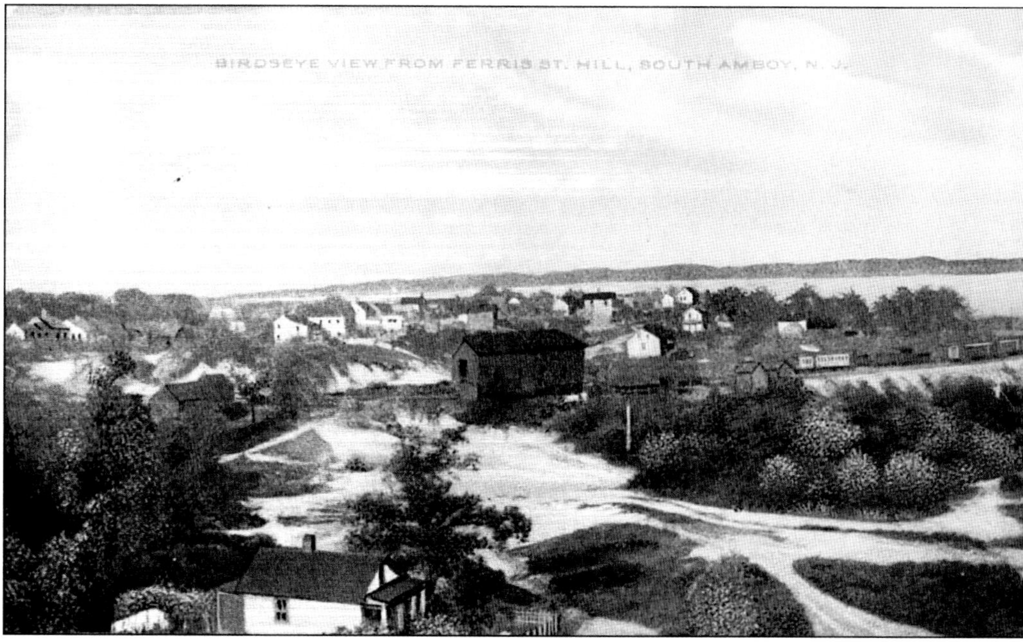

This view is looking north toward the bay. The rail line in the center of the postcard would have been the maintenance yard of the Raritan River Rail Road, which ran under Bordentown Avenue and linked nearby to the Pennsylvania and Jersey Central Railroads.

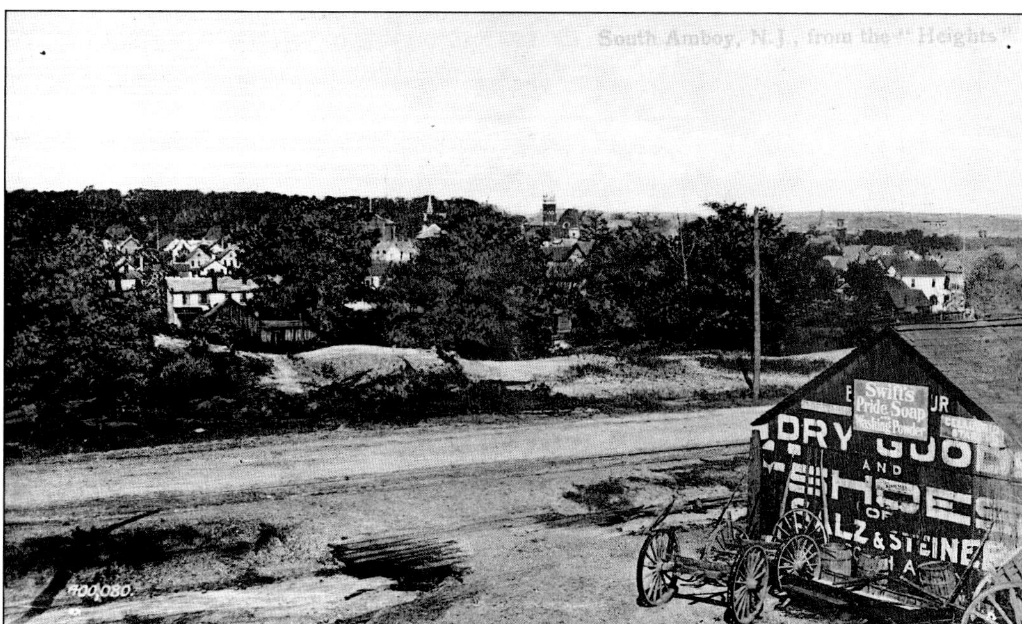

This postcard looks down on Bordentown Avenue near Pine Avenue. The building in the foreground advertises L. Salz and A. Steiner mercantile, which was located on Broadway.

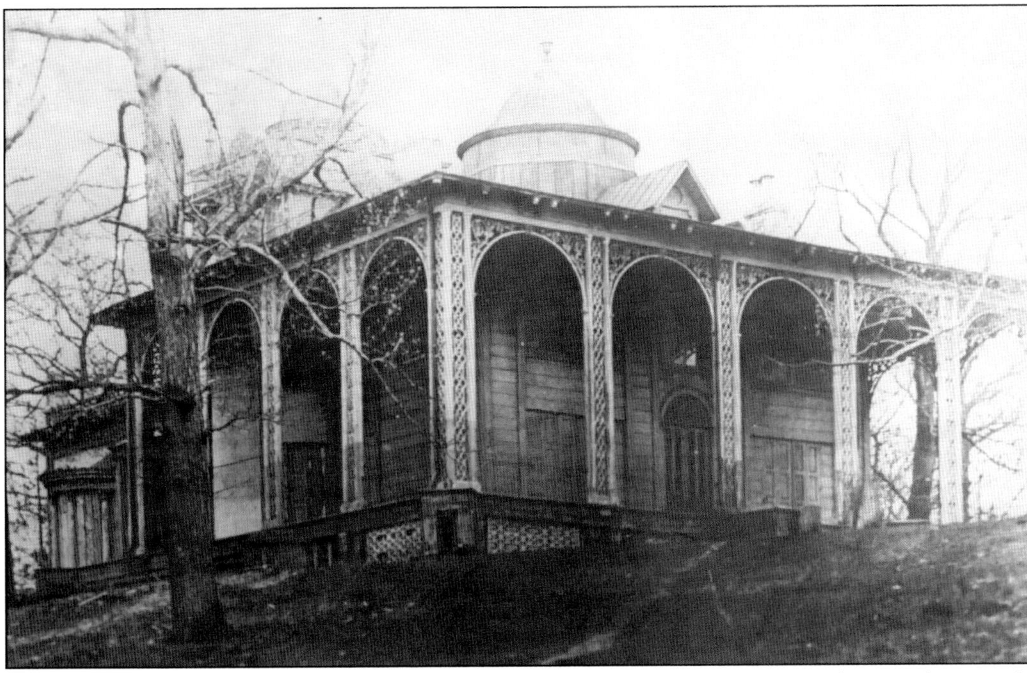

This is a rare photo of the Stevens mansion, which they called Mount Sterling, in honor of a famous relative, Lord Sterling. It was located on Fourth Street across from what is currently the Memorial Hall of Christ Episcopal Church, and reportedly required 25 servants and $80,000 annually for upkeep. In its day, the mansion must have had a commanding view of the bay.

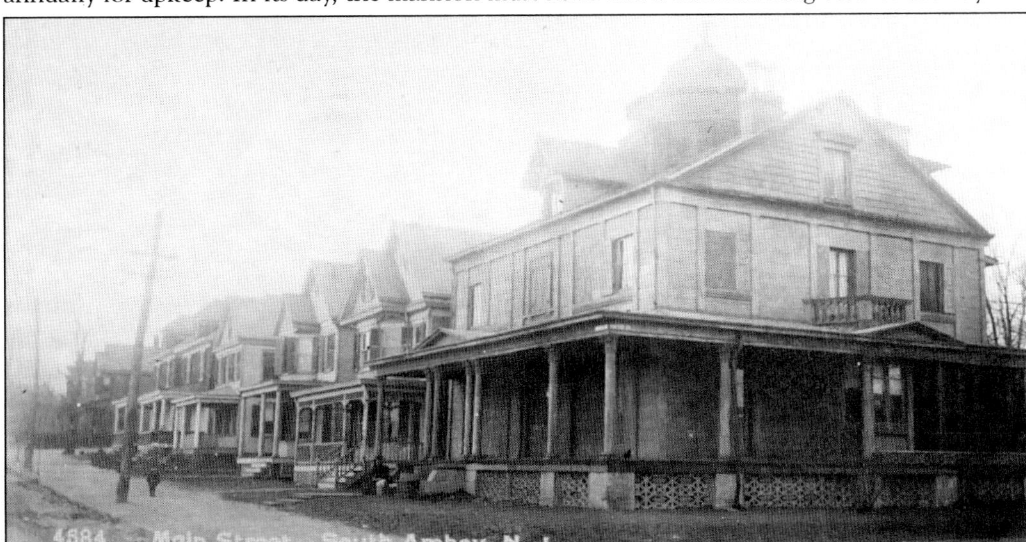

Can it be the same house as above? There is one chronicle of the city's history that says that after the Stevens family moved to Hoboken, the mansion was moved to the corner of Main and Potter Streets. The Burke family started the city's first hospital in the building, and it was destroyed by fire in 1921. The move would probably have meant dismantling the wraparound porch, which is the most noticeable difference between the two buildings. But the similarities include the design on the lattice below the porch, the wide clapboards, and the cupola—perhaps the most distinctive feature.

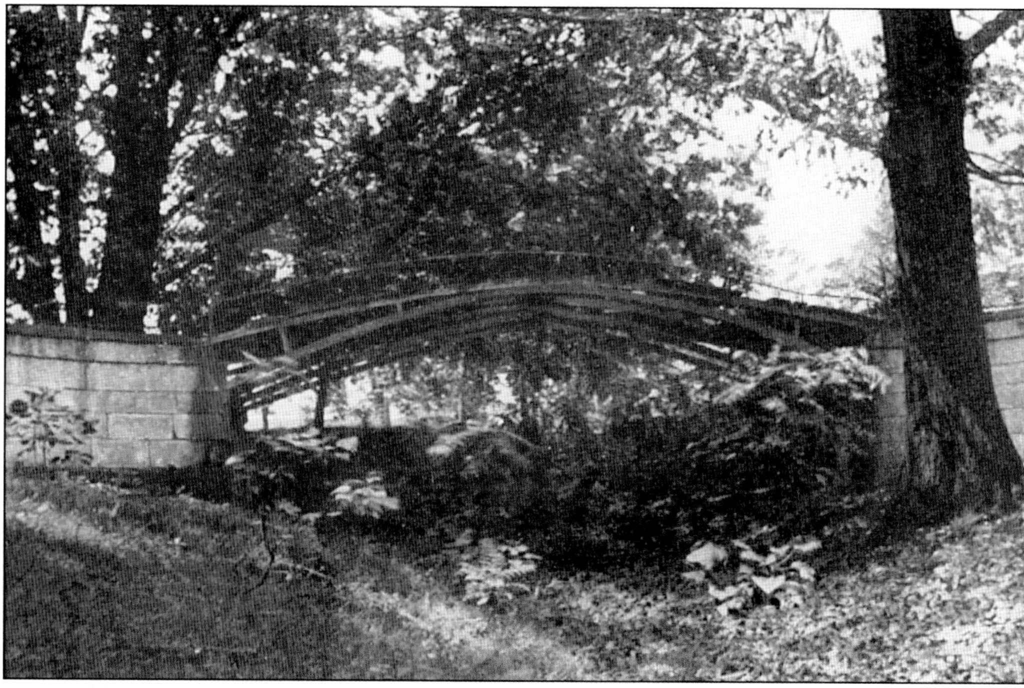

Pictured here is a bridge in Stevensdale, the family's estate. Their pond was reportedly near what is today Pupek Drive and Barkalow Street.

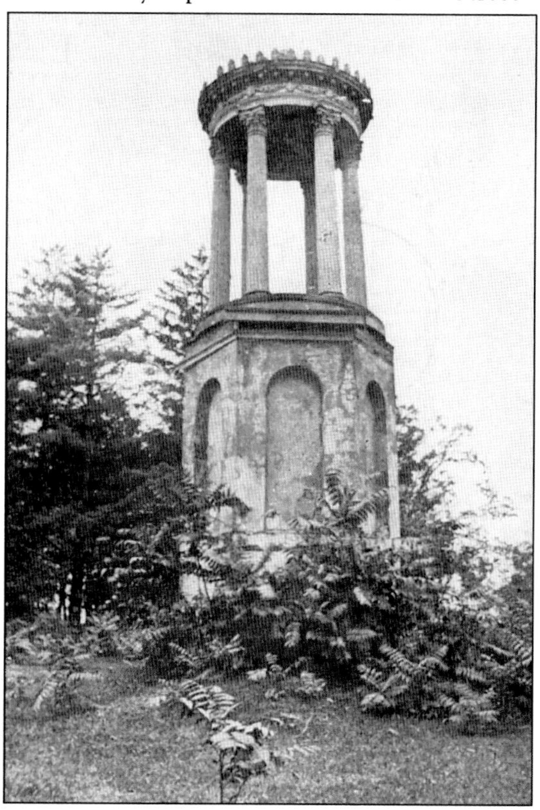

This is the water tower that served the Stevens estate. It was reportedly located just east of the end of what is today Macedulski Terrace.

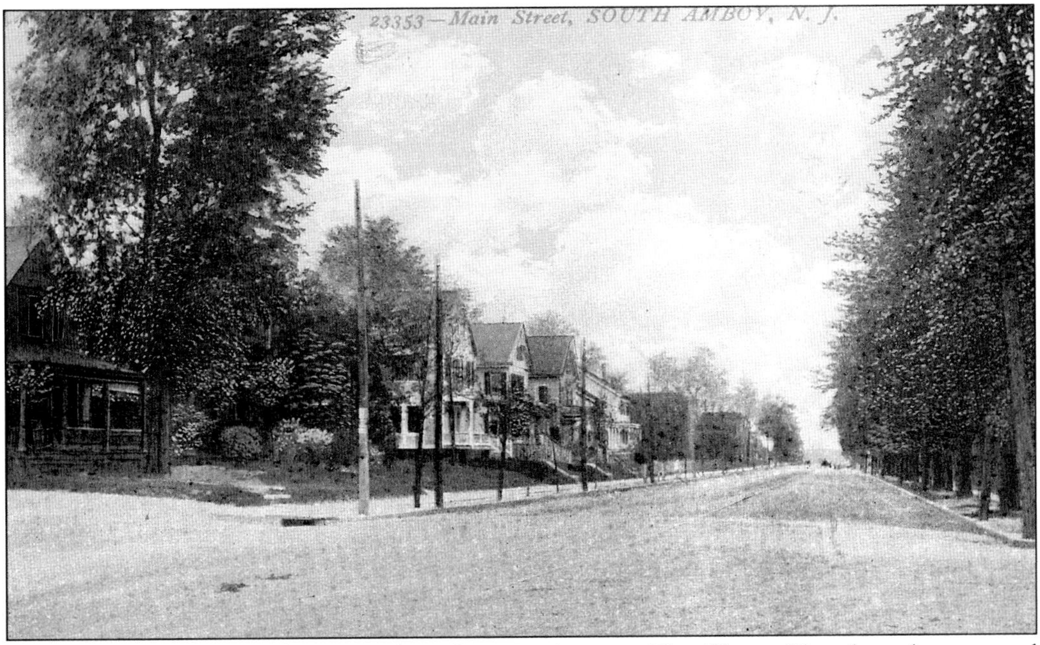

Here is Main Street, looking east from Stevens Avenue. The Christ Church orphanage and church hall (later a thrift shop) are barely visible.

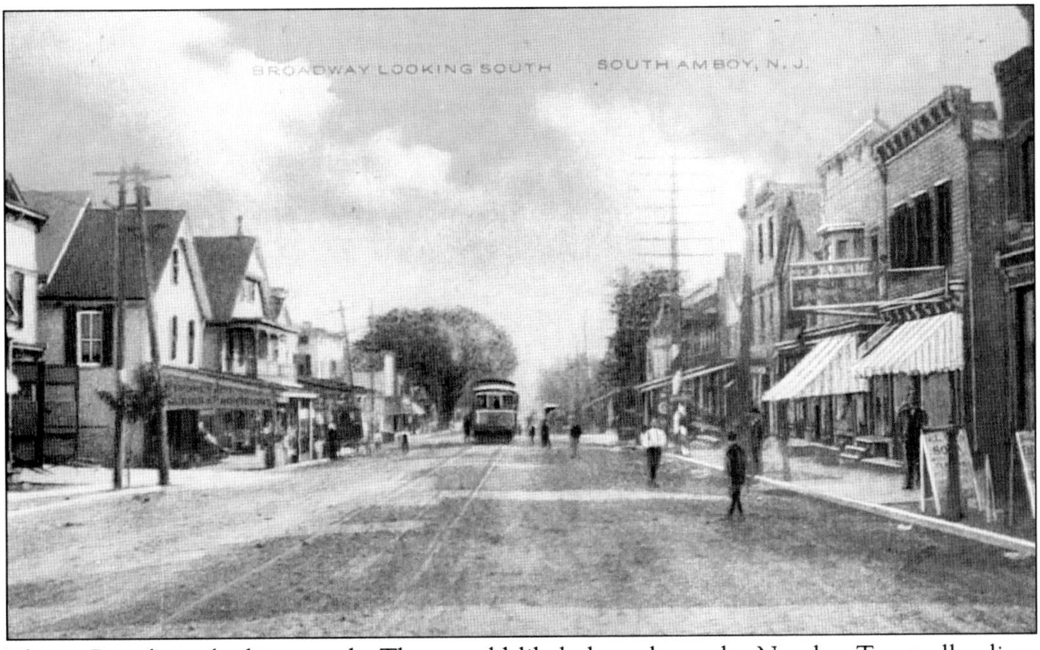

This is Broadway, looking south. That would likely have been the Number Two trolley line, which ran from Division Street down Bordentown Avenue, left onto Broadway and up to Main Street, where it continued on to New Brunswick with a branch to the left down Stevens.

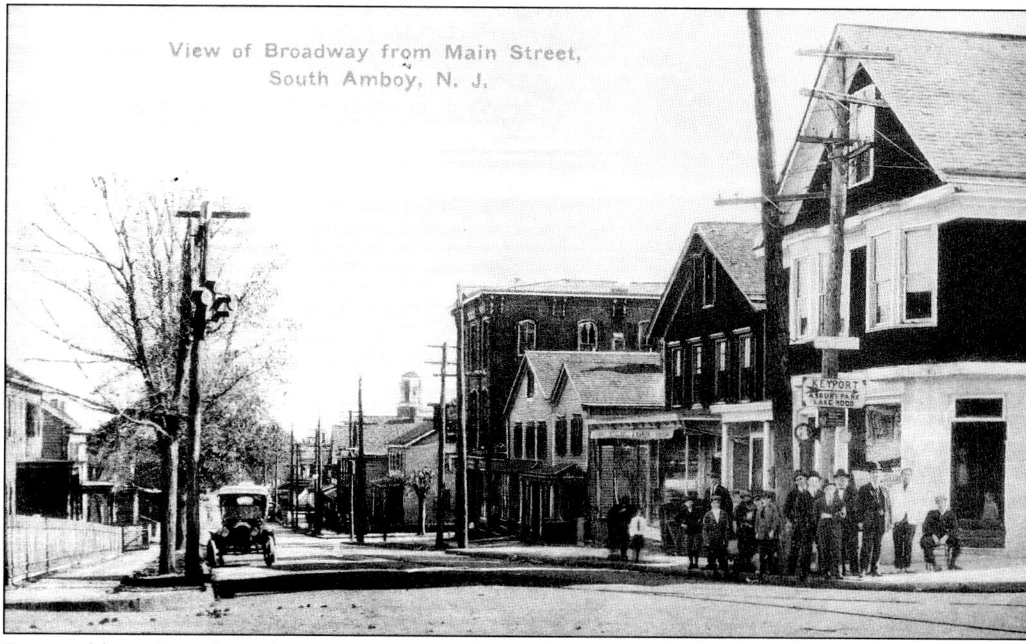

Pictured here Broadway from Main Street, looking toward the spot where there is presently an auto body shop and a Krauszers convenience store. The buildings in the foreground are now gone.

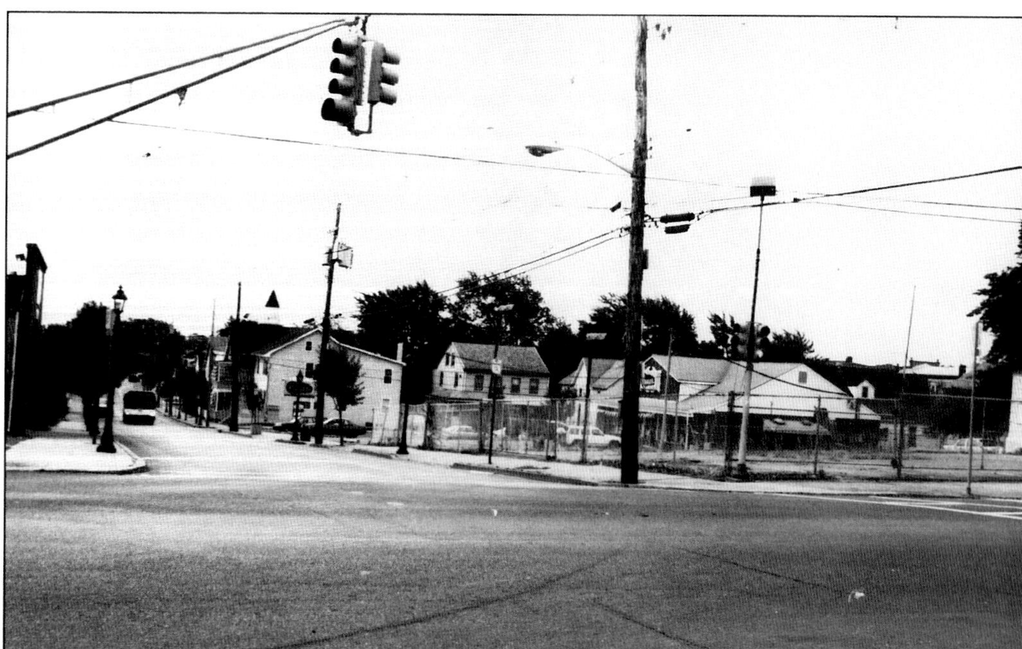

This is a present-day shot of Broadway, as seen from Main Street.

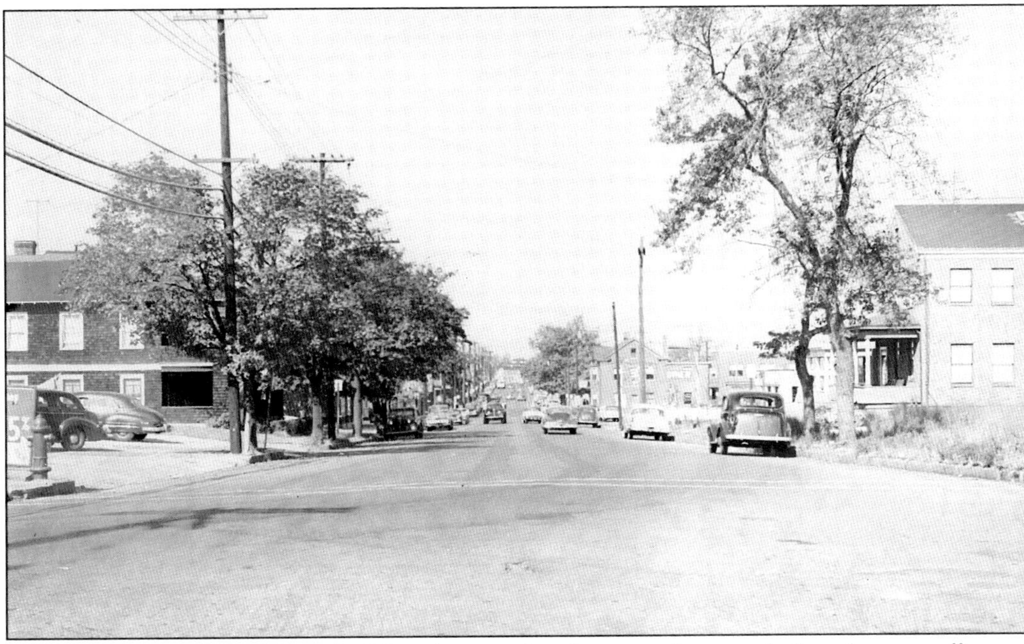

Here is a view at the other end of Broadway, at Bordentown Avenue, before the post office was built. This photograph was apparently taken in the 1950s, when the trolley tracks had already been paved over.

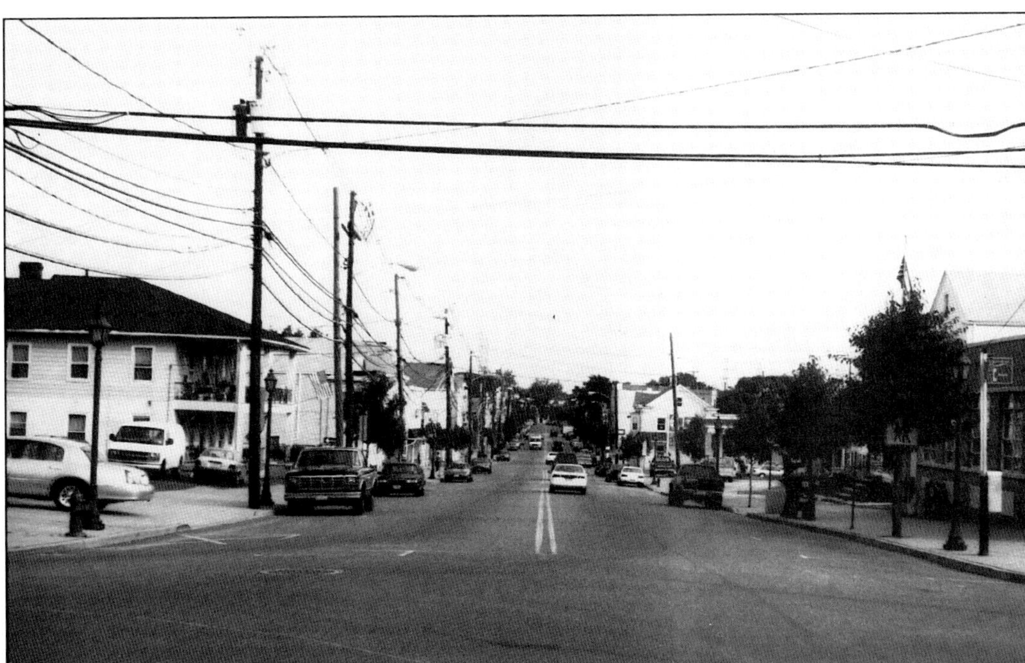

Broadway is seen here from Bordentown Avenue at the same location as the photograph at the top of the page, this time in 1998, with the post office just barely visible on right.

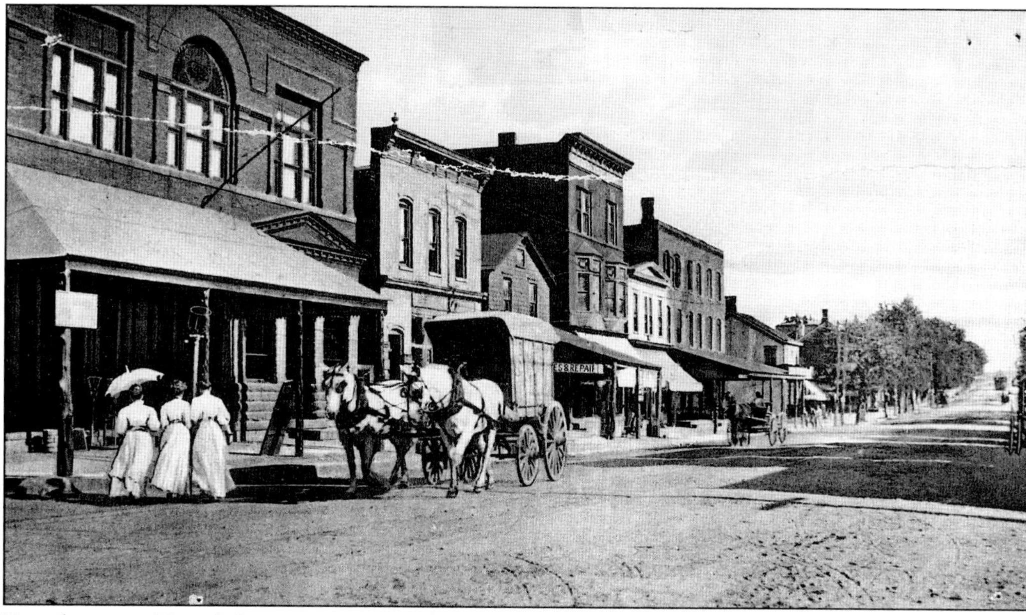

Broadway, at David Street, is pictured here. The building right behind the cart contained the First National Bank, although it is obscured by the awning of the adjacent business. The building still stands, as can be seen in the photo below.

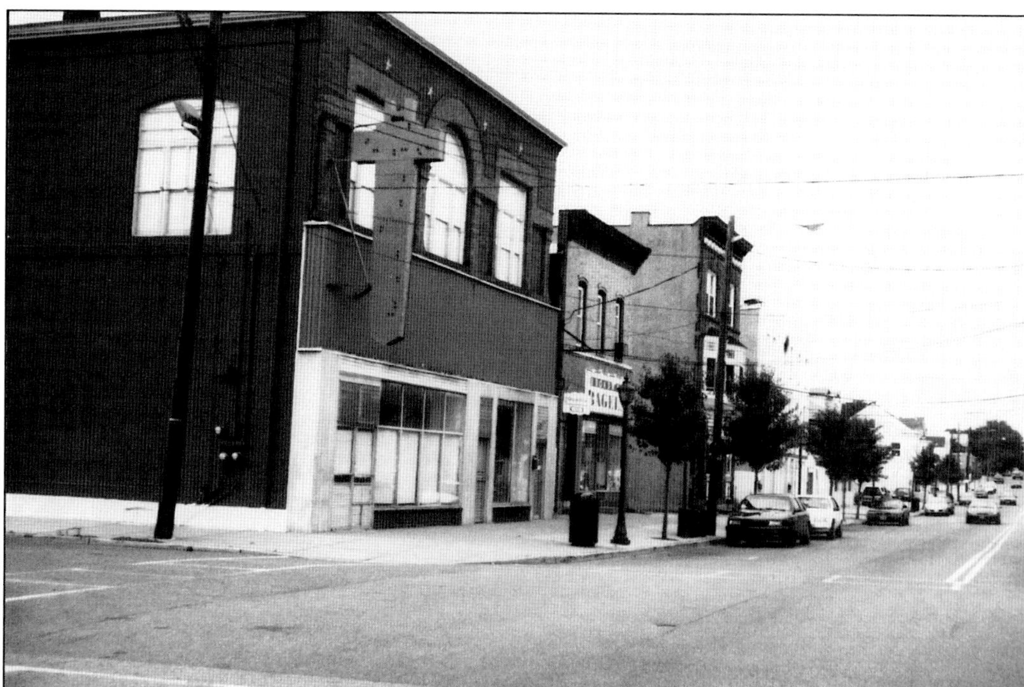

Here is present-day Broadway, at David Street. The top of the former First National Bank is still recognizable.

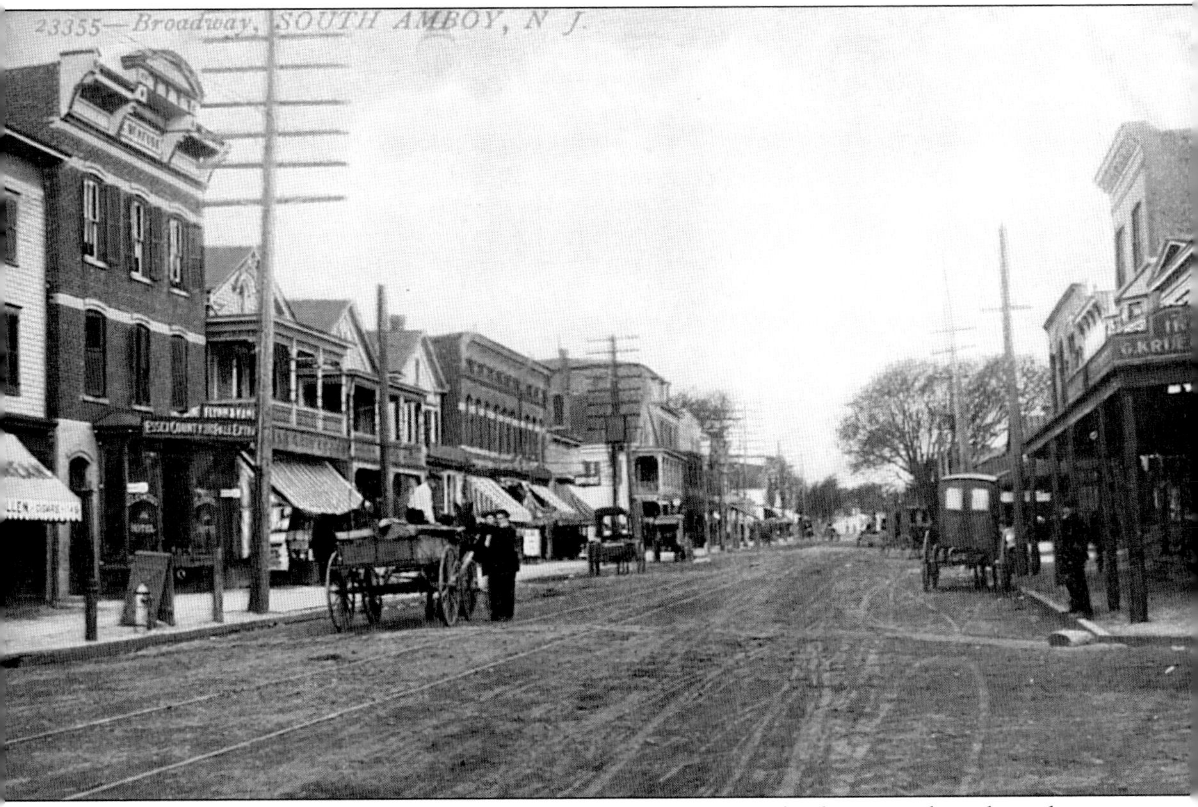

This is a view of Broadway, looking north from Henry Street. In the foreground on the right is the Pimlott House, a hotel and bar operated by Ira B. Martin. Across the street appears to be the Glenwood Hotel. About midway across the picture on the left is the building that would later become Oppenheims five and dime store. Like many of these postcards, the date was not noted, but there are few or no cars, so it likely dates from 1900 to 1920.

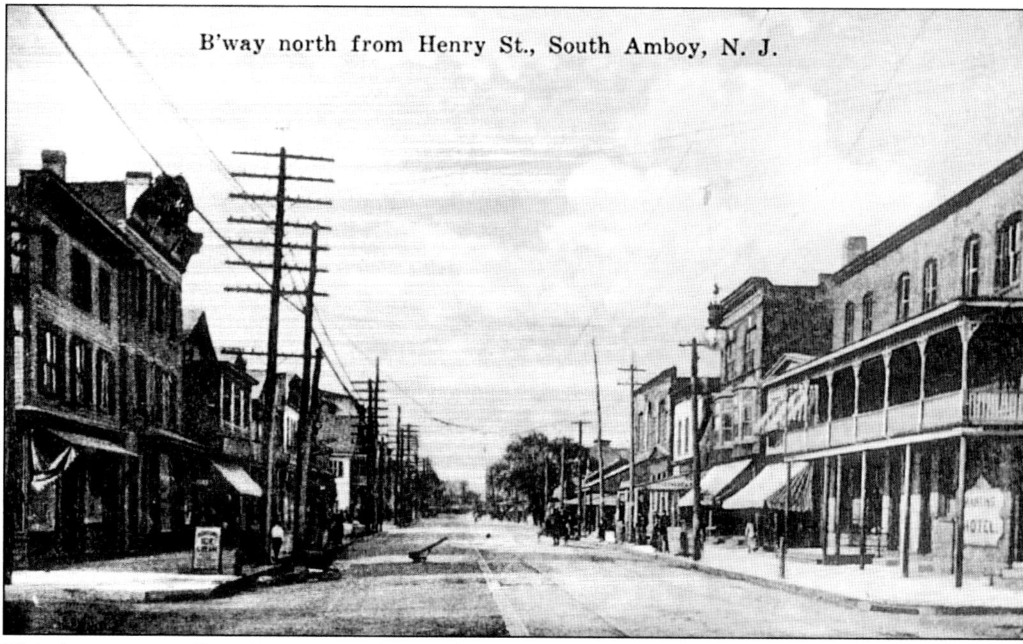

This location on Broadway is similar to the previous postcard, but is looking from a different angle. The sizeable hotel (the first building on the right) is again Martin's. Mr. Martin was also a committeeman (the equivalent of a councilman), treasurer, tax collector, and assessor.

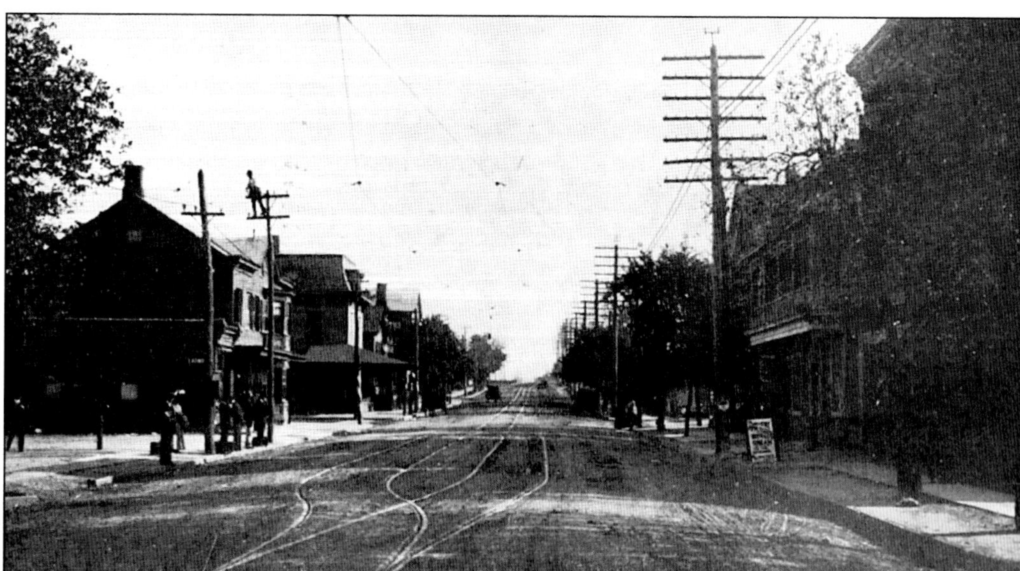

This view is looking in the opposite direction from the image at the top of the page, south on Broadway. The gap on the left was a courtyard entrance to the old train station.

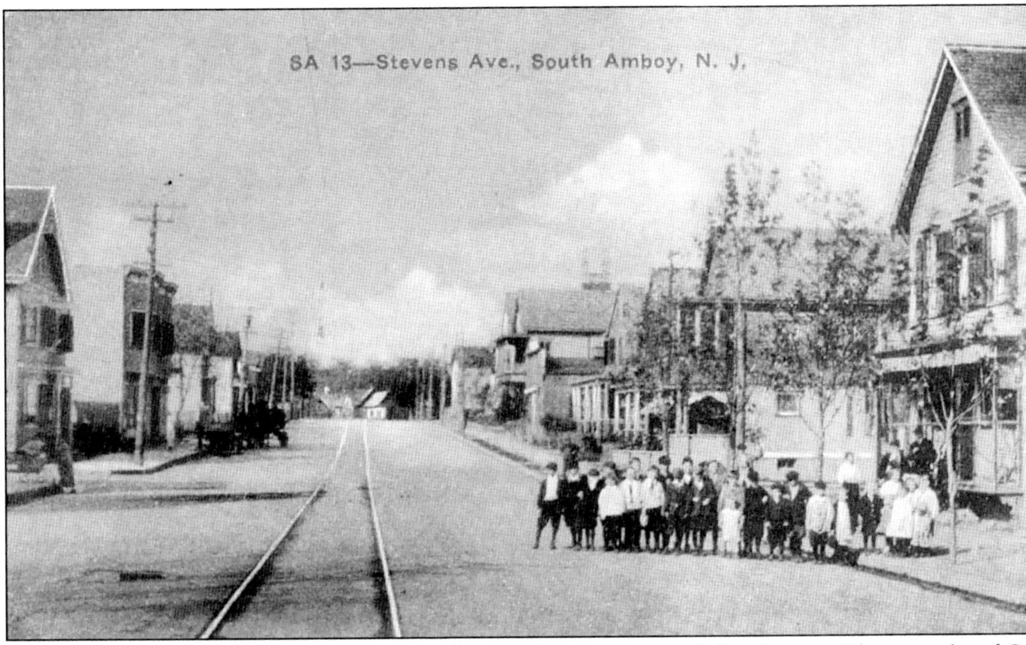

Stevens Avenue is visible here with trolley tracks, from near John Street. The steeple of St. Mary's Church can be seen just above the roof line slightly to the right of center.

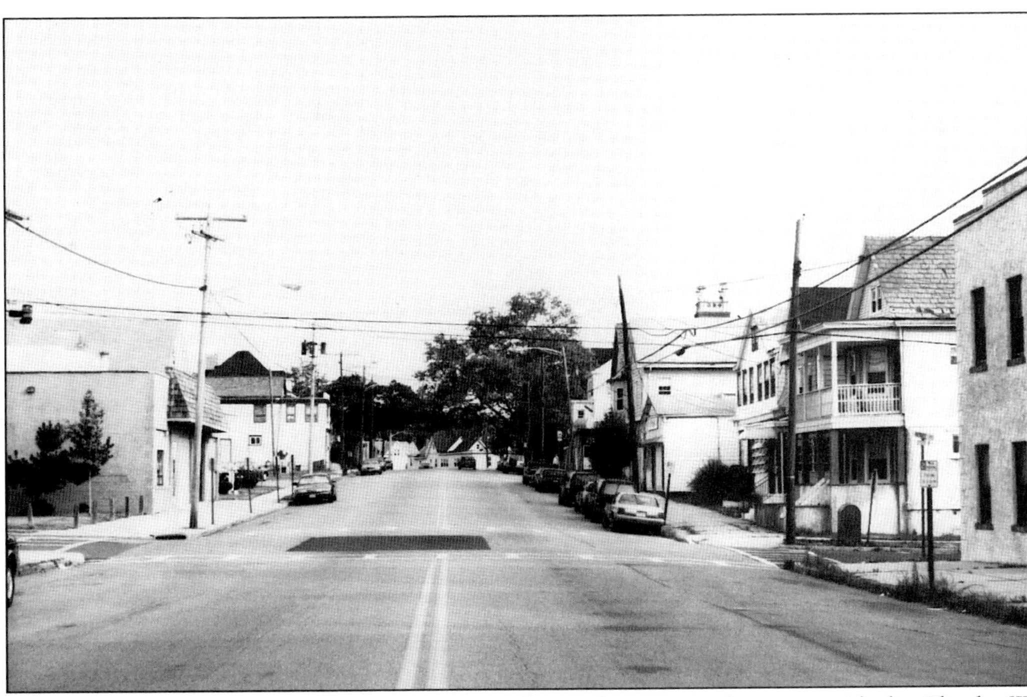

This is the same location as the previous image, but is the present-day view, with the Charles W. Hoffman Senior Citizen Center visible on the left.

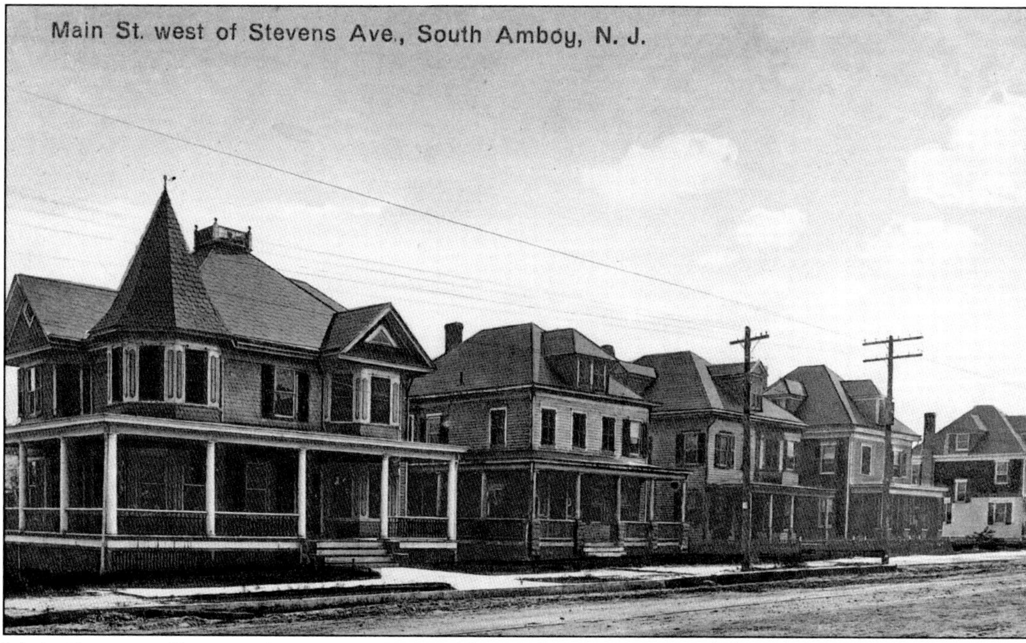

Main Street at Stevens Avenue is pictured here, showing some of the impressive houses on the city's main drag.

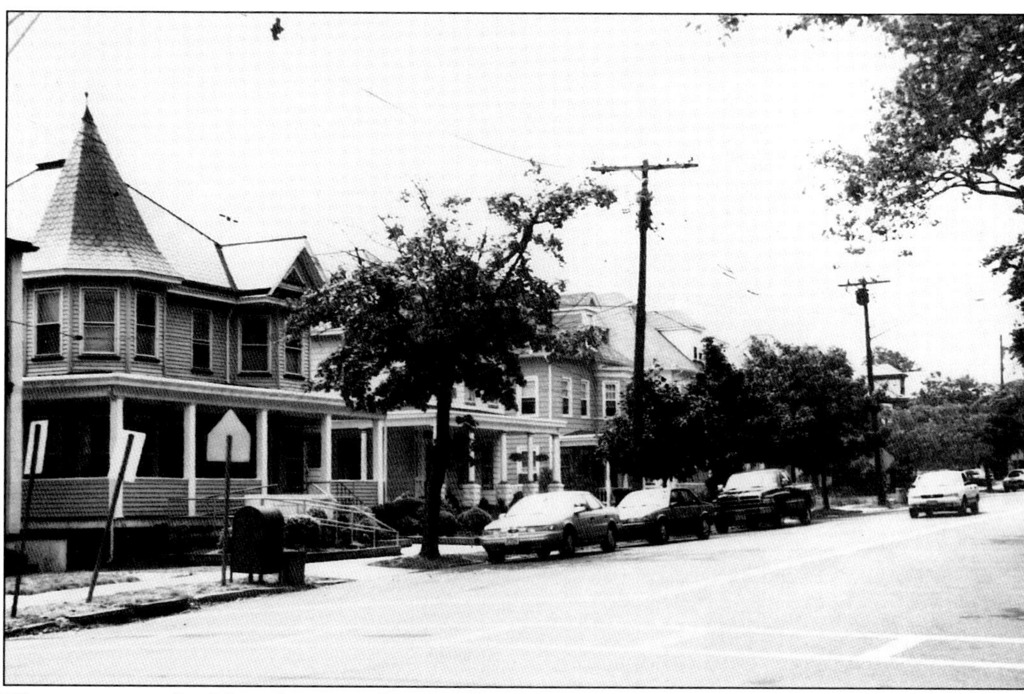

This is present-day Main Street at the same location as in the photograph at the top of the page, with the offices of Dr. Harold McKenna in the first building.

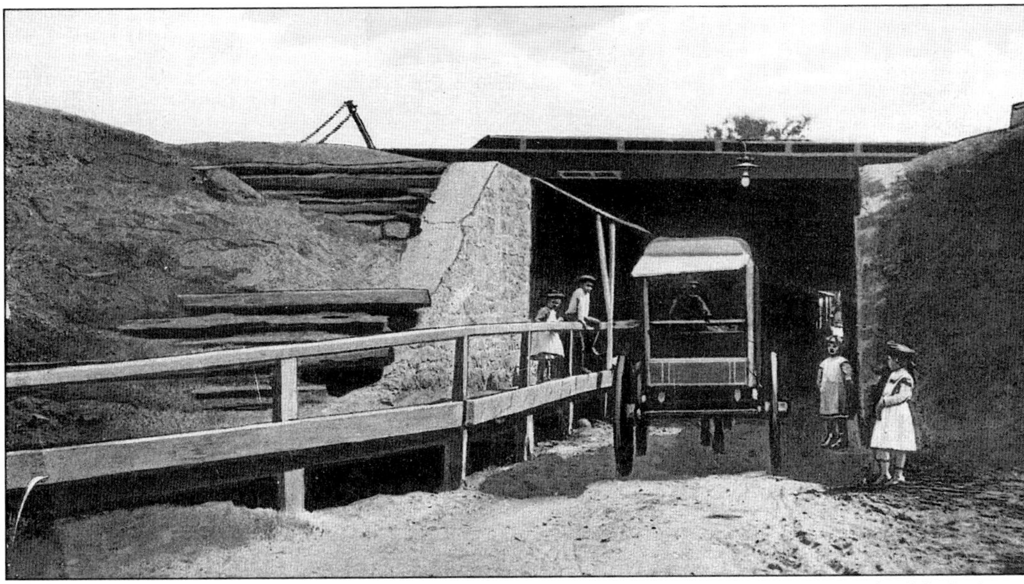

They did not choose the term "tunnel" or "underpass," but rather the more colorful "hole-in-the-wall." This is where Stevens Avenue runs under six or eight sets of train tracks to emerge on the other side as Ridgeway Avenue. The view is looking south from the Mechanicsville neighborhood toward the rest of the city. It was obviously a very early and narrow version of the hole-in-the-wall.

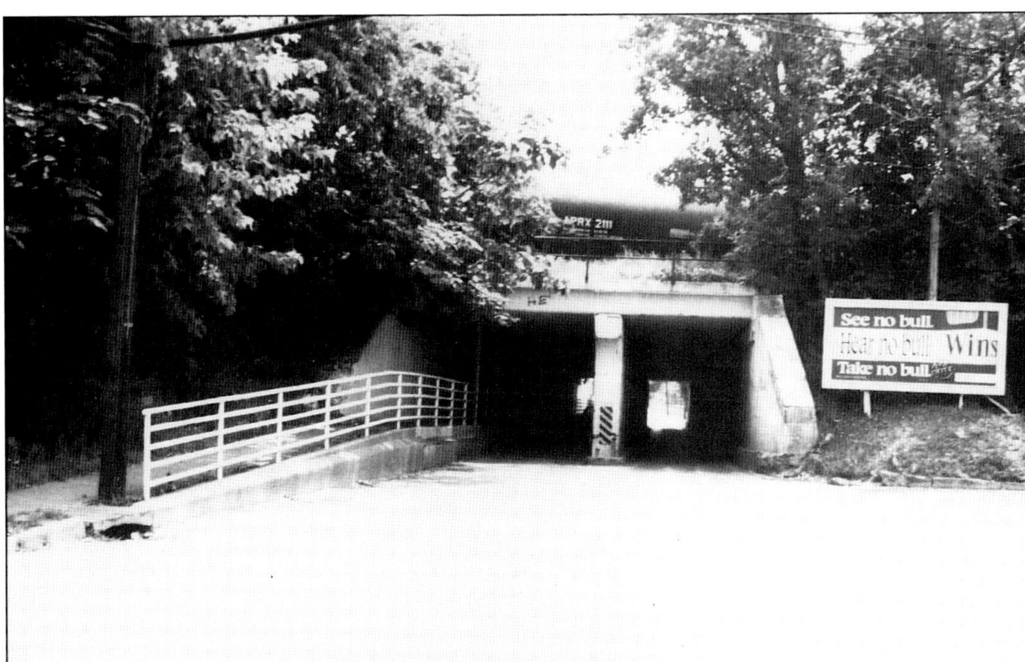

Here is the hole-in-the-wall today, with train, also seen from Mechanicsville.

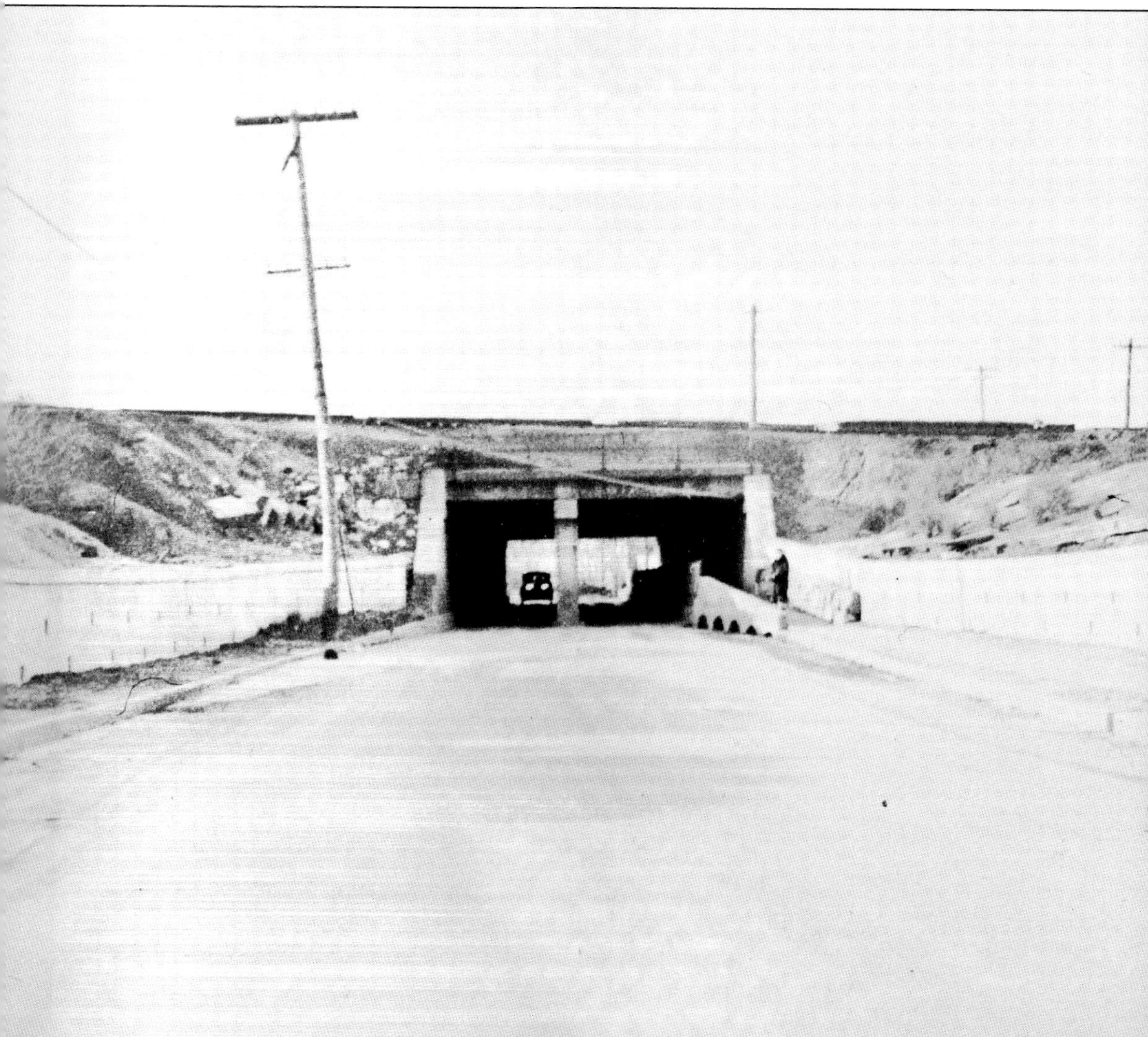

The hole-in-the-wall is seen here from the south, looking north toward Mechanicsville. What is also noticeable here is that this is a pre-1950s photograph, and Amboy Gardens, the development containing Barkalow, Pupek, and nearby streets, has not been built.

Two

WORKING

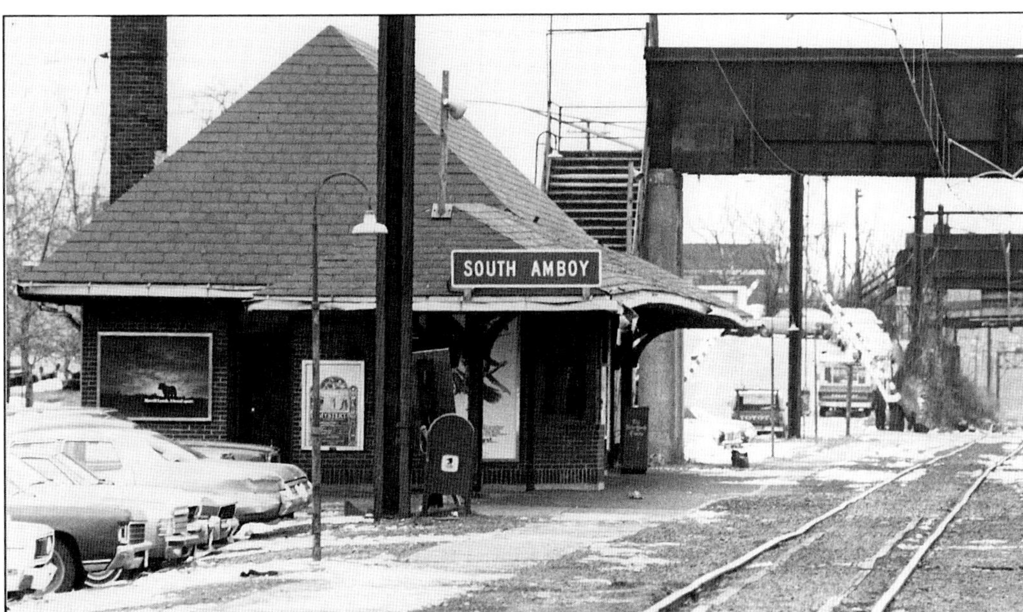

This chapter explores some of the city's industries and businesses. Of those, the rail line is perhaps most important. This is the current train station, on Mason Avenue, which in 1998 carries about one thousand commuters daily to New York City, from a half-dozen neighboring towns that do not have rail service.

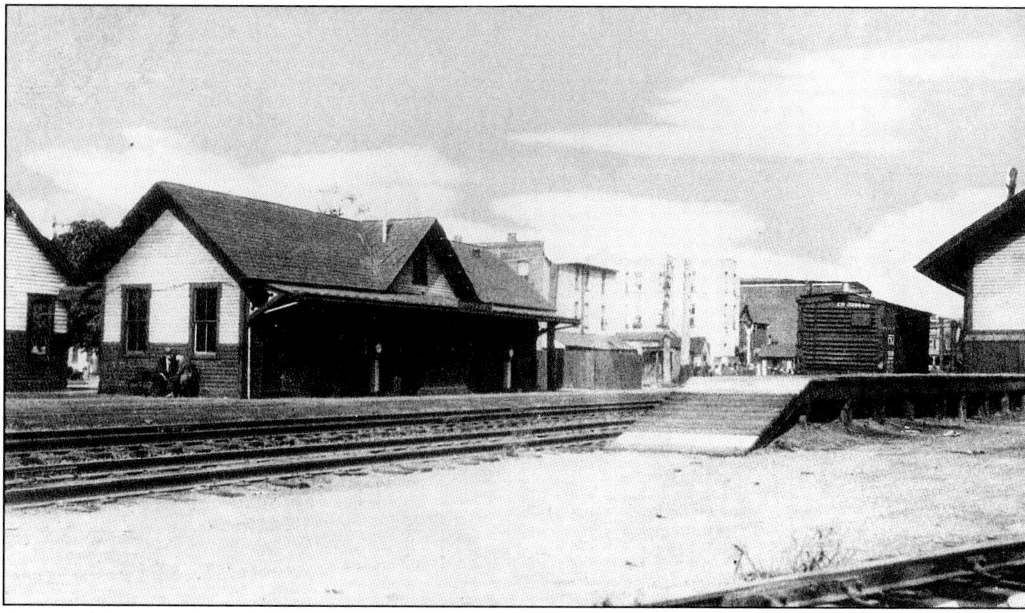

Pictured here is the former passenger train station seen from Mason Avenue, which was across the tracks and just south of the present terminal. On the right is the freight terminal.

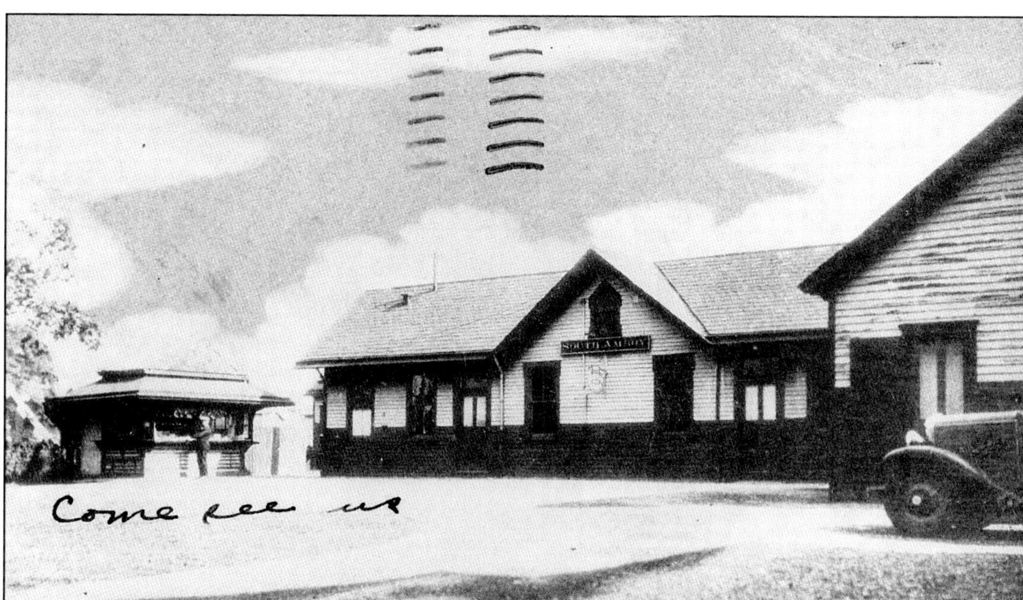

The entrance to the passenger terminal is seen here from the Broadway side, with the newsstand on the left. The green in front of the station was called "Whiskey Park," at least unofficially. It was torn down in 1935 when the railroad was electrified, which was also when Mason Avenue was created.

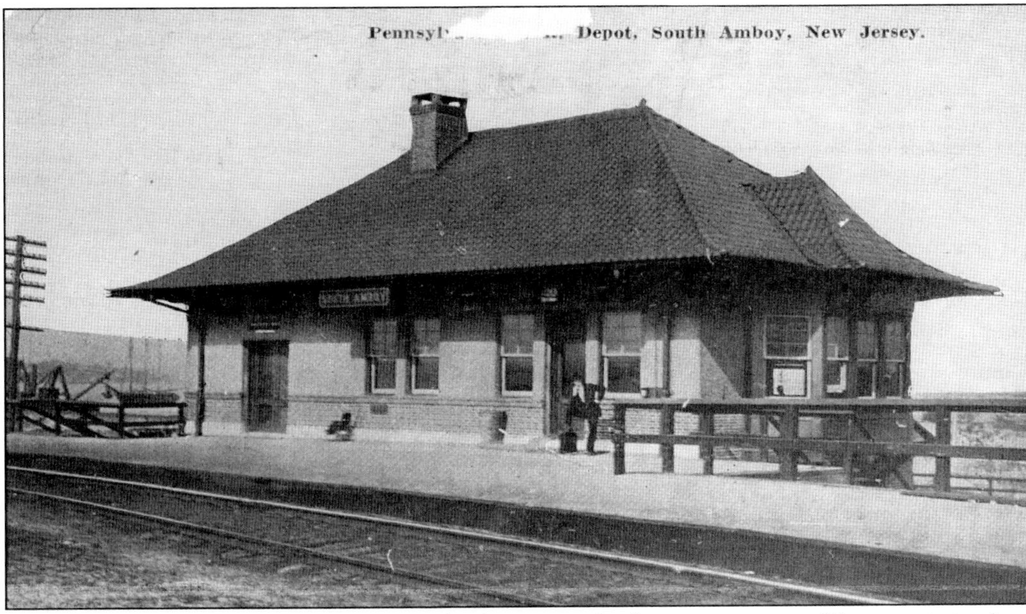

The Pennsylvania Railroad station was also known as the "junction station," because it is where the Camden & Amboy branch of the PRR and the New York and Long Branch Railroad came together. It was located where the northbound tracks curve east, roughly where the overpass to the Jersey Central Power and Light plant is on Main Street. Passengers from here would go down one flight to the New York and Long Branch tracks, which followed a southerly course to the Jersey Shore.

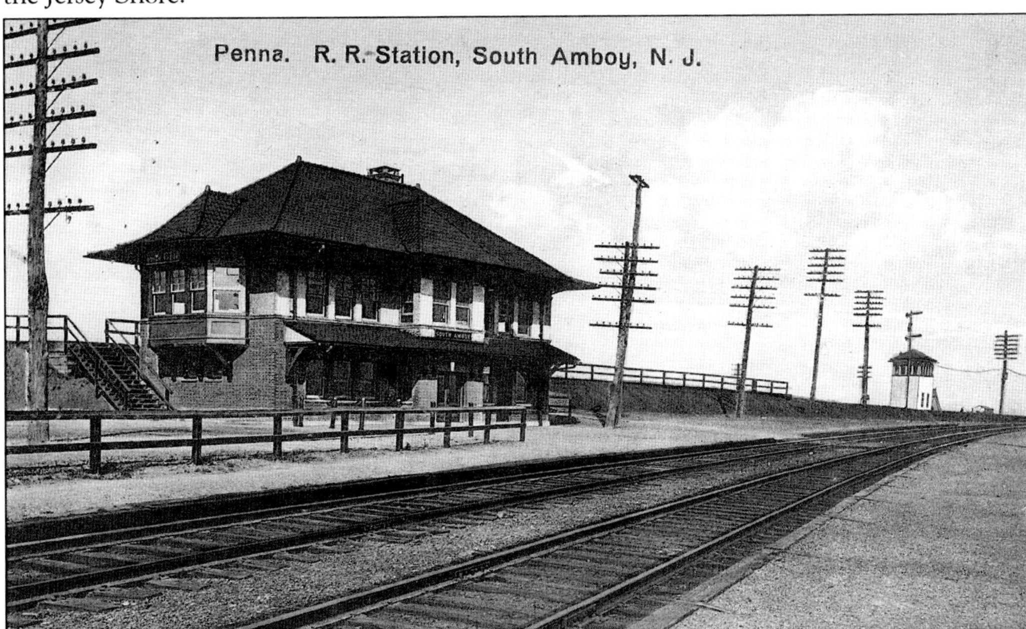

Here is the other side of the junction station, with New York and Long Branch tracks in the foreground. Passengers would go up one flight to the Camden & Amboy tracks, which followed a southwesterly route toward Jamesburg and ultimately Camden. The station was nearly destroyed by the 1950s munitions explosion.

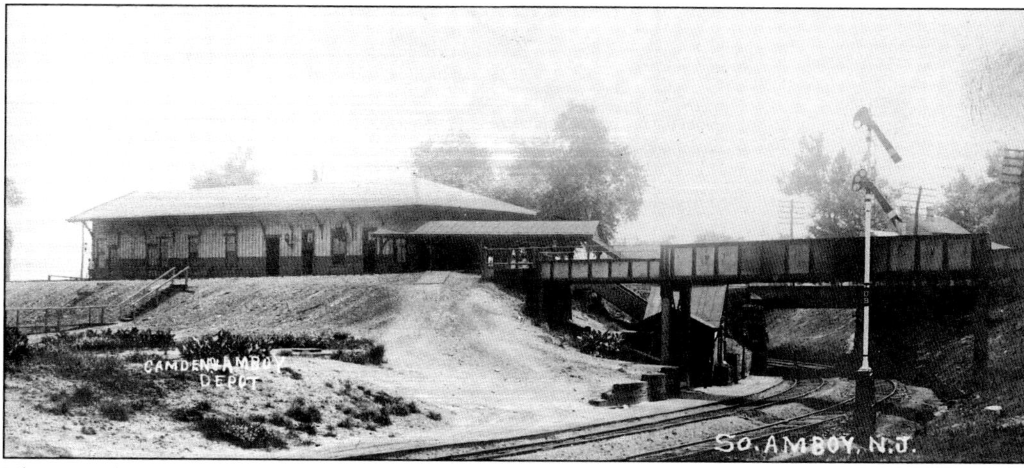

The Camden & Amboy depot, now long gone, was located near the Jersey Central Power and Light plant, near the foot of Main Street.

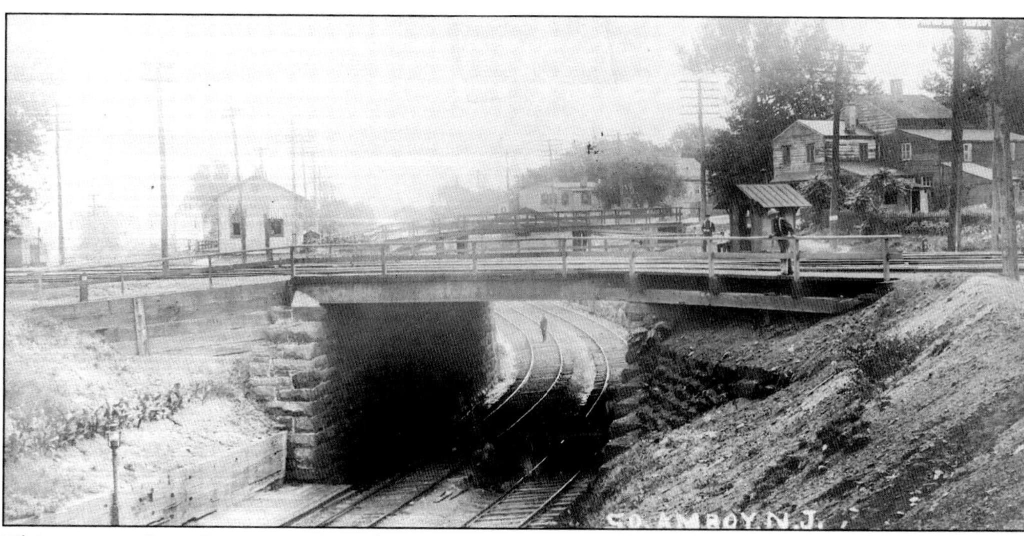

This is an early rail overpass near the junction station, roughly at the curve at the foot of Main Street, where Main Street runs under the tracks in a short tunnel.

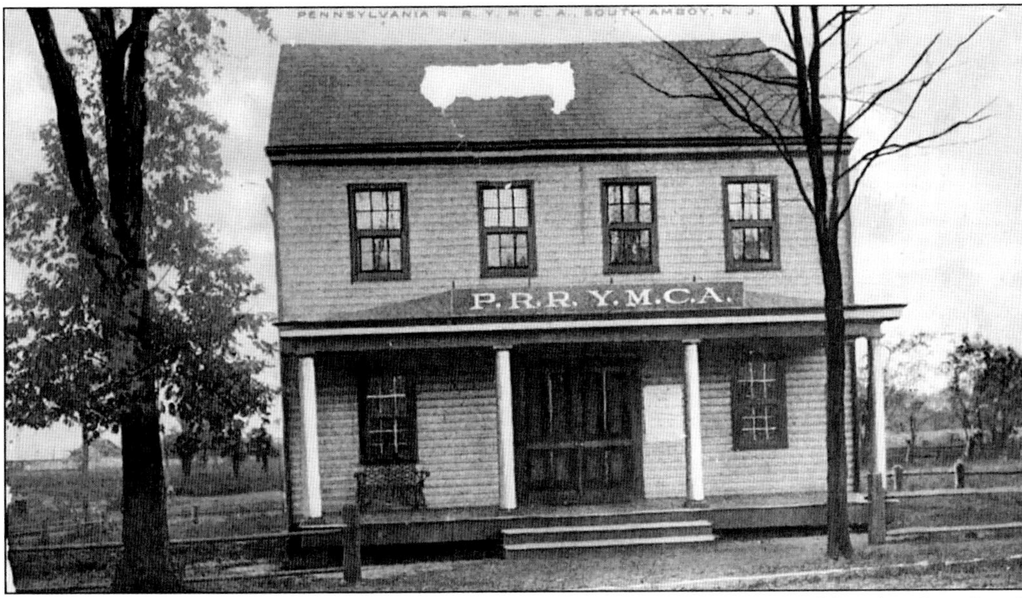

This is a close-up shot of the Young Men's Christian Association, started by the Camden & Amboy Rail Road to give its workers housing and an alternative to the local taverns. It was located east of the present-day Miller, Bergen, & Welsh lumber yard, along the tracks.

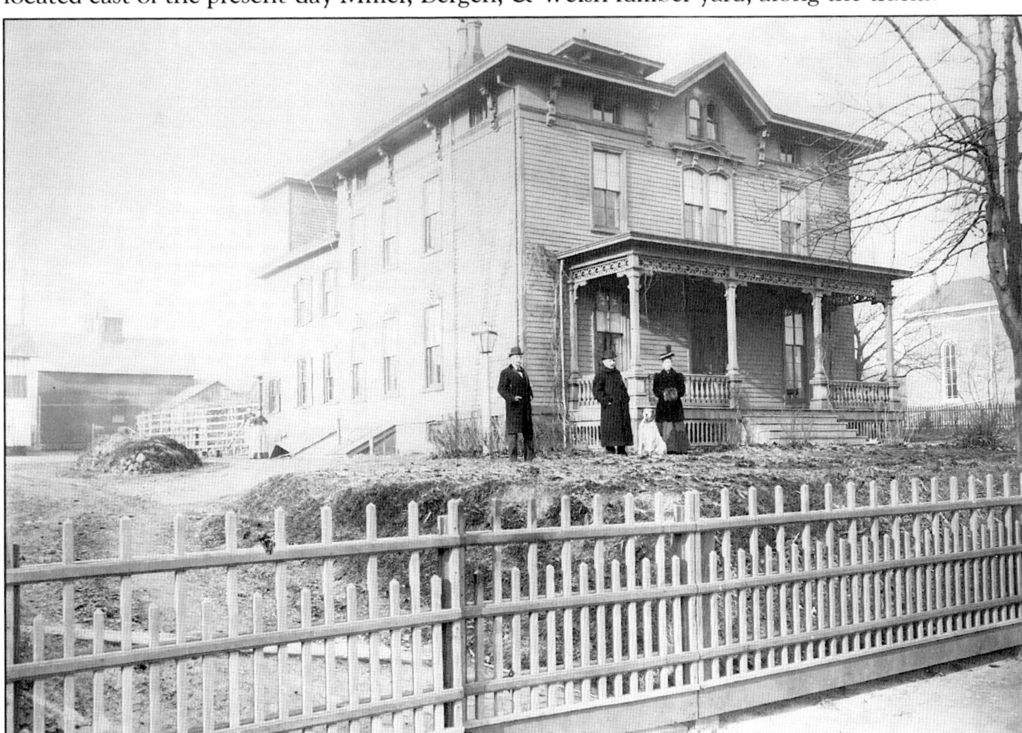

This home was located where city hall currently sits. It was a railroad company home at this point in the 1890s, occupied by Railroad Superintendent Alexander C. Davis, who is pictured on the left next to his son-in-law, Allan C. Parisen, and Fannie Davis Parisen, Davis's daughter and Parisen's wife. The dog's name was "Baron." The building later became the second YMCA.

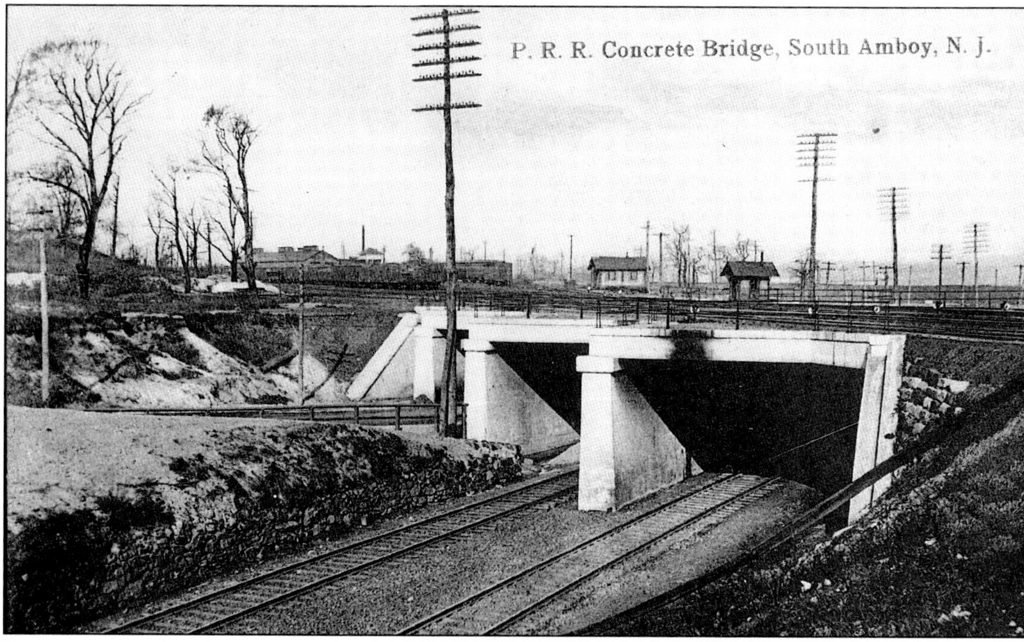

Here is a view heading out of town, on lower Main Street. This overpass still looks basically the same. To the left of the overpass the Camden & Amboy rail yard can be seen, where freight and coal cars waited to be taken to or from the docks, out of view to the right of this photograph.

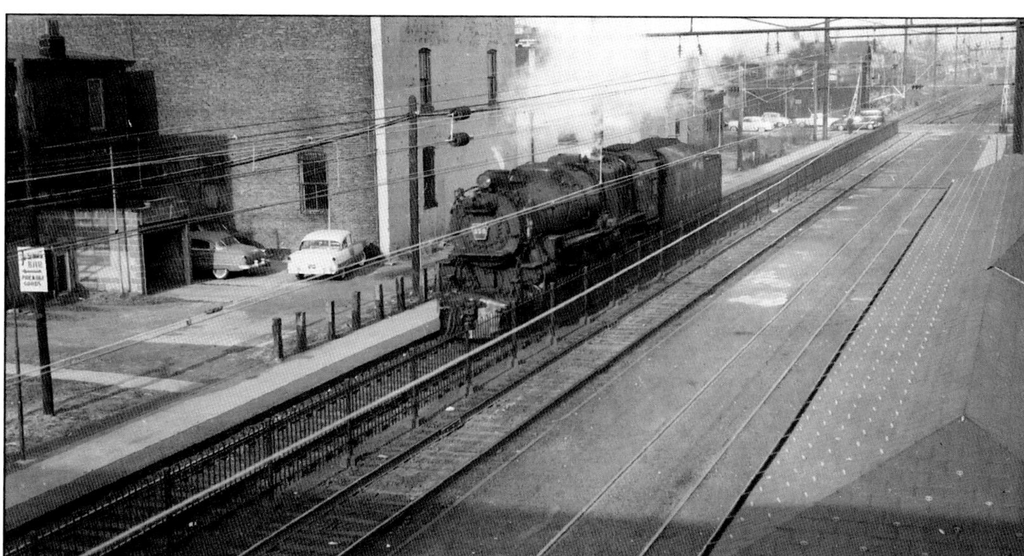

A K-4 locomotive is leaving South Amboy, southbound. The sign for Joe Jerome's Bar (now Lagoda's) is barely visible on the far left.

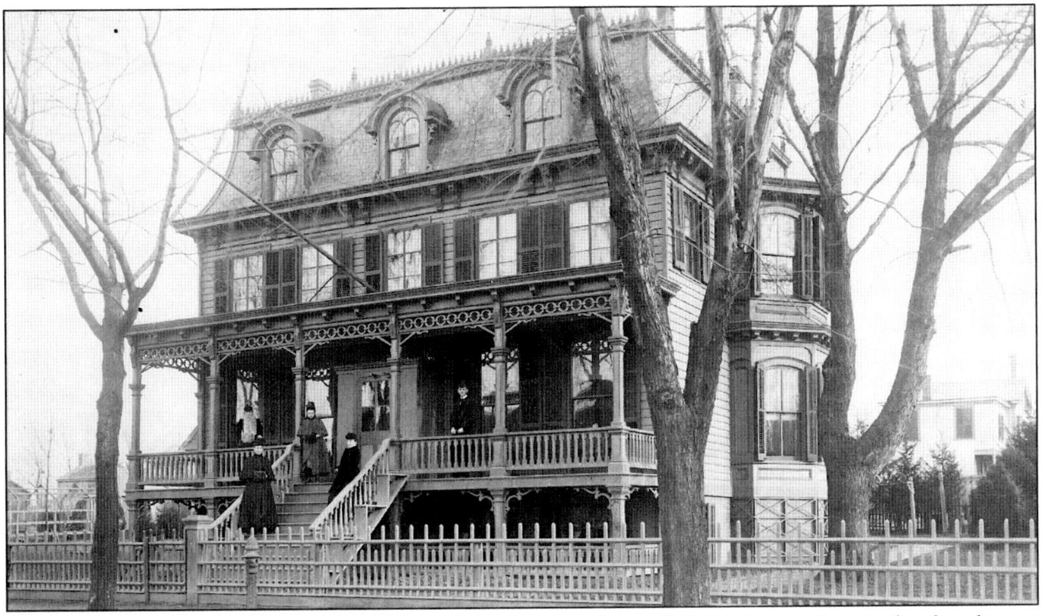
This was the home of Alexander C. Davis, superintendent of the railroad. It was the first house "below," or east of the tracks, on John Street.

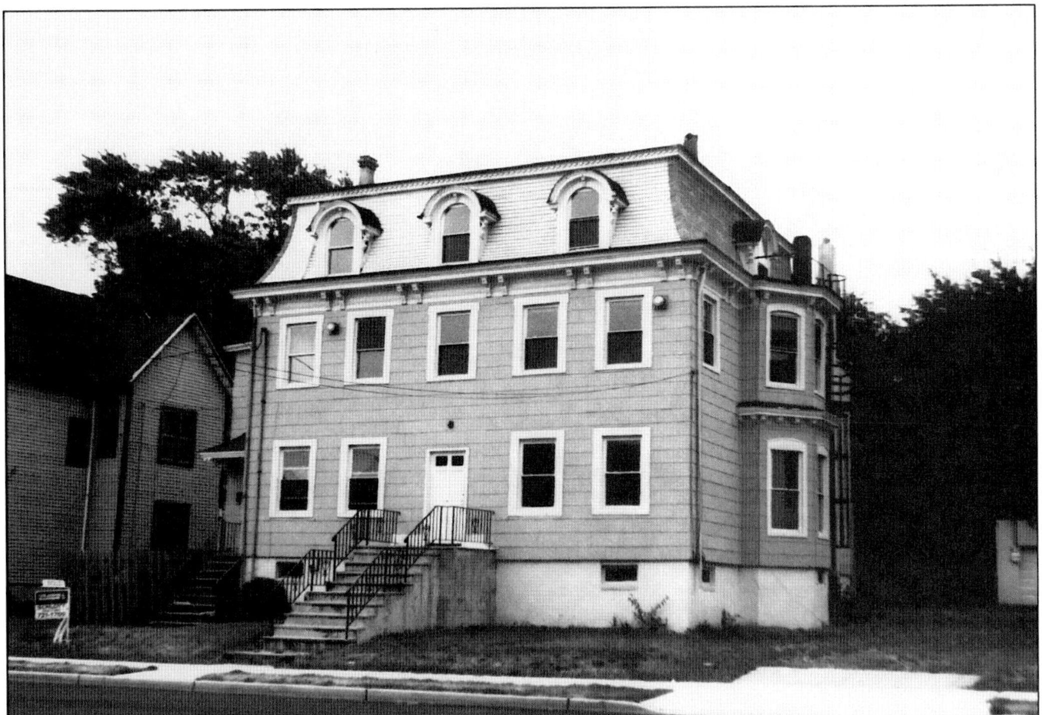
Here is a present-day shot of the Davis house.

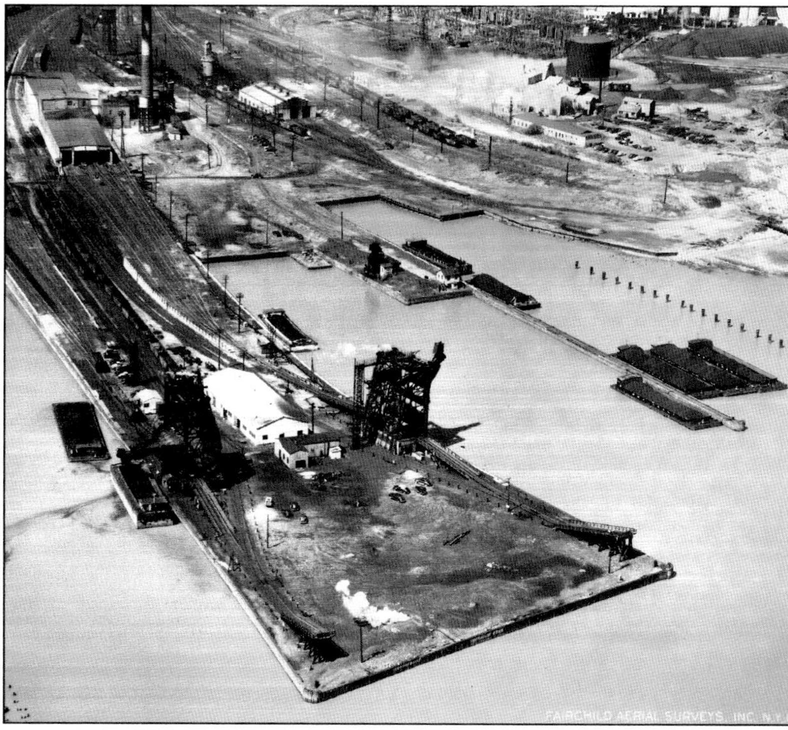

The coal pier was used to load coal barges for transport to New York City.

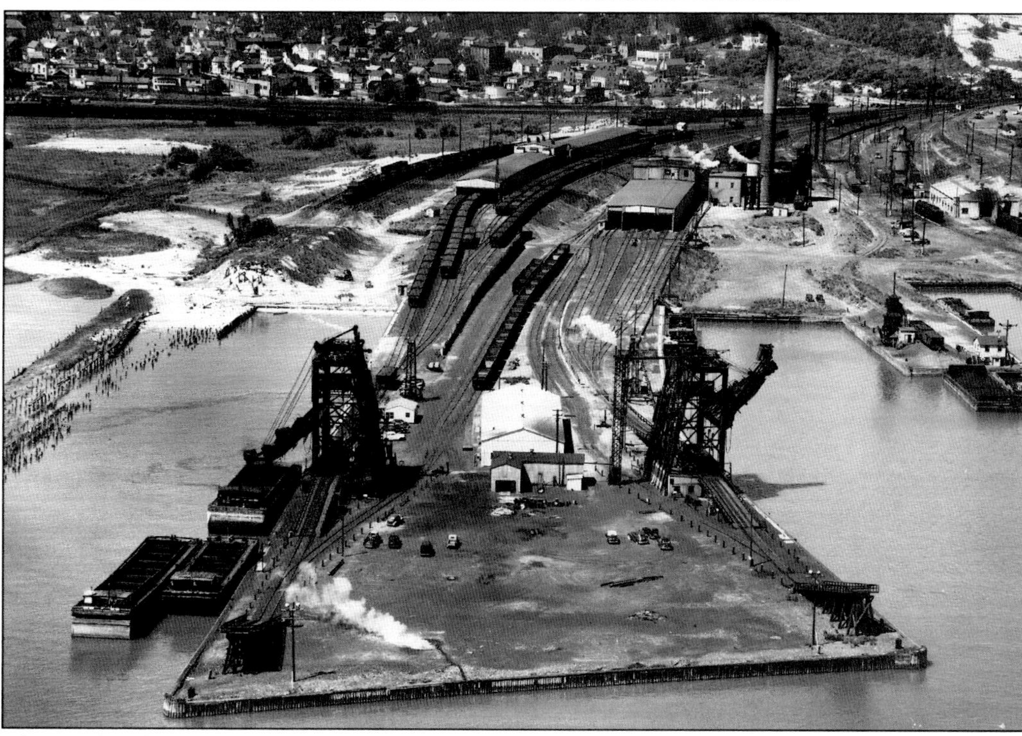

This is a head-on view of the coal dumpers, with most of the city in the background. The photo was taken around 1953, as evidenced by the bare pilings to the left of the property at the powder pier, which exploded in 1950.

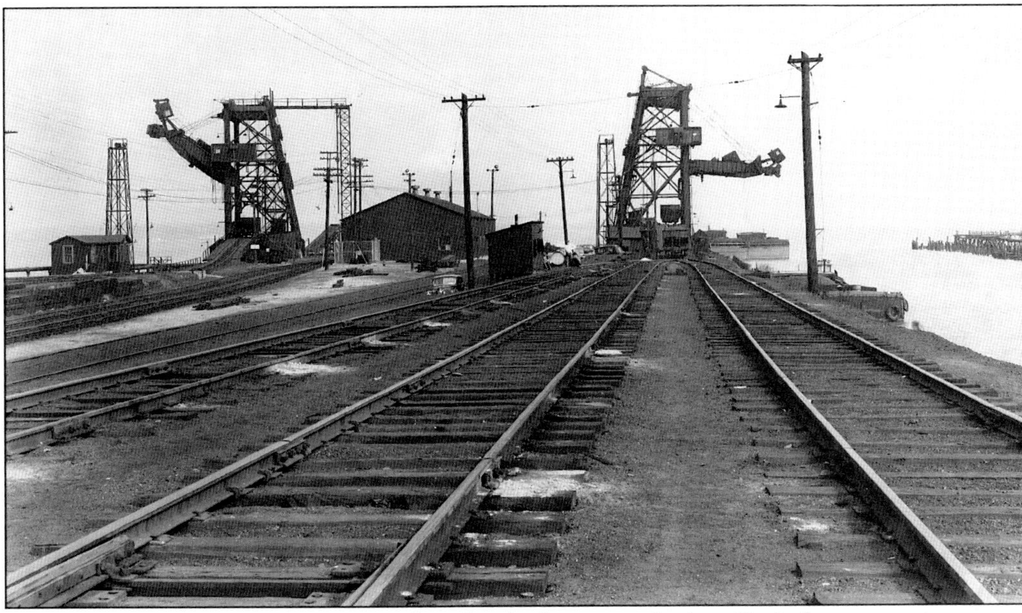

The coal dumpers are seen here in a shot that looks out to the bay. Each dumper in this picture has a coal car either ready for unloading or recently unloaded. It worked by pushing the cars up an incline to a point under the tower. The entire car would be hoisted and tipped on its side so that the contents spilled into the pan, the long piece protruding out from the structure. The pan was then lowered to spill the coal into the barge waiting below.

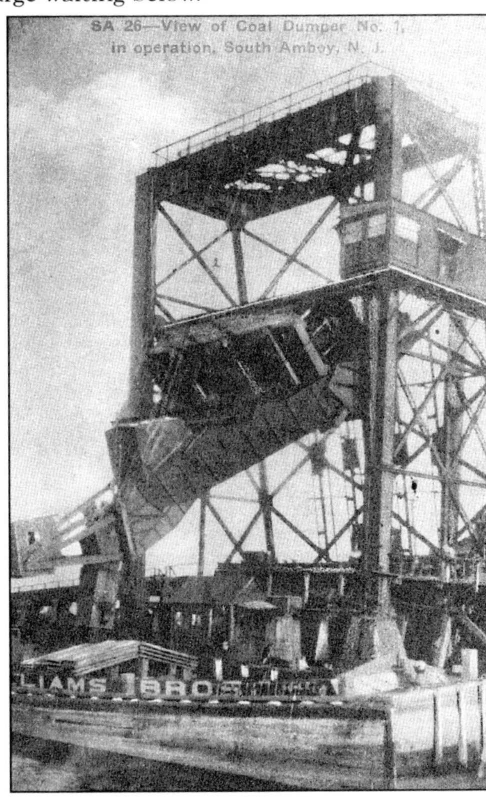

This postcard shows the pan, with a coal car, being tipped toward a barge.

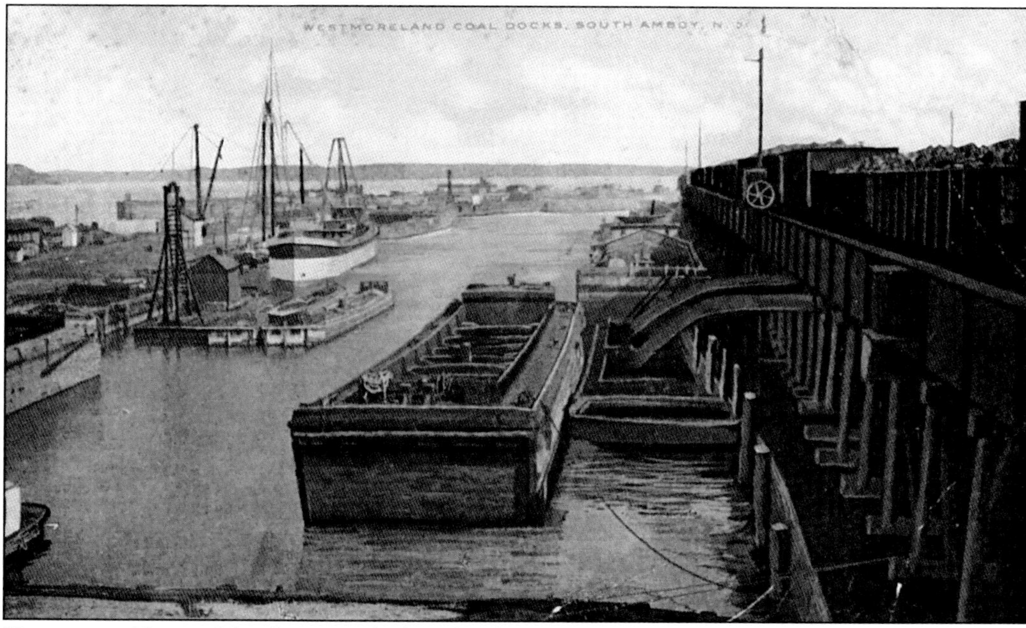

Here is an older coal-loading pier, before the dumpers were constructed. The hoppers under the coal cars would be opened from the bottom, a dangerous job, and the coal would spill out into the chute to the barge.

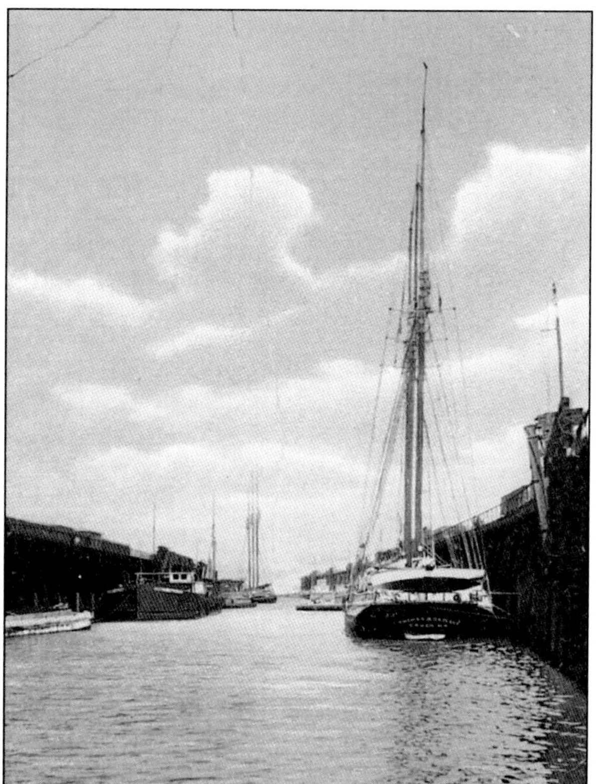

These barges are docked along the coal docks. They are sailing vessels, which could not have been efficient for shipping heavy loads like coal.

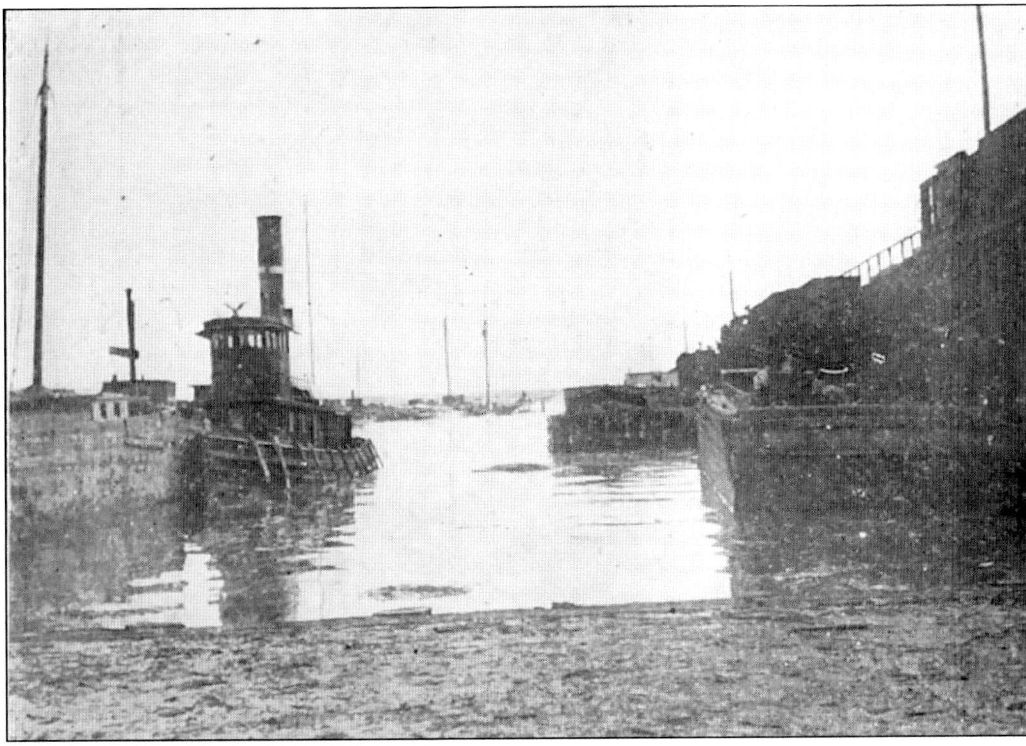

This tug is waiting to take away a barge.

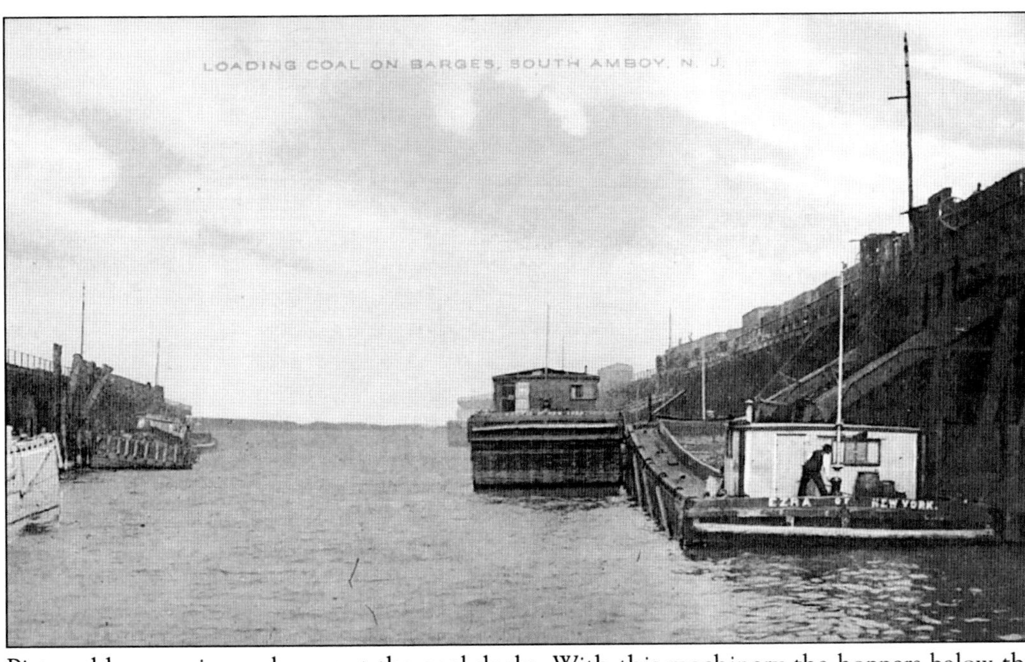

Pictured here again are barges at the coal docks. With this machinery the hoppers below the coal car were opened and the rocks spilled out to a chute and onto the waiting barge. This could be a hazardous method, because when the hopper became clogged, workers had to crawl under and bang the chutes clear.

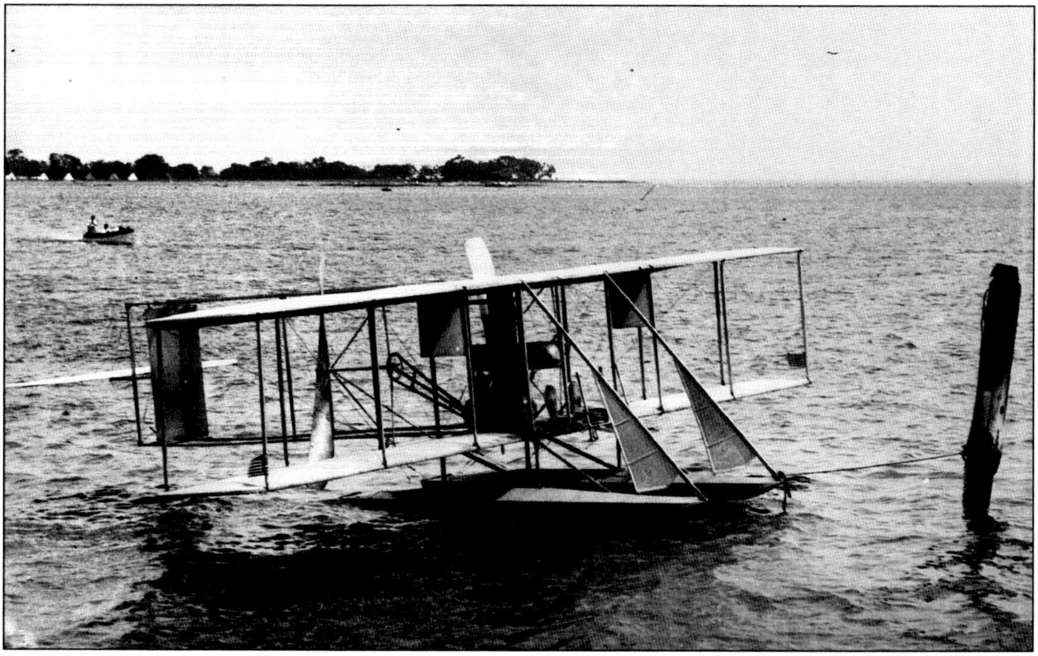

South Amboy was the scene for the first airmail flight in New Jersey on July 4, 1912. The flight was from the foot of Henry Street to the foot of Lewis Street in Perth Amboy, a journey of about 1.2 miles. It was the idea of South Amboy Postmaster Edward C. Roddy and was put together by the publisher of *Collier's* magazine, Robert Collier, with O.G. Simmons as pilot and Perth Amboy Mayor Ferd Garretson on the first official flight, carrying 16 pounds of mail. Thousands gathered to see it.

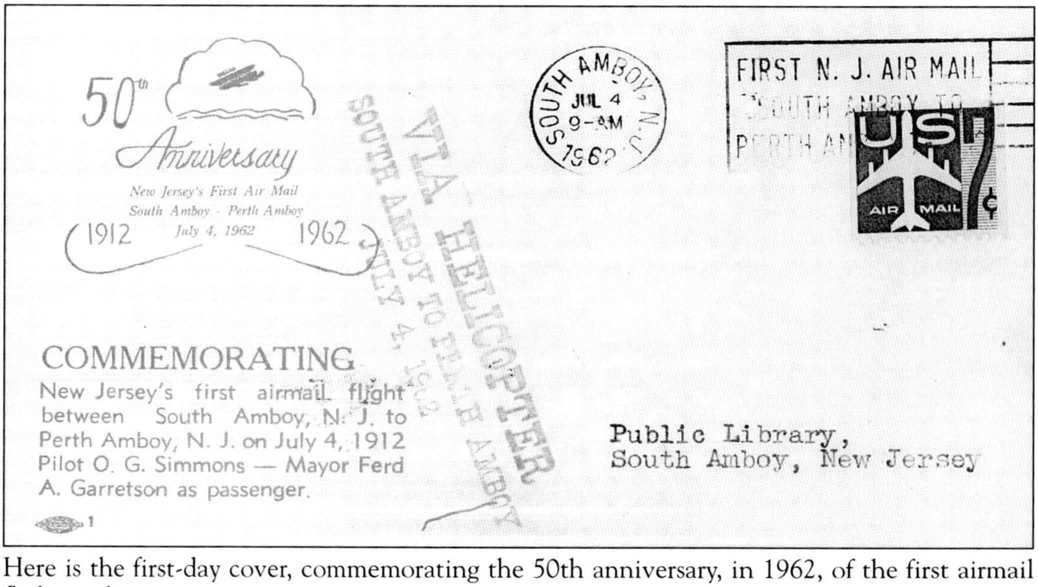

Here is the first-day cover, commemorating the 50th anniversary, in 1962, of the first airmail flight in the state.

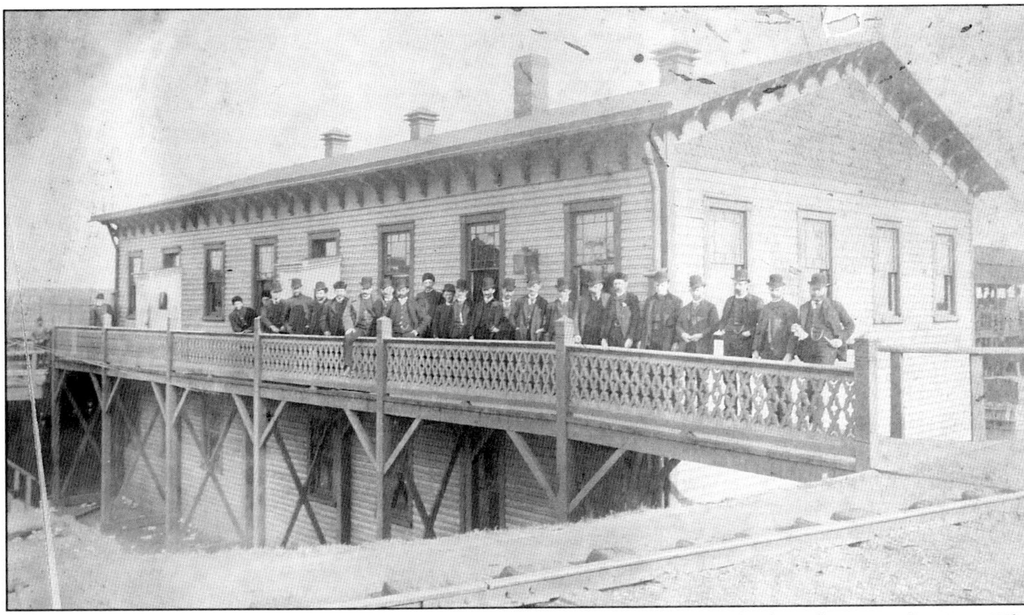

This was one of the railroad or coal offices near the waterfront, but little is known about it. The coal brokering business in South Amboy was started by John Scully, whose son Thomas was a congressman.

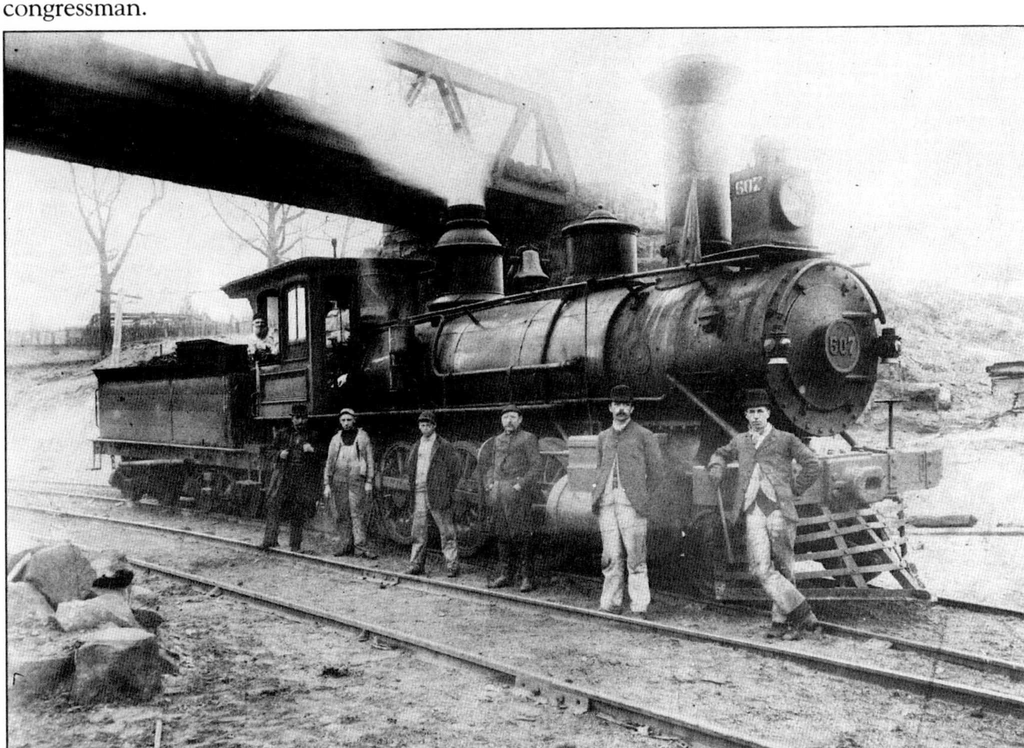

Here is an early locomotive, possibly at the overpass where the railroad travels through. Pictured second from right is Elias Clayton, an ancestor of Anna Harris Friberg, who lives in Sayreville and is a proud repository of South Amboy history.

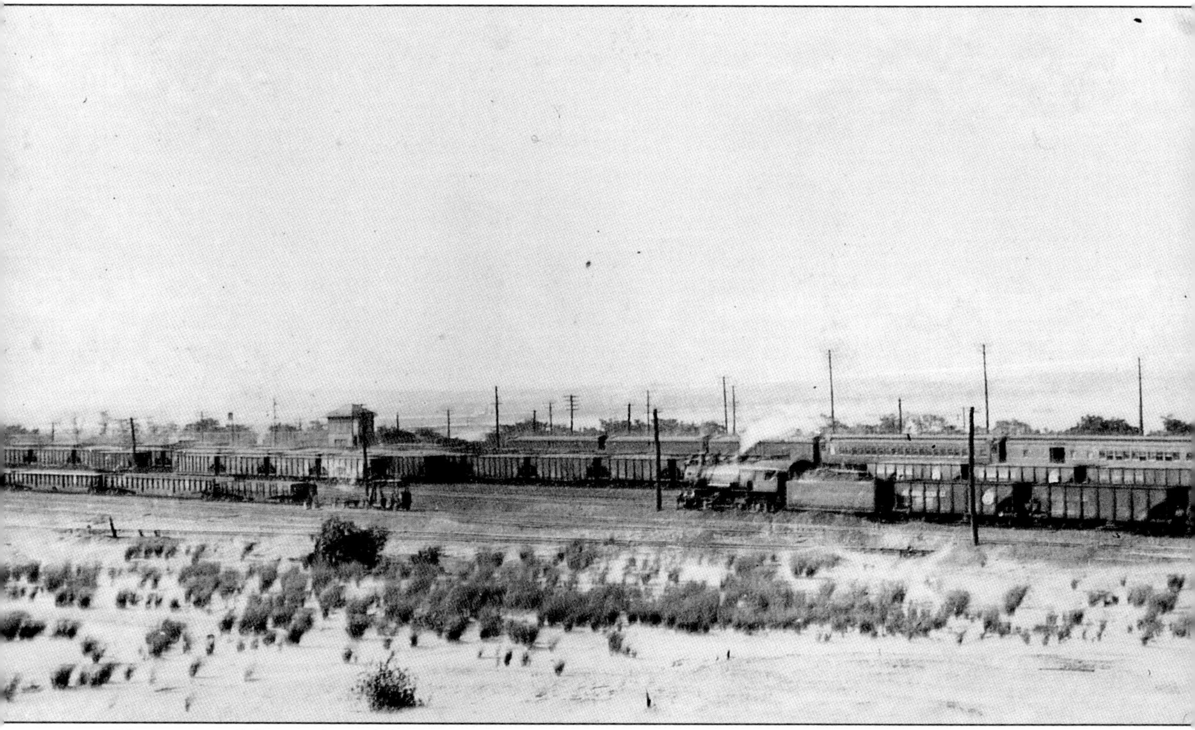

This view of the rail yard looks north, with the Jersey Central plant on the far right. Coal cars

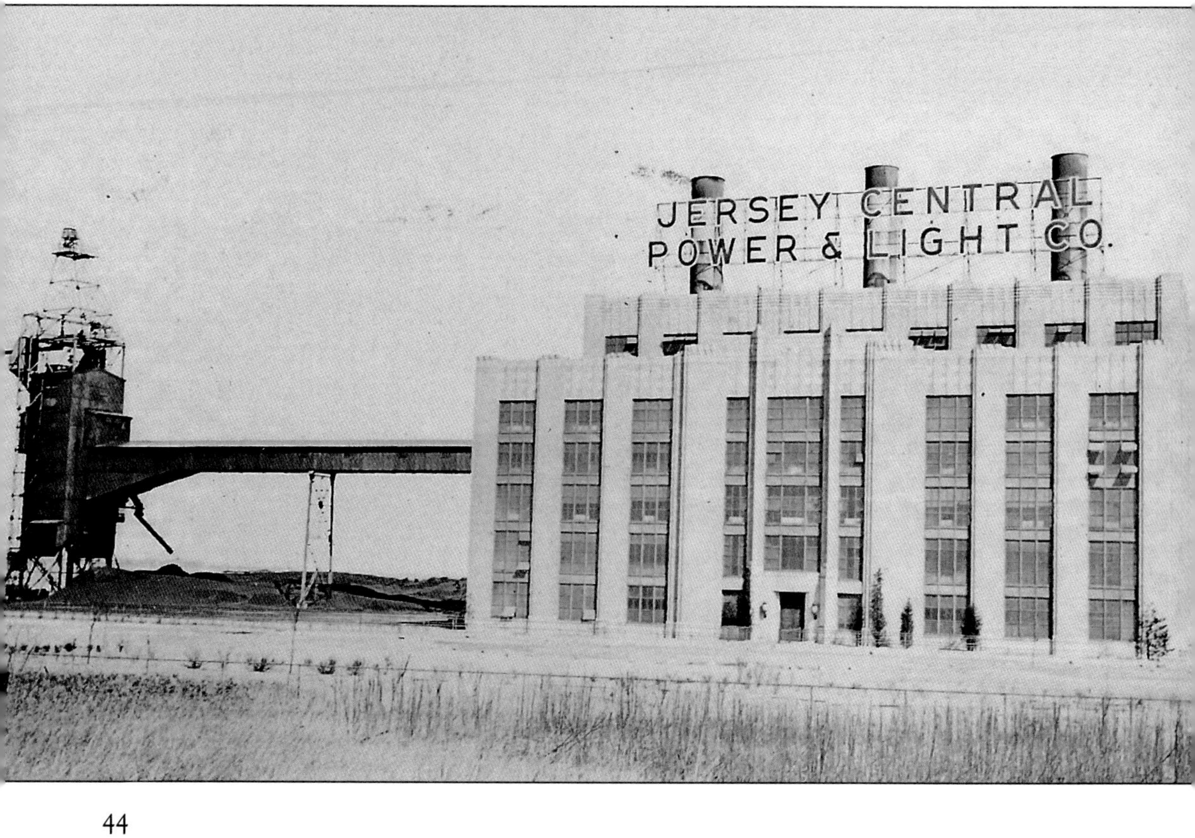

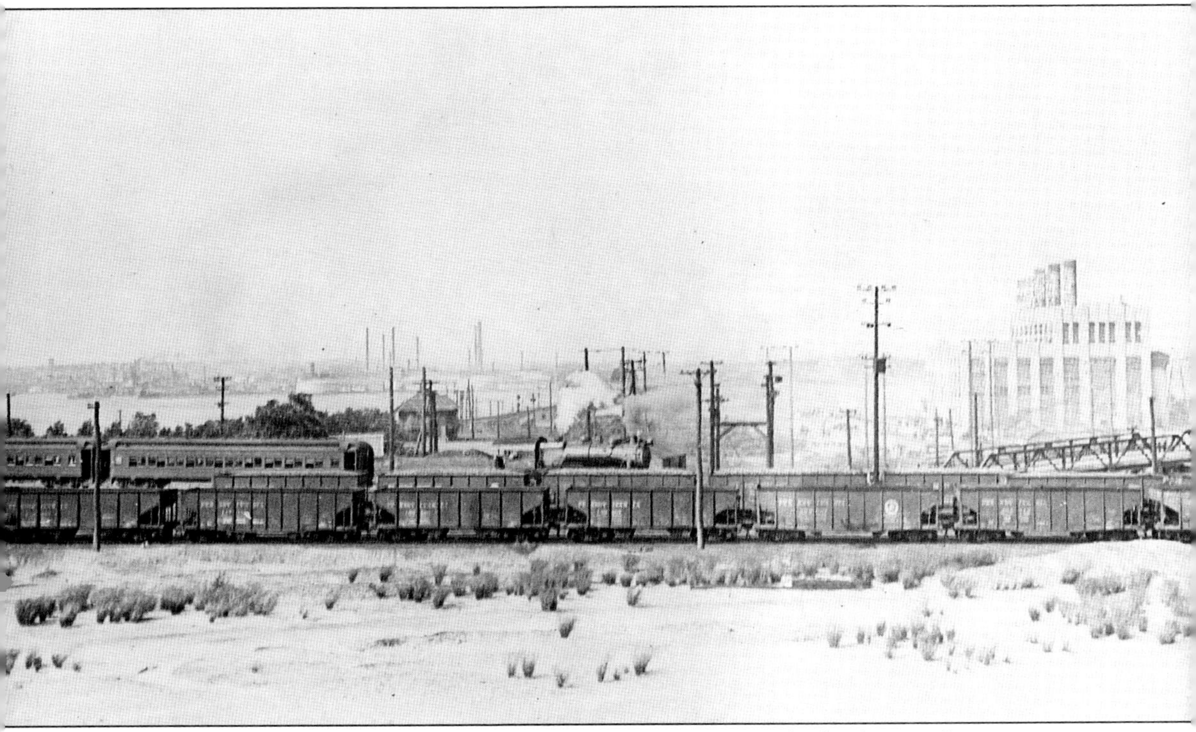

wait to be emptied or pulled away, and there are passenger cars in the background.

Opposite: The Jersey Central Power and Light Company is shown here in an earlier day. Now defunct, it bears almost no resemblance to this image, as the company has added on to the sides and up.

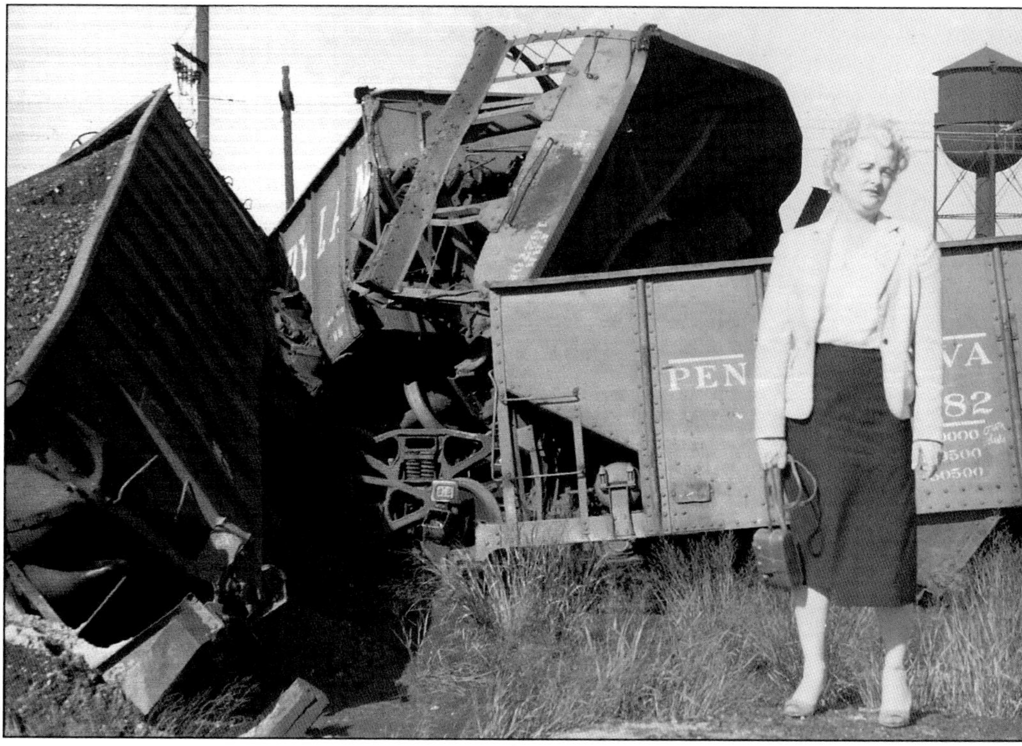

The trains rarely derailed, as in this photograph from the 1950s, probably at the Camden & Amboy rail yard. Pictured is Eva Houmiller of New York, a relative of Ken and Joyce Elyea, former South Amboy residents and avid postcard collectors.

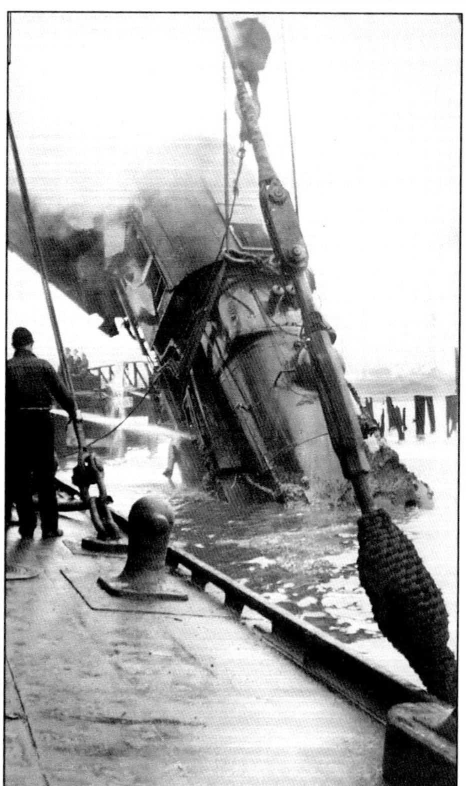

This locomotive went off the end of one of the piers and into the bay. A huge crane, towed by tugboat down to South Amboy from New York City, lifted the engine out of the water. They had the engine running again within a few days.

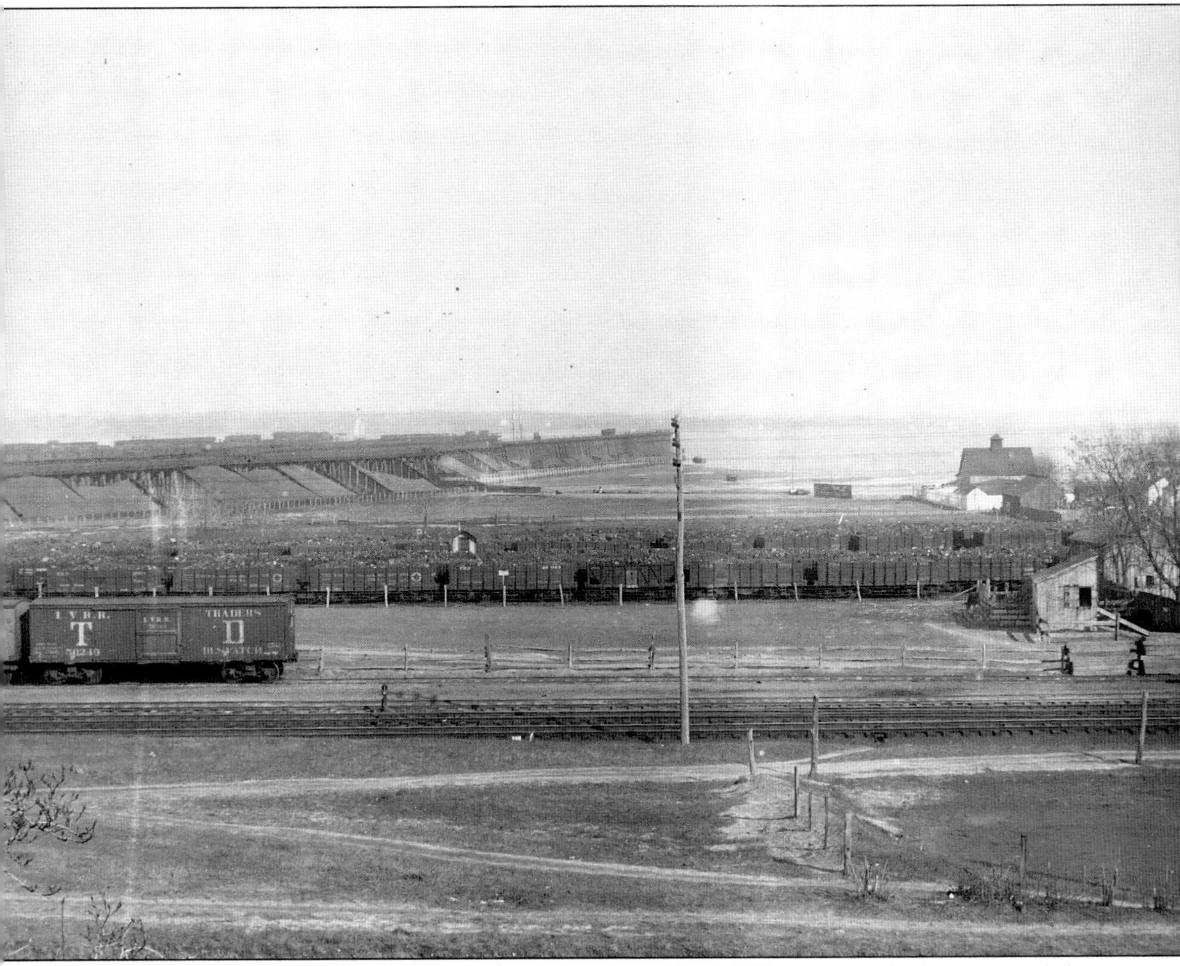

Dozens of coal cars are waiting to be unloaded at the rail yard. The view is looking toward the bay and Perth Amboy.

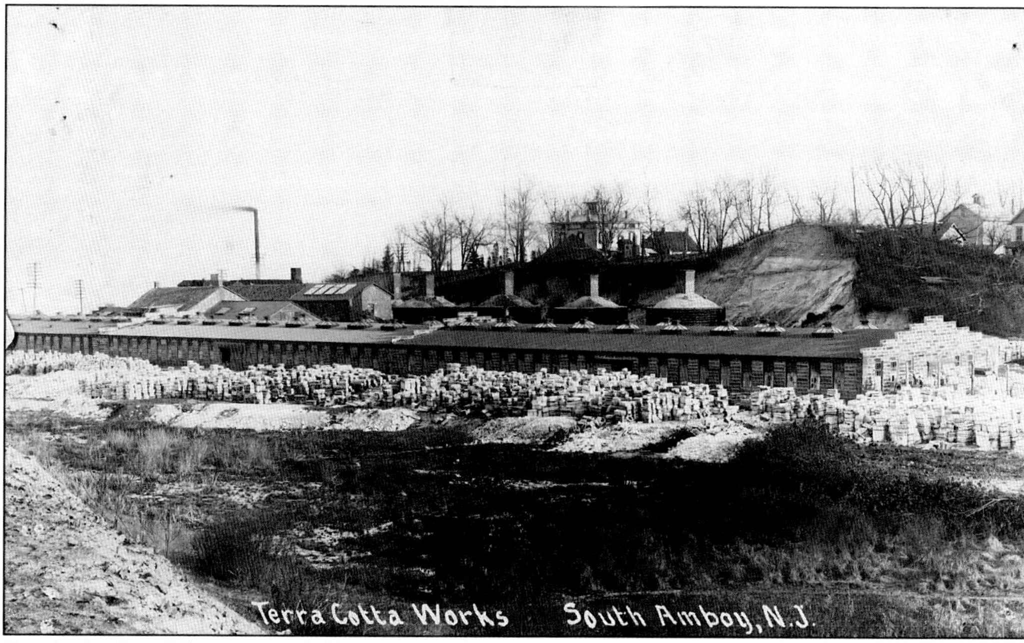

South Amboy, like many of the surrounding towns, made a major industry out of the natural clay that lay beneath its surface. There were three major companies, all located at the south end of Broadway, on a rise called Swan Hill. Although it was one of the major industries, there seem to be few remaining pictures of it.

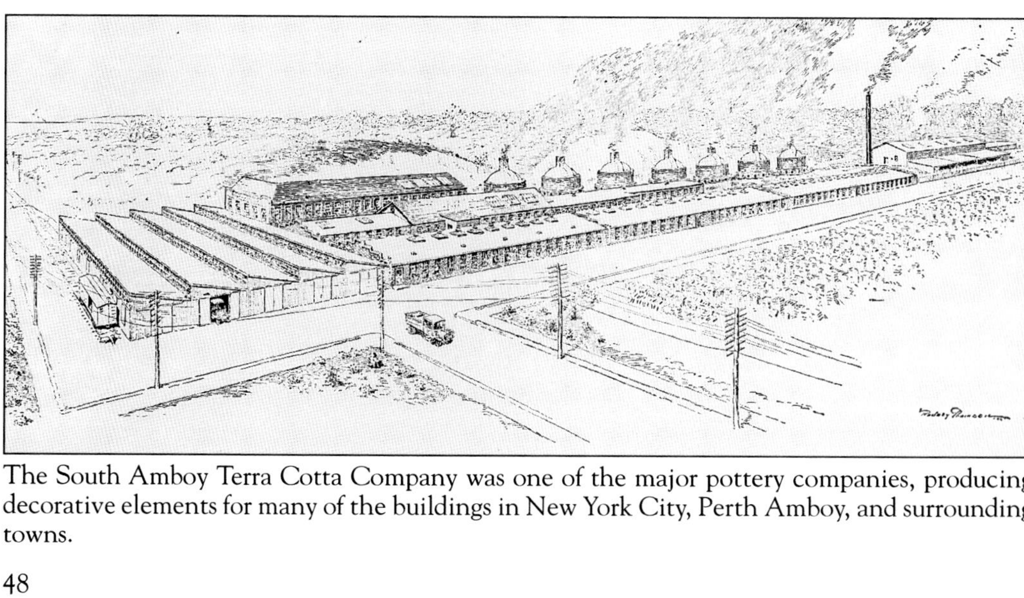

The South Amboy Terra Cotta Company was one of the major pottery companies, producing decorative elements for many of the buildings in New York City, Perth Amboy, and surrounding towns.

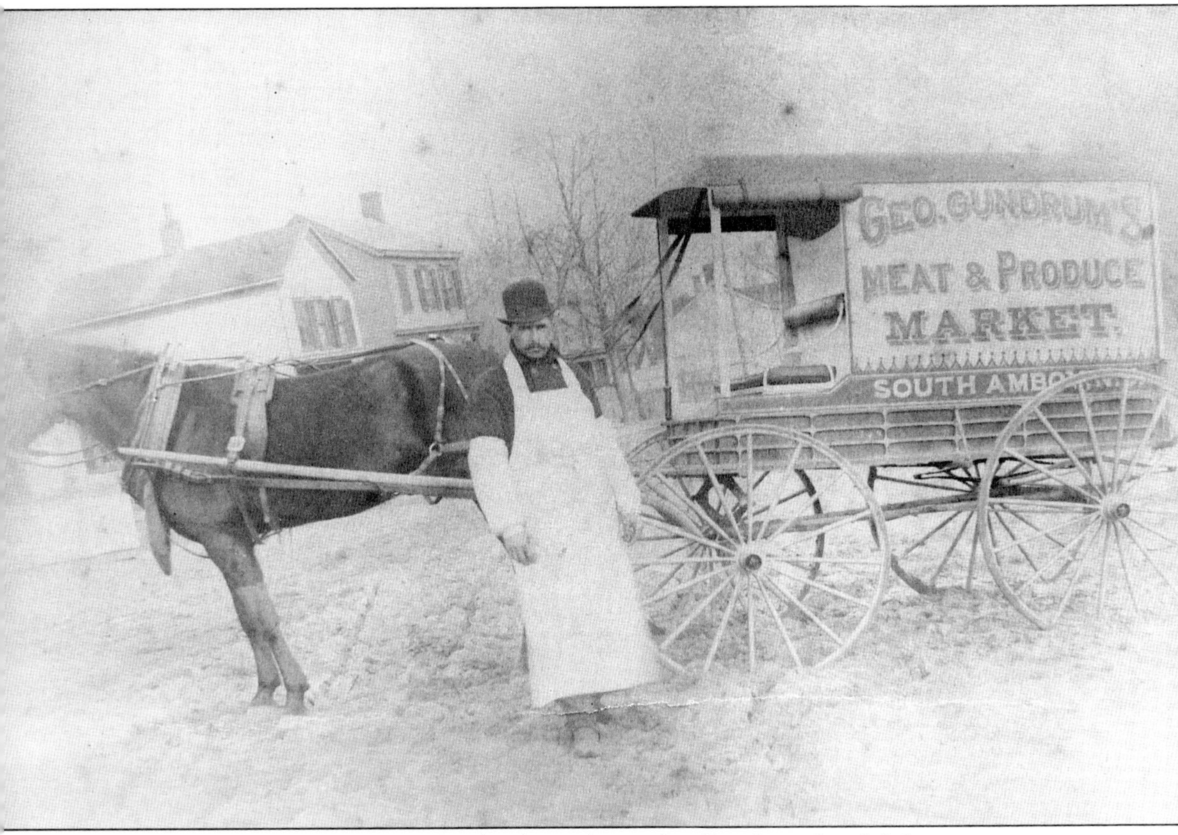

This may be the oldest photo in this book. It shows the Gundrum family's business in meats before the one they are famous for today, the funeral service business. George Gundrum Sr. was called "Butch" for the butcher shop he ran on John Street, just off of Stevens Avenue. He also ran a home repair and contracting business. His son, George Jr., started the funeral home in 1919. It was located on David Street and Broadway before its present location on Bordentown Avenue.

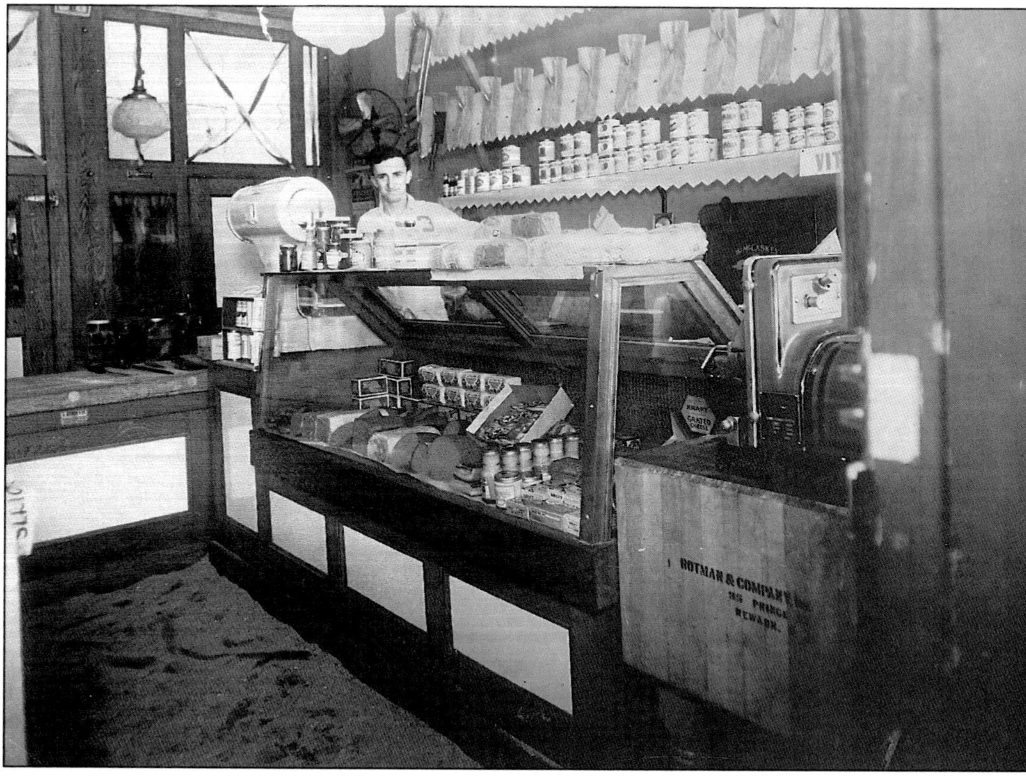

This is Frank Paczkowski inside his first market on Bordentown Avenue, where the offices of Dr. Andrew Tanchyk, dentist, are today. It was an A&P market before Frank started the dynasty that continues as Foodtown, which is owned by his son Edmund.

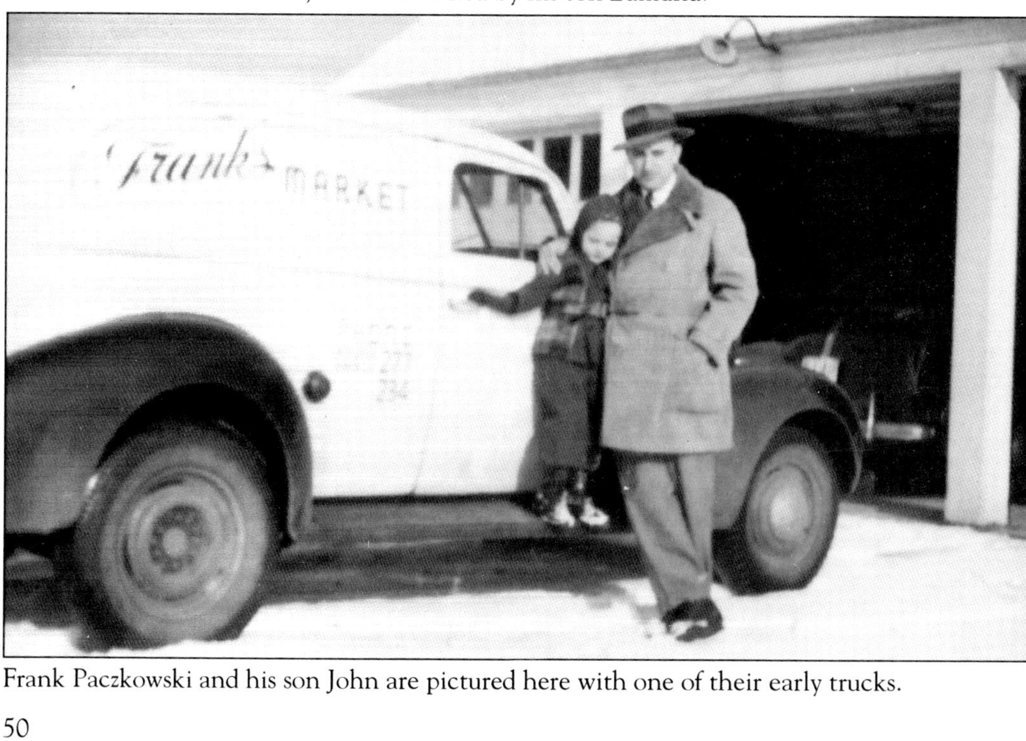

Frank Paczkowski and his son John are pictured here with one of their early trucks.

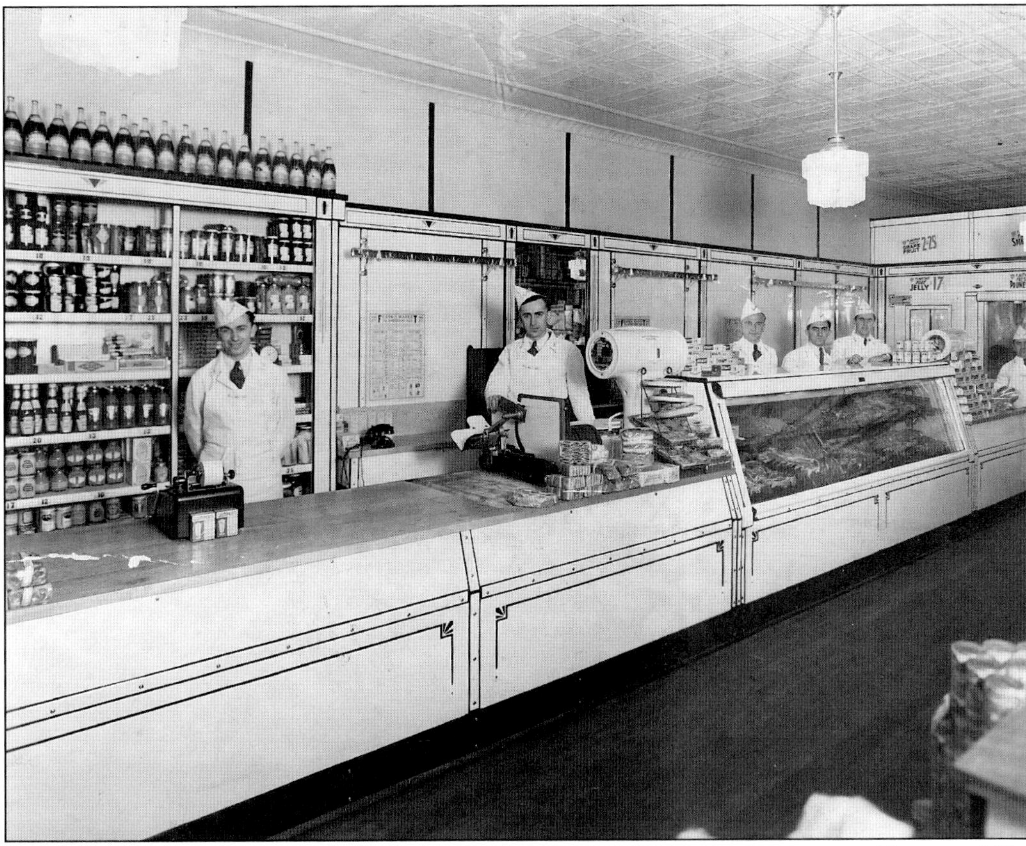

The meat counter at the second Frank's Market (today's Foodtown) is pictured here in 1934, with, from left to right, Gus Potts, Frank Paczkowski, John Kaboski, Stanley Paczkowski, Jack Rose, and Louie Gardner.

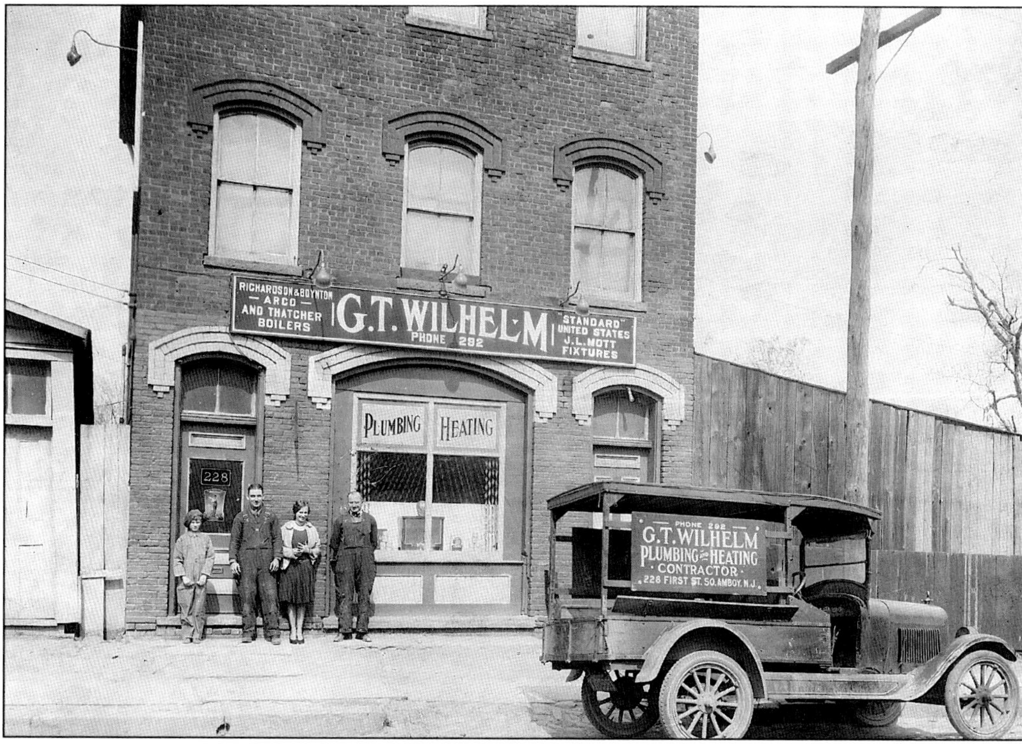

The Wilhelm Building, then a plumbing and heating business on First Street, is in the middle of the block between Stockton Street and Broadway. The child is unknown, but the adults are Dory Wilhelm (the son of founder G.T. Wilhelm), Maude Tice, and John Brennan. The evolution of this building continues in the next picture.

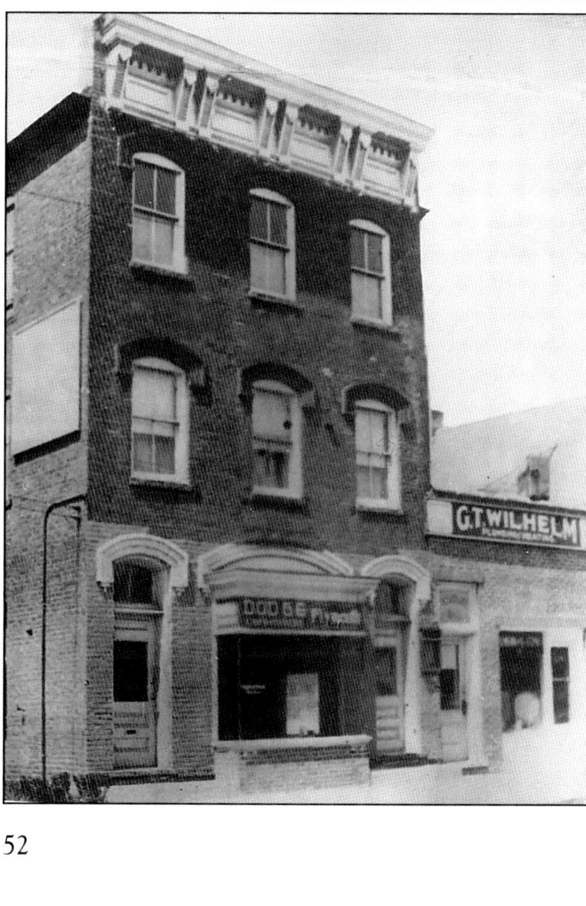

In this photo, a Dodge car dealership has taken up the original building (somewhat off the beaten path, half a block from Broadway), and Wilhelm's has moved to an addition on the right side.

This is the original First Aid Squad headquarters, as indicated by the sign over the garage door to the right. It was located at the Wilhelm Building on First Street. It was also the home of the Rotary Club in Welsh's Hall, upstairs, as well as a heating and air conditioning business.

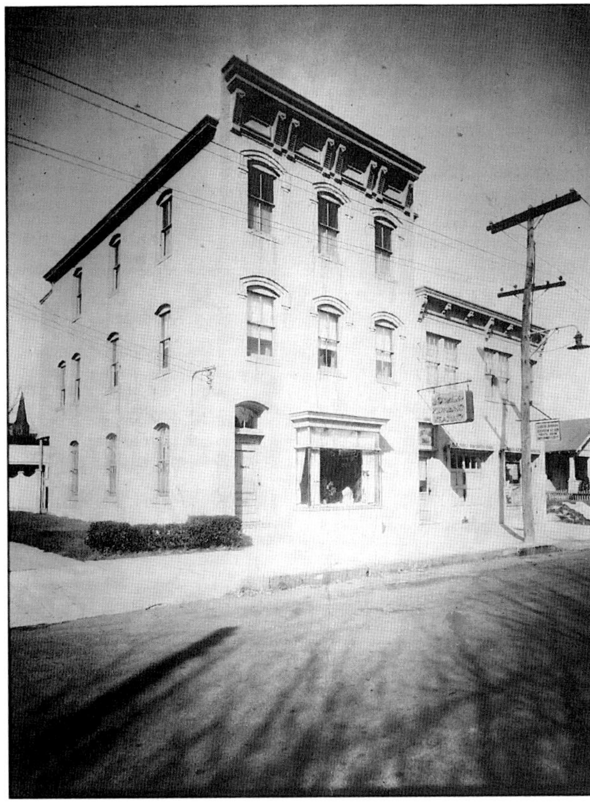

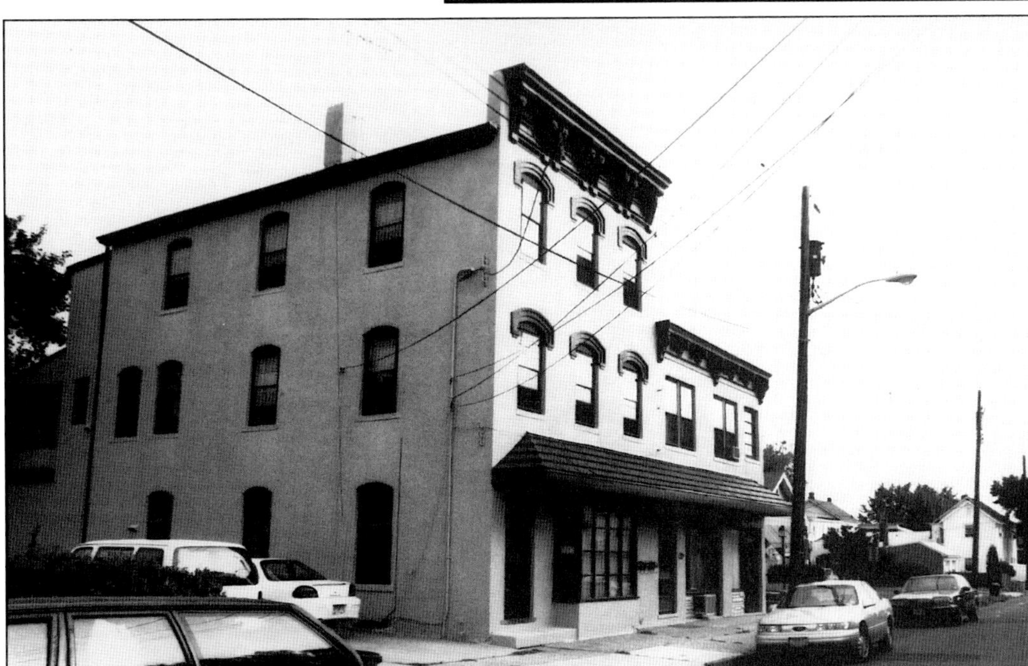

The Wilhelm Building is shown here in 1998, now occupied by Joe Sumski, J and J Aluminum, and apartments.

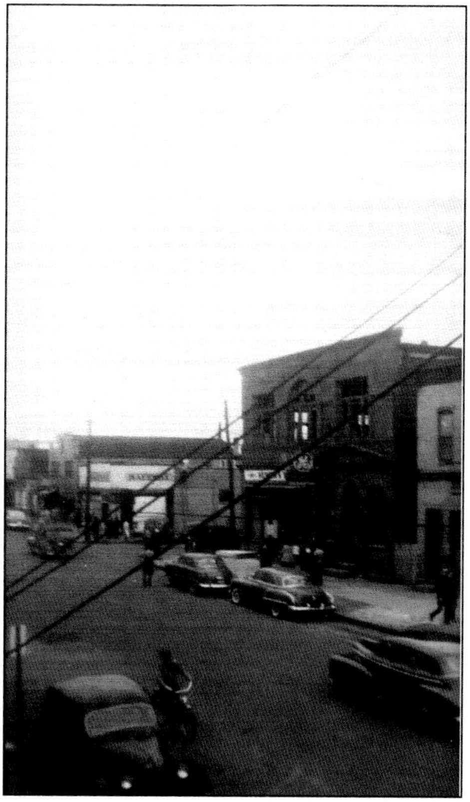

This photo was actually taken just after the 1950 explosion, and shows Broadway looking north toward the Safeway and the former offices of the First National Bank, the storefront with the three arched windows and the peaked-roof facade.

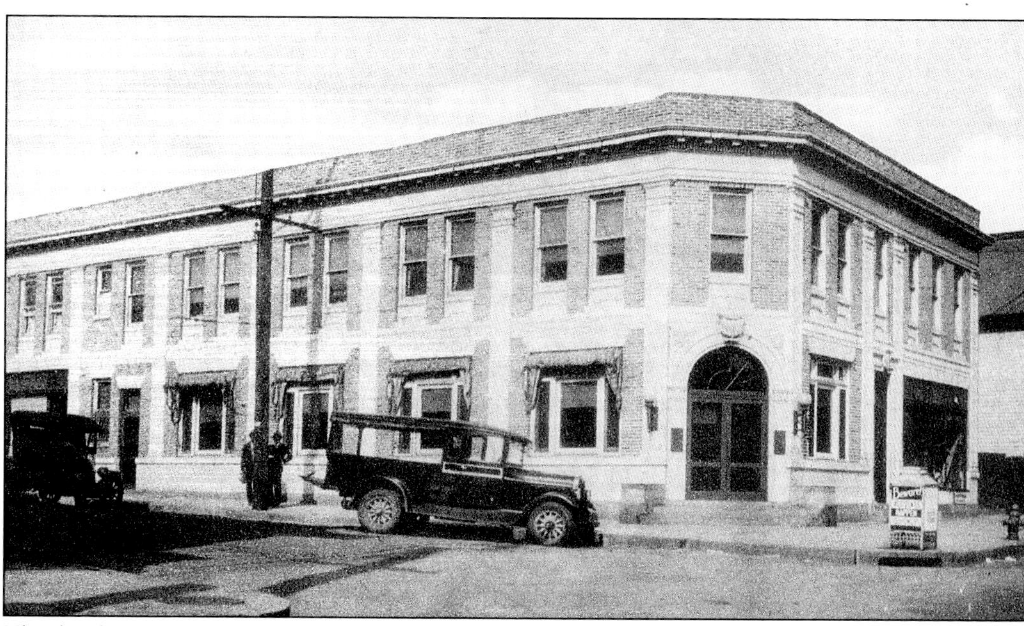

This bank on Broadway at Augusta Street became a branch of First Union Bank in 1997. It has gone through several changes, but started out as the South Amboy Trust Co. It was built by Allen C. Parisen, who had a drug store on the right.

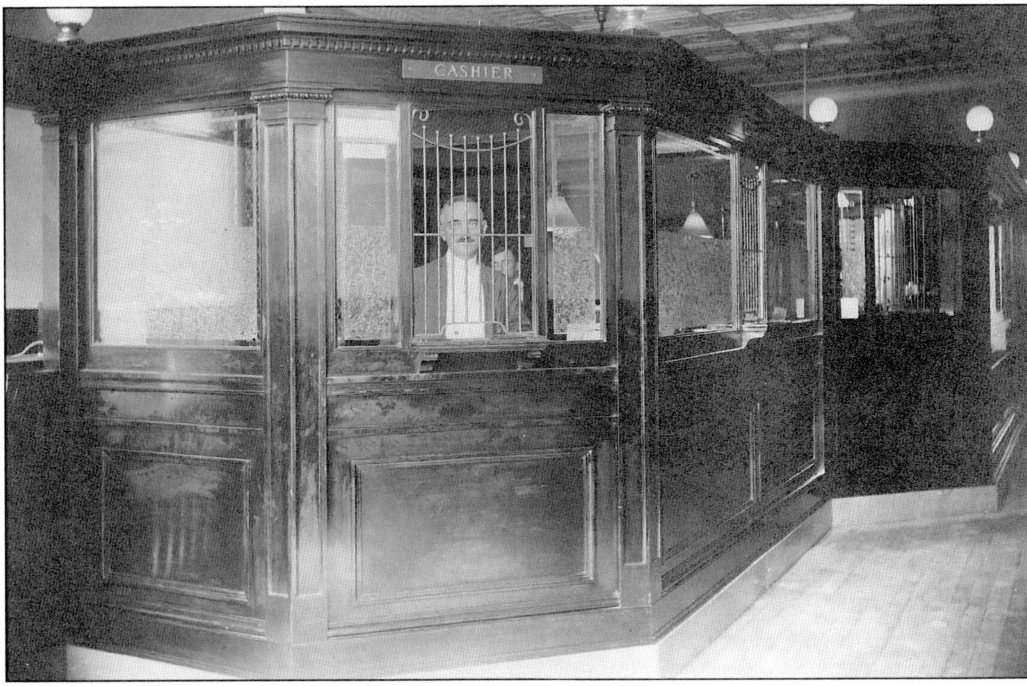

This is the teller's window inside the First National Bank when it was on Broadway at David Street, as seen in the photograph at the top of the previous page.

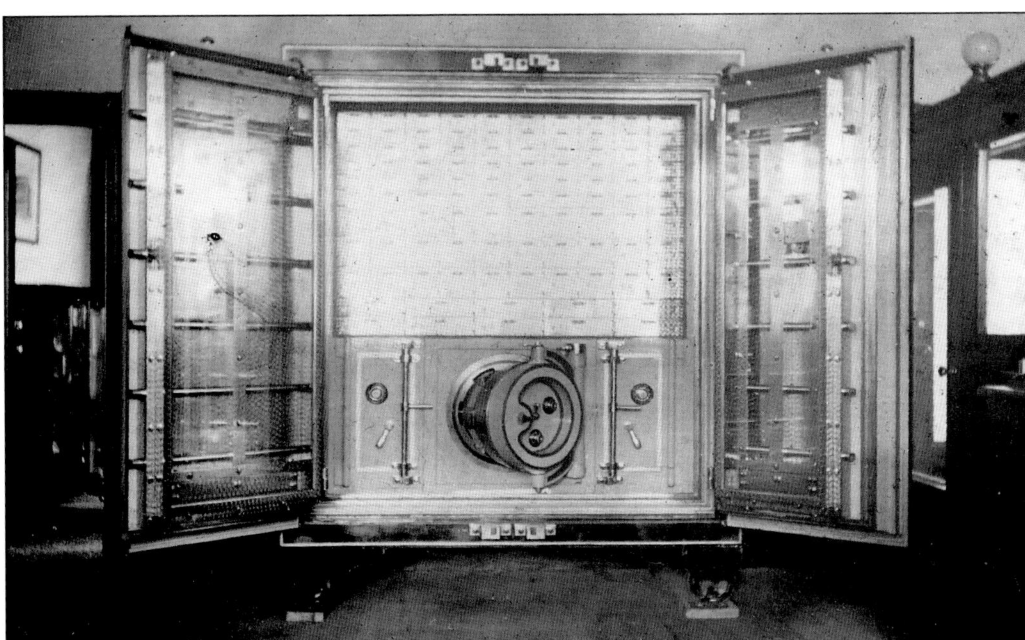

Here is the vault inside the First National Bank.

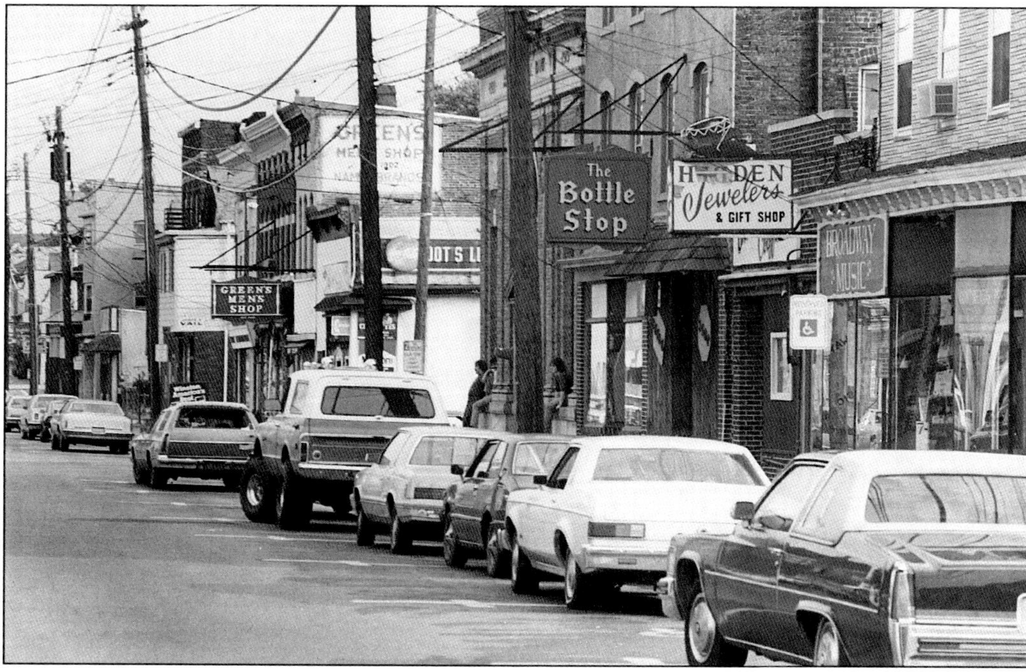

Although this photo was only taken in 1983, much has changed already. Green's Mens Shop, Reiner's Hardware, the Bottle Stop, Holden Jewelers, and Broadway Music are all gone, and the facades are being redone in the turn-of-the-century-look restoration project started by Mayor John T. O'Leary.

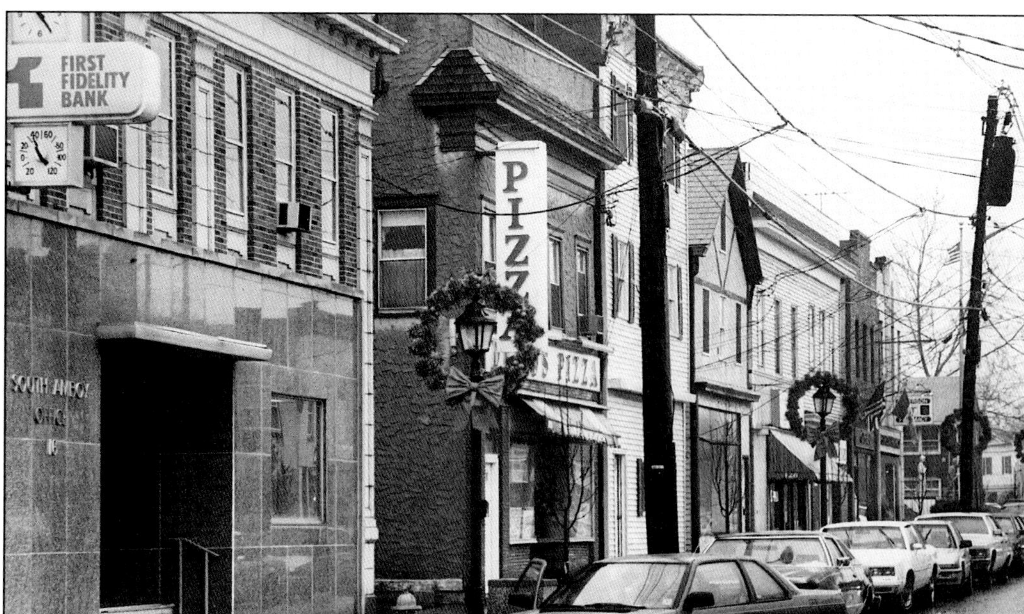

This photo, also from 1983 at Christmas, shows the Trust Co., at the time a First Fidelity bank, at the corner of Broadway and Augusta. It sports a marble facade that has since been removed.

The A.C. Parisen Pharmacy is pictured here, where Green's Mens Shop was later located, on Broadway near David Street.

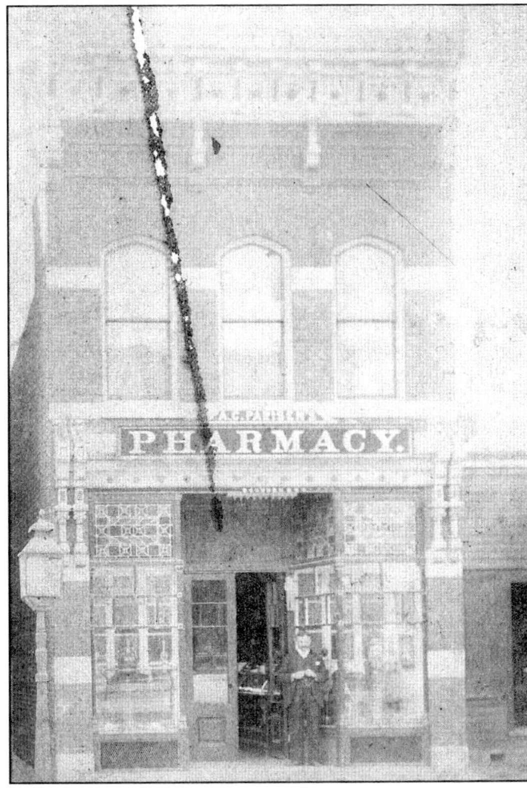

This is a view of the interior of Parisen's pharmacy, *c.* 1900, with Allen C. Parisen on the far right. His father was killed at Antietam during the Civil War.

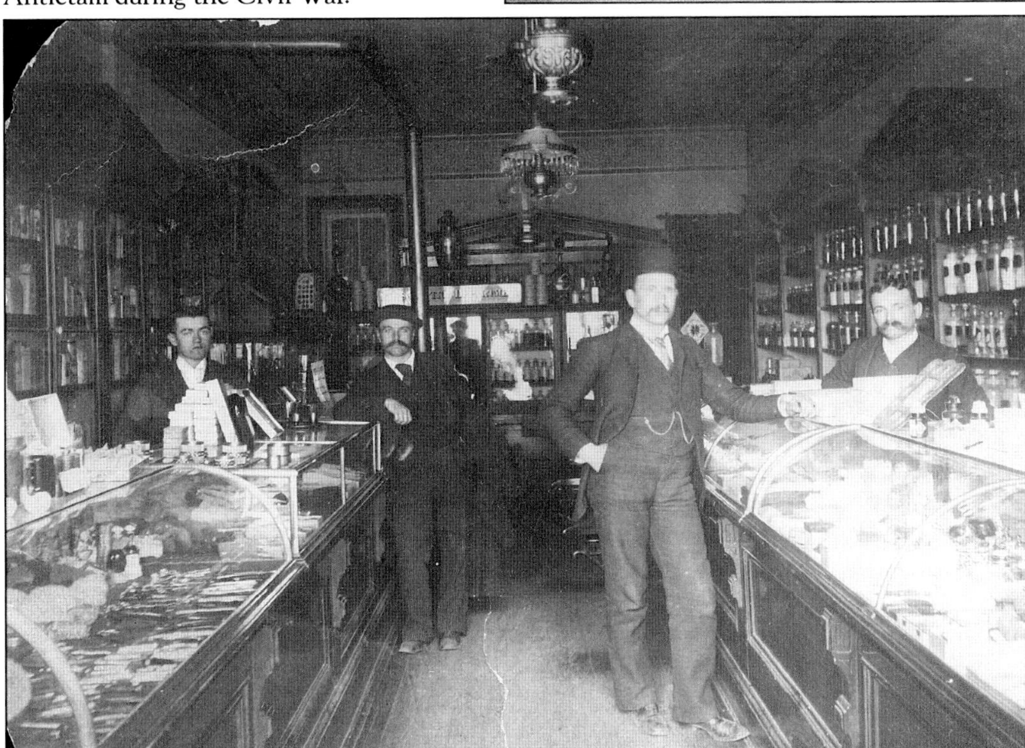

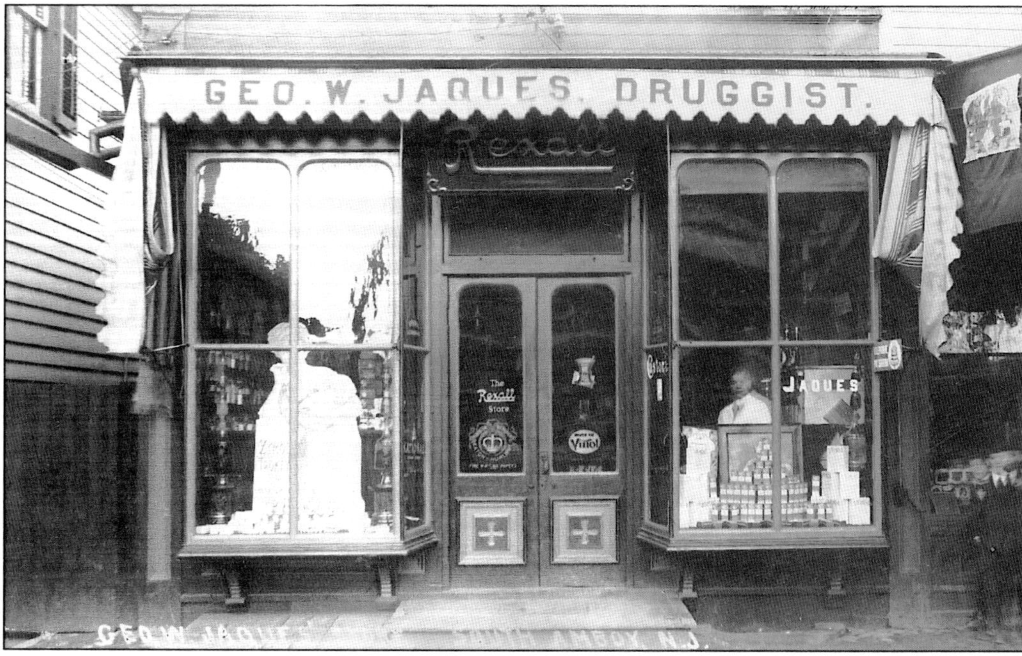

Here is Jaques Drug Store, c. 1908, located next to the present-day Landmark Tavern on Broadway, near Augusta Street. In the window is Walter Peterson, who later started the pharmacy that bears his name, shown in the photograph below when it was still owned by Dr. J.C. Albright.

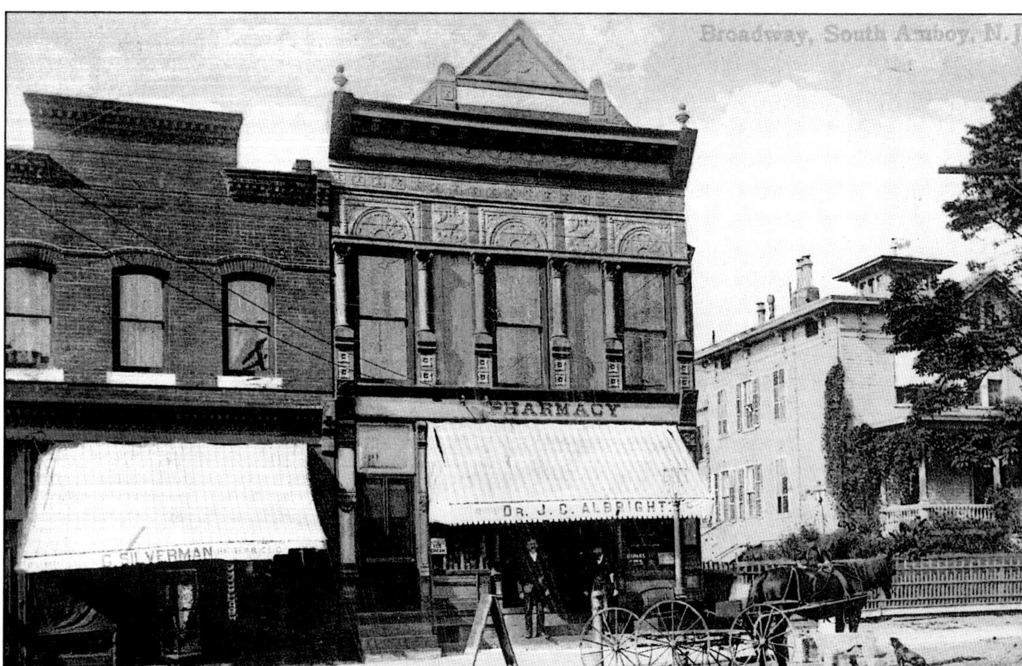

Albright's Pharmacy, the predecessor to Peterson's, was next to city hall. To the right is the building that preceded city hall, which was once a YMCA.

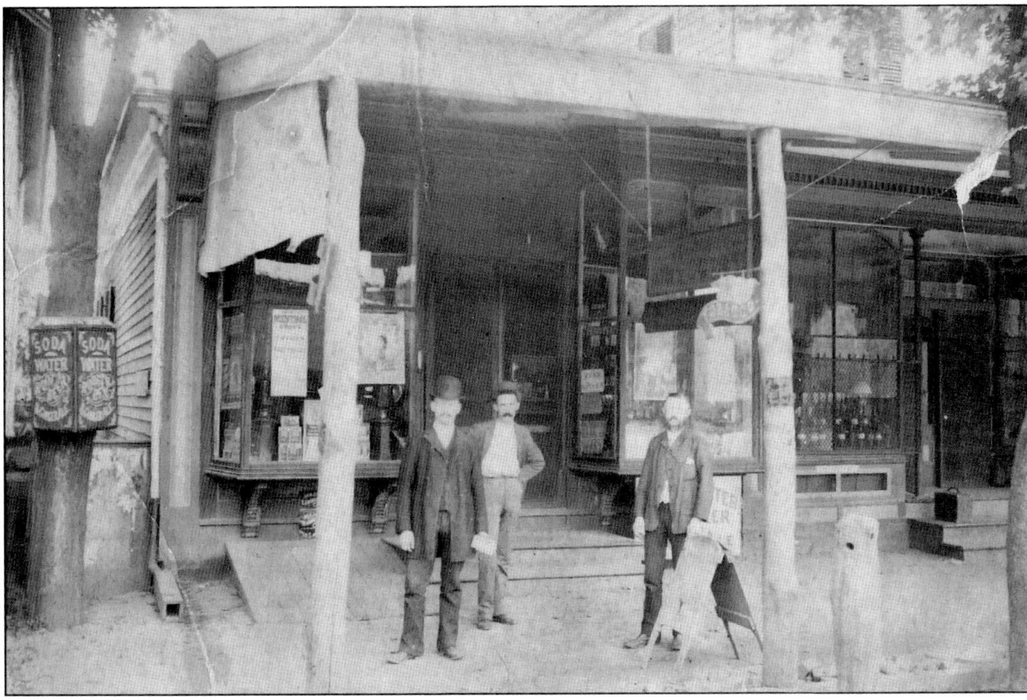

This is another shot of Jaques Drug Store, next to the Landmark Tavern.

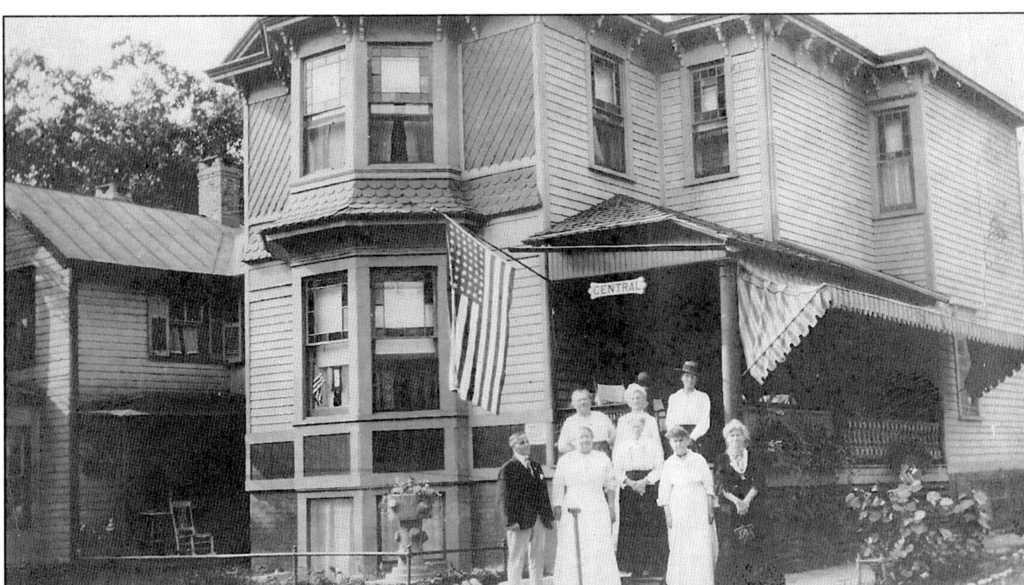

Central House, one of the city's many hotels around the turn of the century, was located on the corner of Augusta Street and Broadway, on what is now a parking lot across from the First Union Bank.

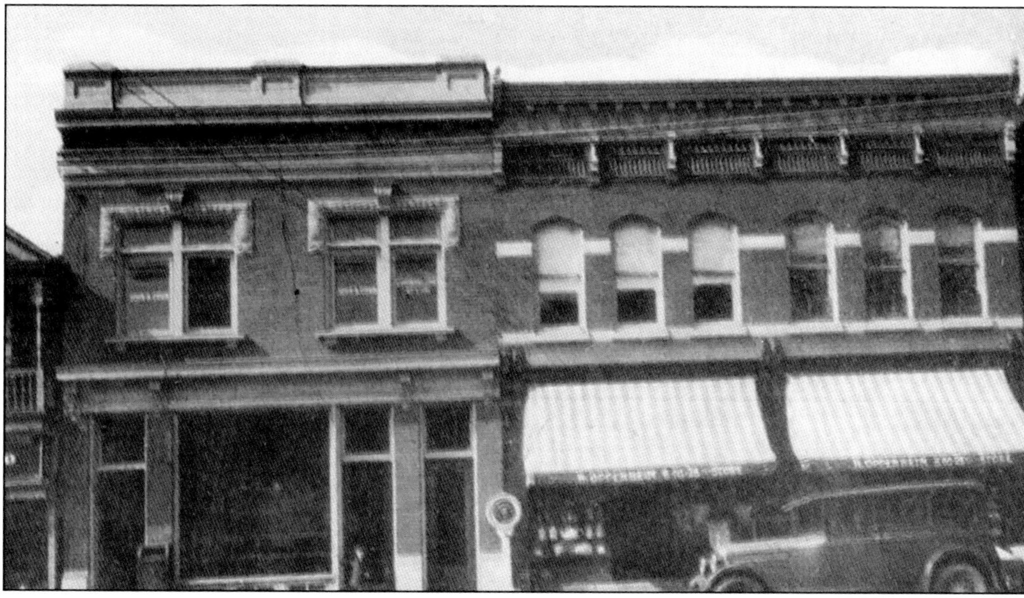

These buildings still stand in the middle of Broadway between Henry and David Streets. In this *c.* 1920s photo, Oppenheim's Five and Dime and the city's second post office occupy the buildings. The second floor of the building on the left housed the city's first library from 1914–16, when it was operated by the South Amboy Woman's Club.

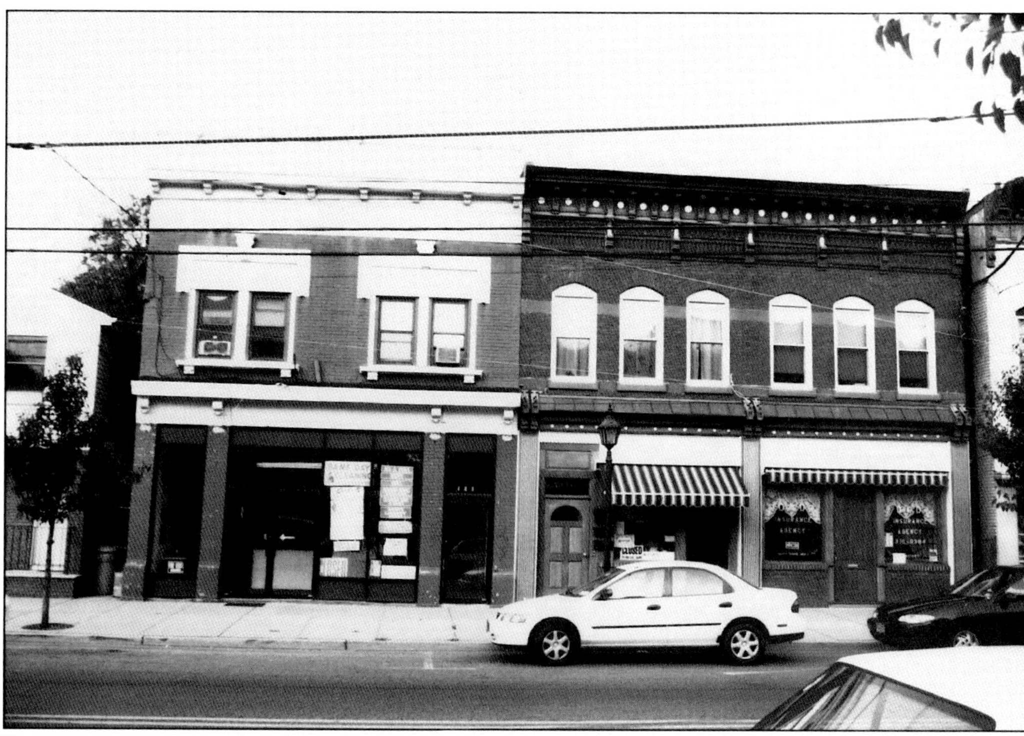

Present-day shops in the above building include an insurance agent and dry-cleaning business.

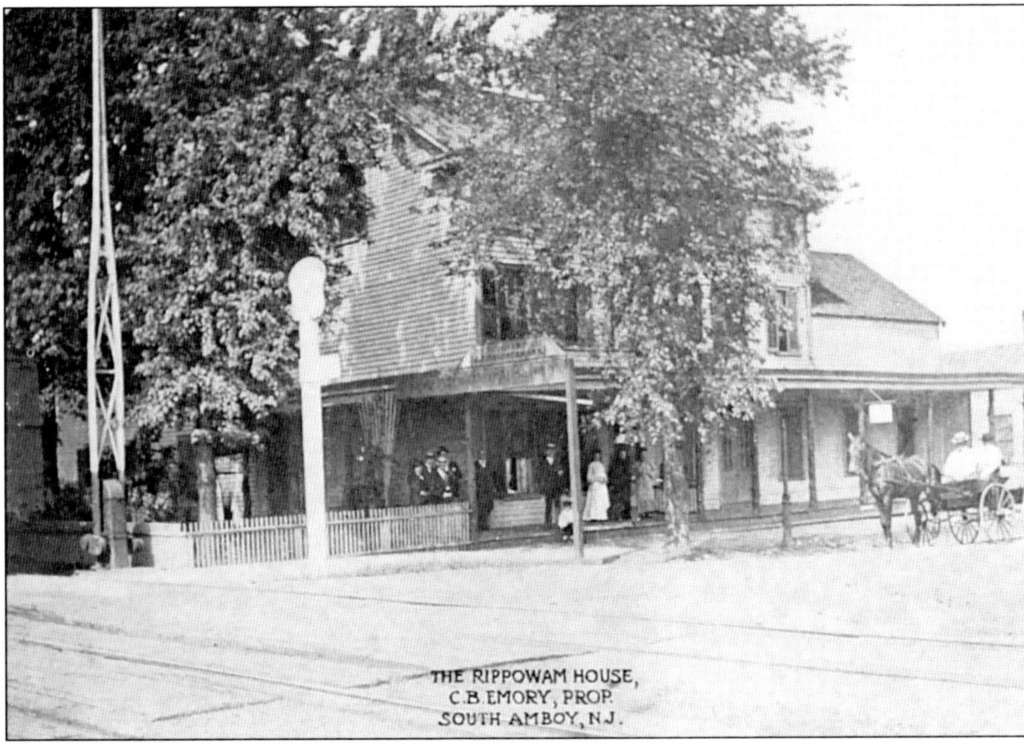

Here is Rippowam House, which was located on Augusta Street at the end of Mason Avenue. There is currently a commuter parking lot at this location.

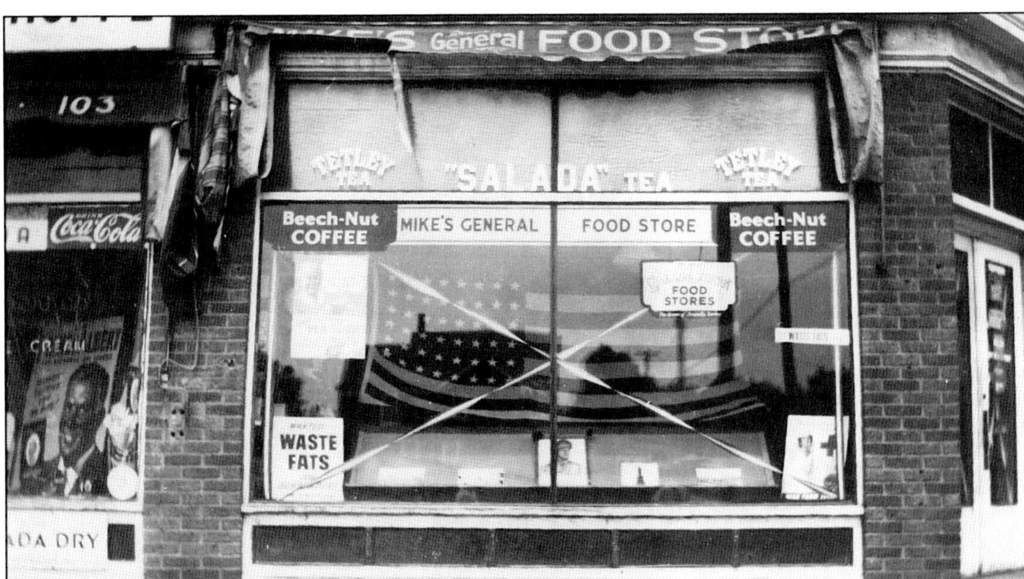

Mike's General Store, on Stevens Avenue at the corner of David Street, was owned by Mike Rzepka. The store essentially sold meats and groceries. It opened in 1936, and this photo was taken that year. Today it is the South Amboy Deli.

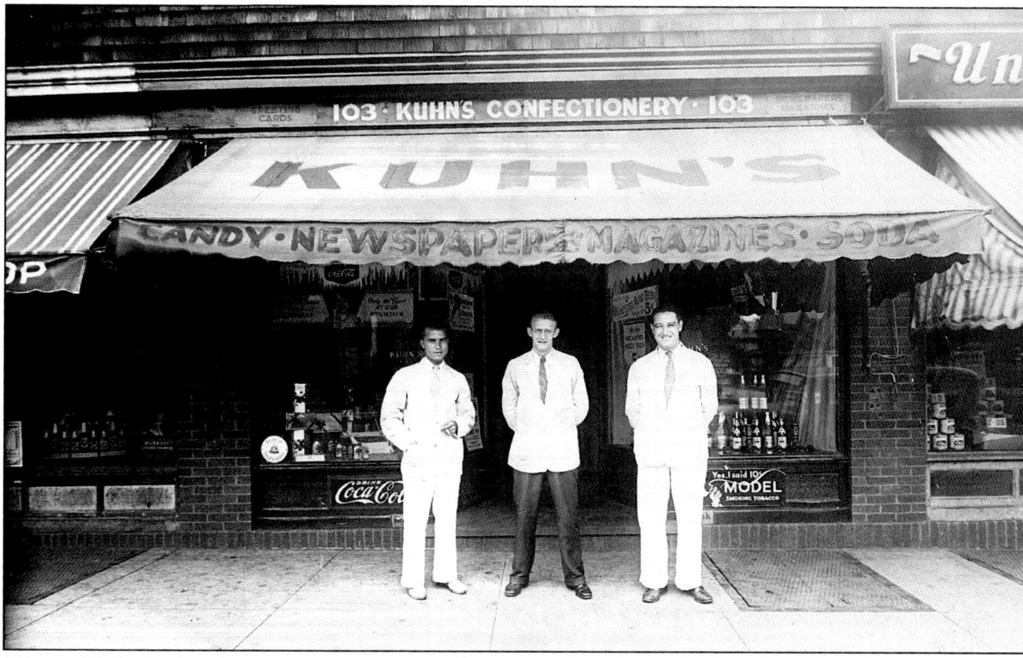

This is Kuhn's Confectionery, next to Mike's General Store on Stevens Avenue. The men in the photo are Pete Gretico, who owned a barber shop next door on the left, Ed Grimley, and Frank "Ruby" Kuhn.

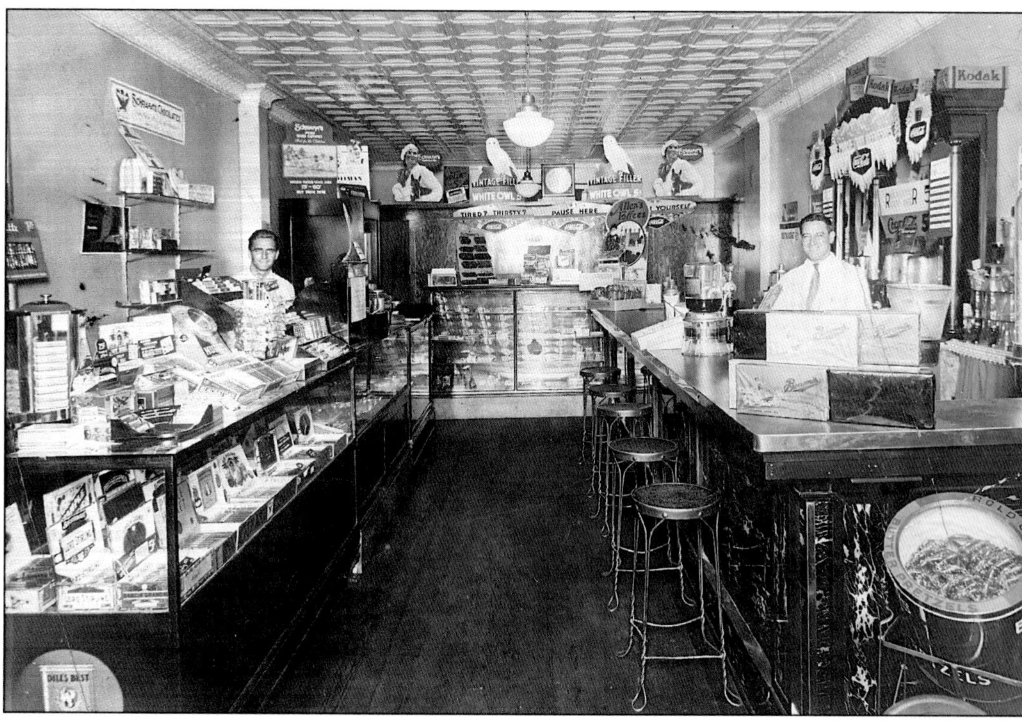

Here is a look inside Kuhn's Confectionery, with John Grimley on the left and Frank "Ruby" Kuhn, the proprietor, on the right. There is a substantial selection of cigars in the case on the left, demonstrating that what is old will be new again, considering the cigar fad of the 1990s.

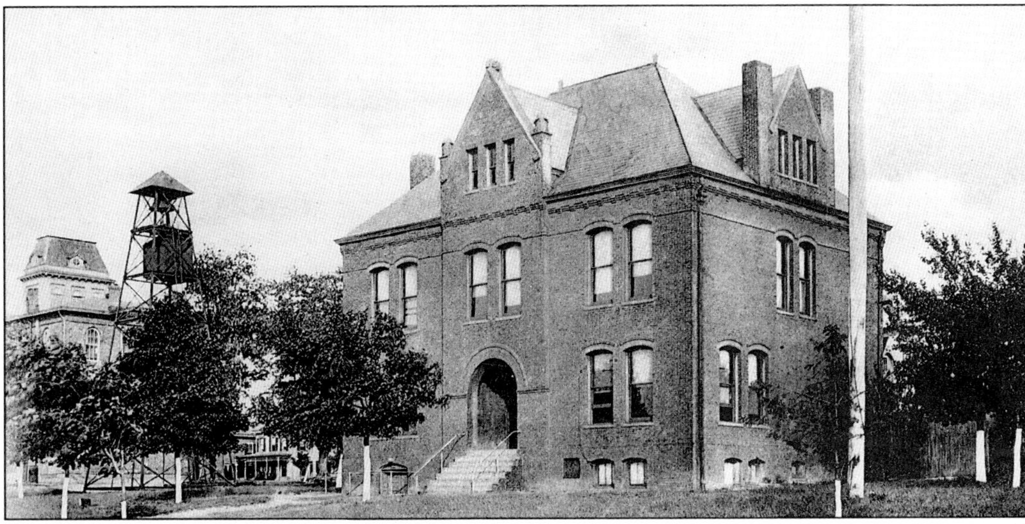

The original city hall was located on the corner of Stevens Avenue and John Street. The cupola of School Number One is barely visible at the far left.

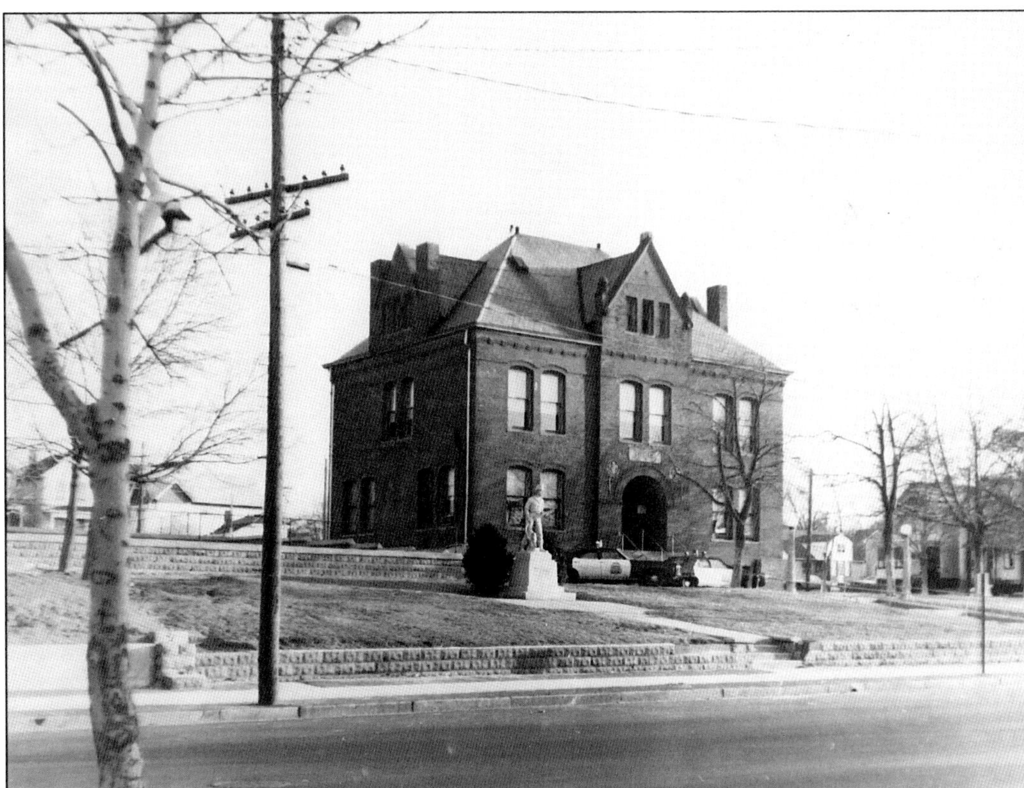

Here is the first city hall from another angle, taken in 1970.

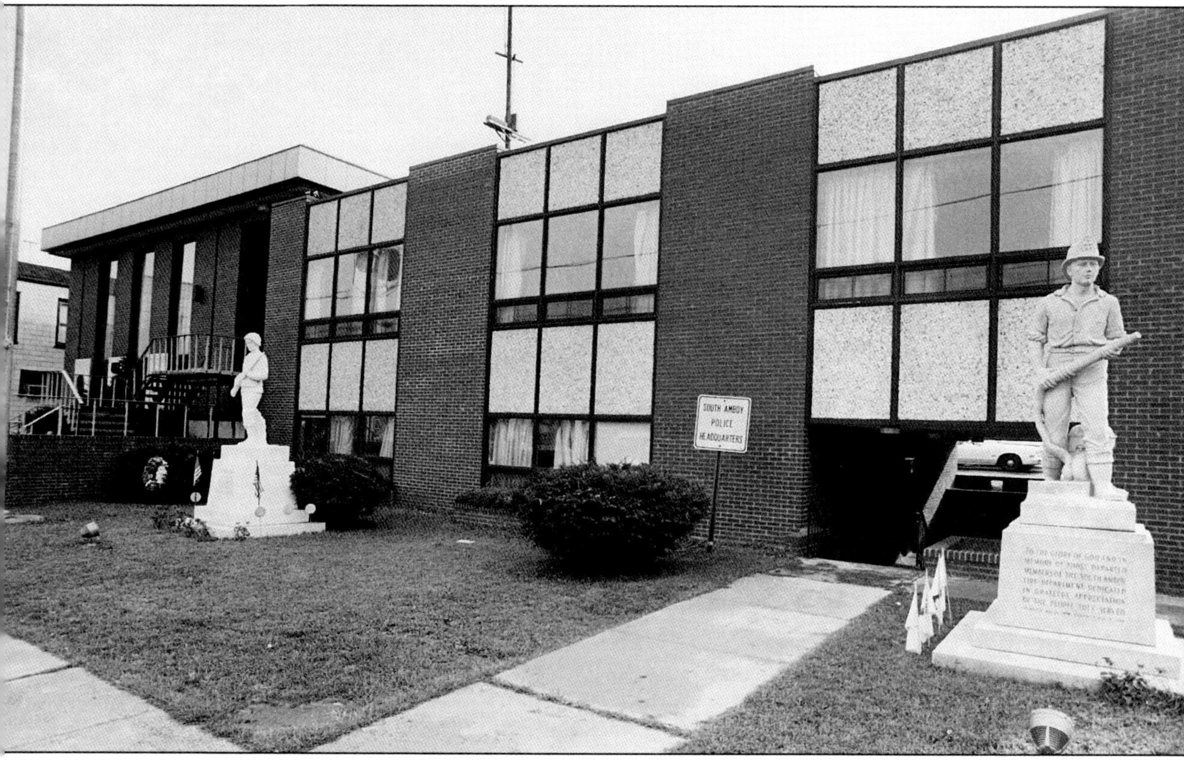

The present city hall was built in 1971. This photo was taken in 1983, before the renovations that would give it the same turn-of-the-century look as the rest of downtown.

Three

PROTECT AND SERVE

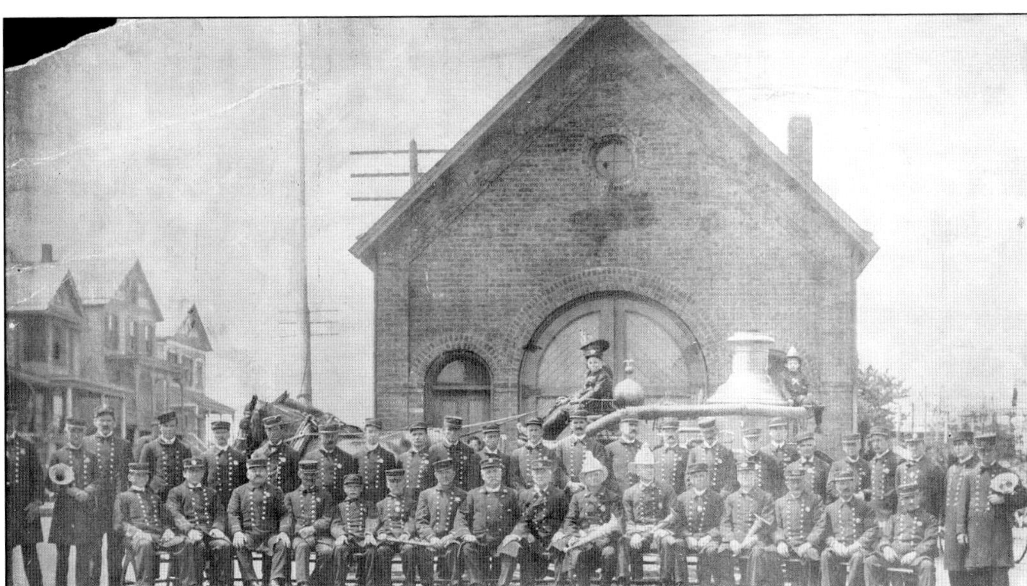

This chapter explores South Amboy's fire, police, and first aid services, and some of the disasters they faced. This the original Protection Fire House, in 1910, which was located on what is today a concrete island, at the intersection of Main and Feltus Streets, across from Jag's White Eagle bar.

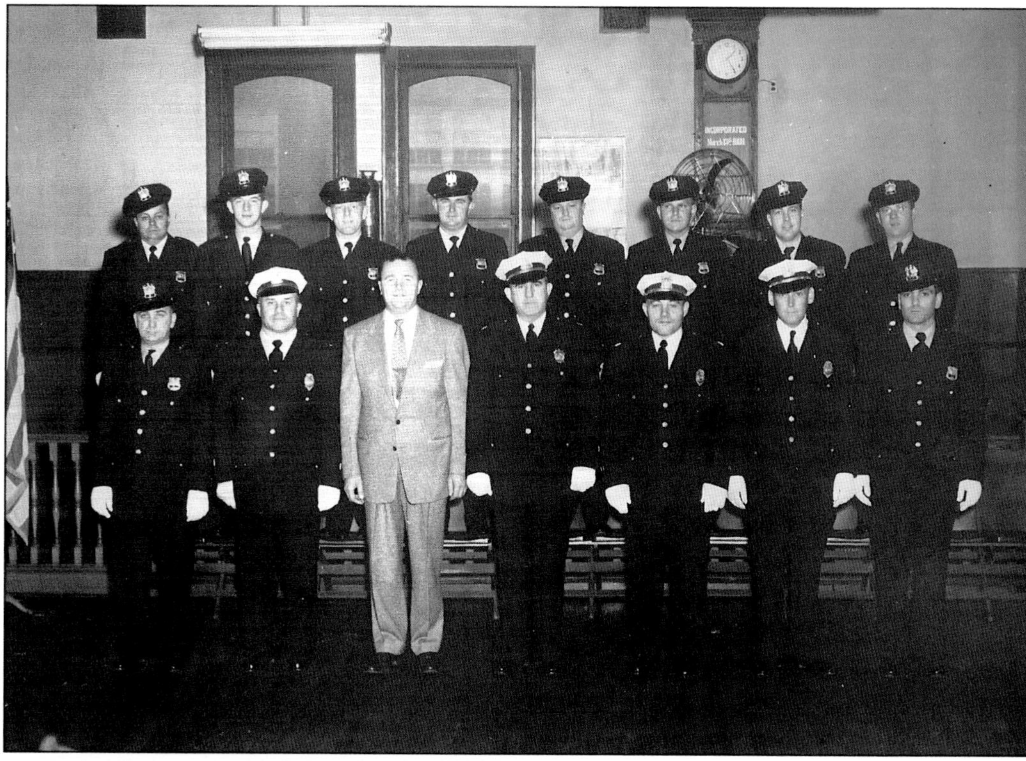

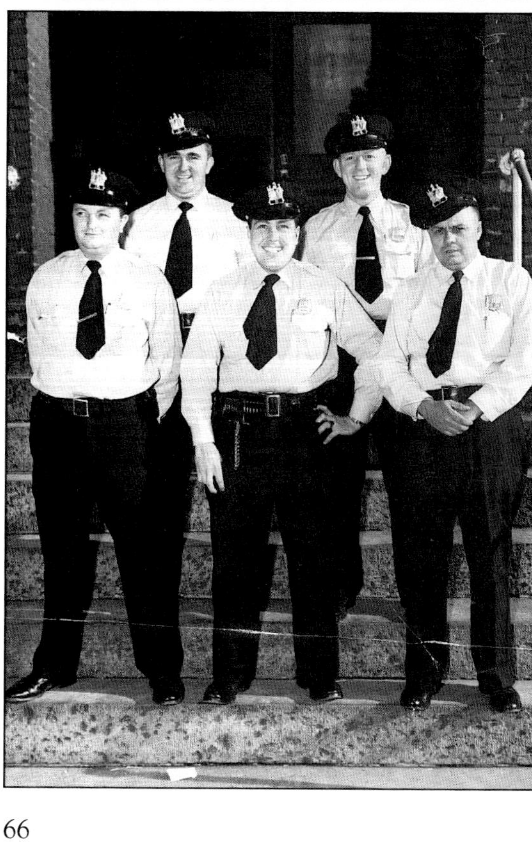

Surprisingly, not many photos exist of the police force. This is one of the few. From left to right, they are as follows: (front row) Edward McKeon, Walt Rogers, Councilman Al Jankowski, Vincent Abatiello, unidentified, Ray Mundy, and Anthony Tarallo; (back row) Charles Rea, James Tedesco, Leroy Kurtz, Edward O'Leary, Bill Schwarick, Ed Orzulski, Charles Travinsky, and Jack Duggan.

On the steps of city hall, from left to right, are the following: (front row) Charles Travinsky, Leroy Kurtz, and Charles Rea; (back row) William Schwarick and Edward O'Leary.

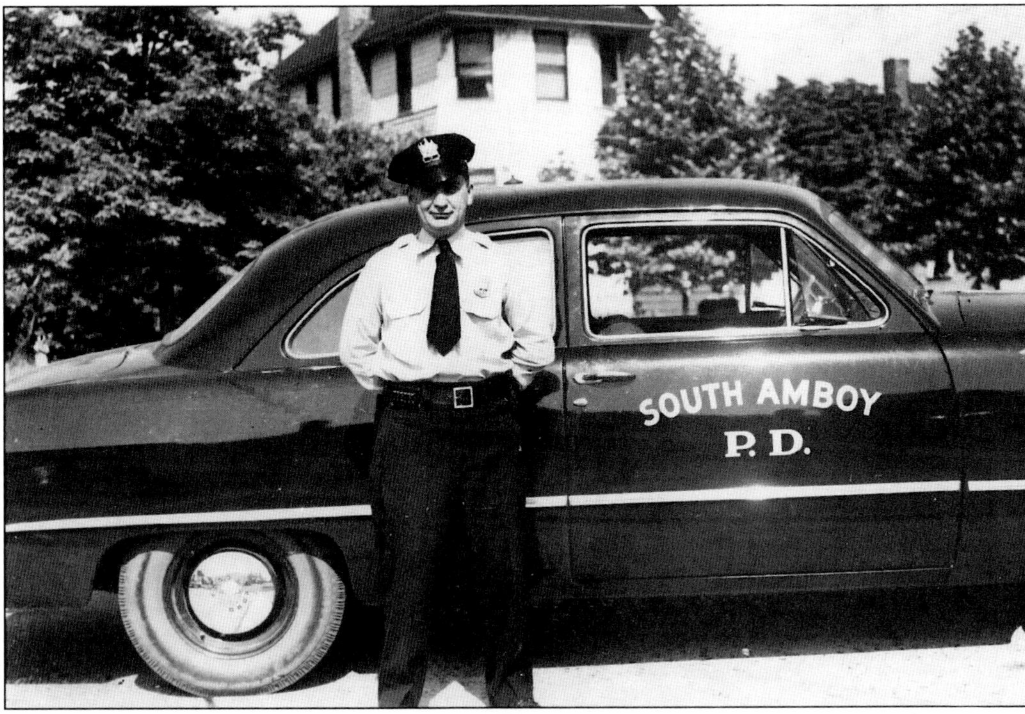

Captain Edward McKeon is pictured here with a vintage car, *c.* 1940s, at Pine Avenue and Portia Street.

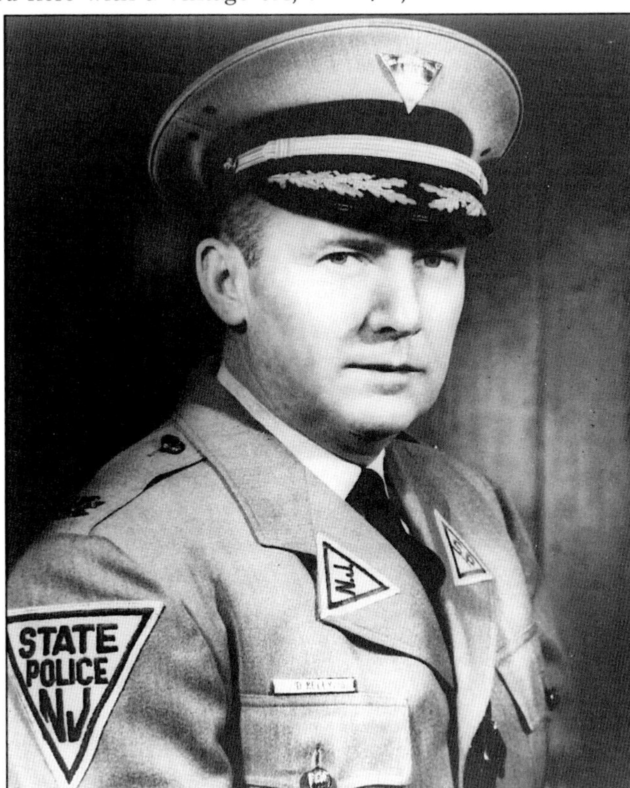

Colonel David B. Kelly was the seventh superintendent (or head) of the entire New Jersey State Police from 1965 through 1974. His distinguished career included attaining the rank of brigadier general in the U.S. Army Reserve, earning two Silver Stars, two Purple Hearts, and a Distinguished Service medal for his military service. He founded D.B. Kelly Associates, a security and investigations firm. Colonel Kelly died in 1997.

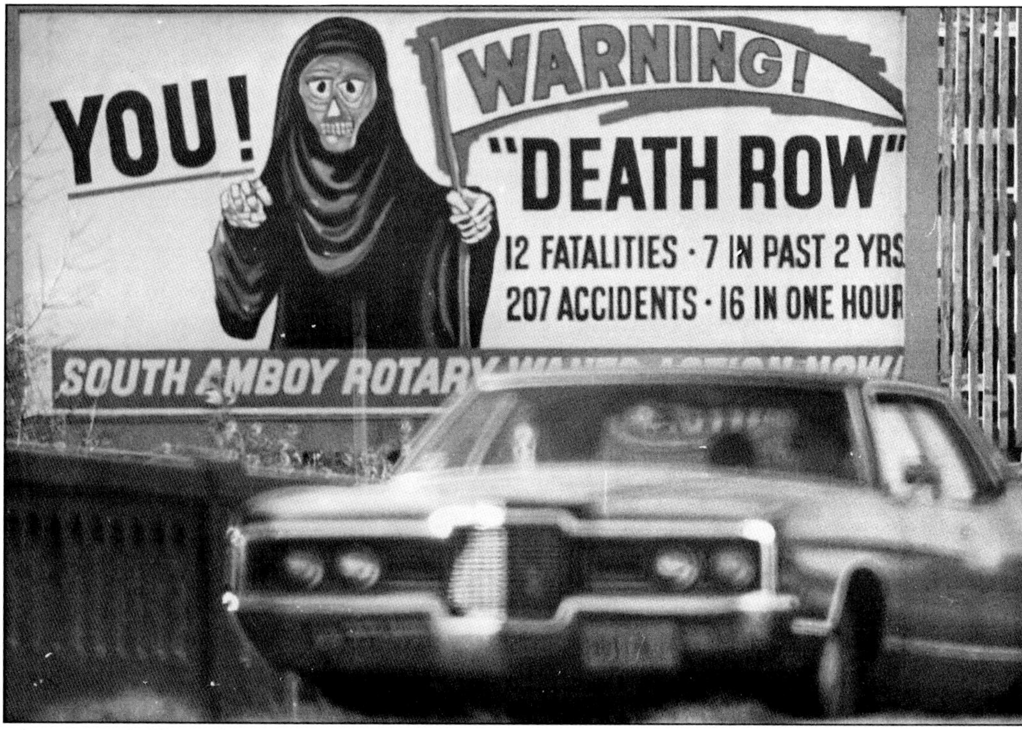

This was a billboard on Route 35 at the junction with Route 9 in late 1974. With little or no subtlety, it was intended to warn motorists of a hazardous turn.

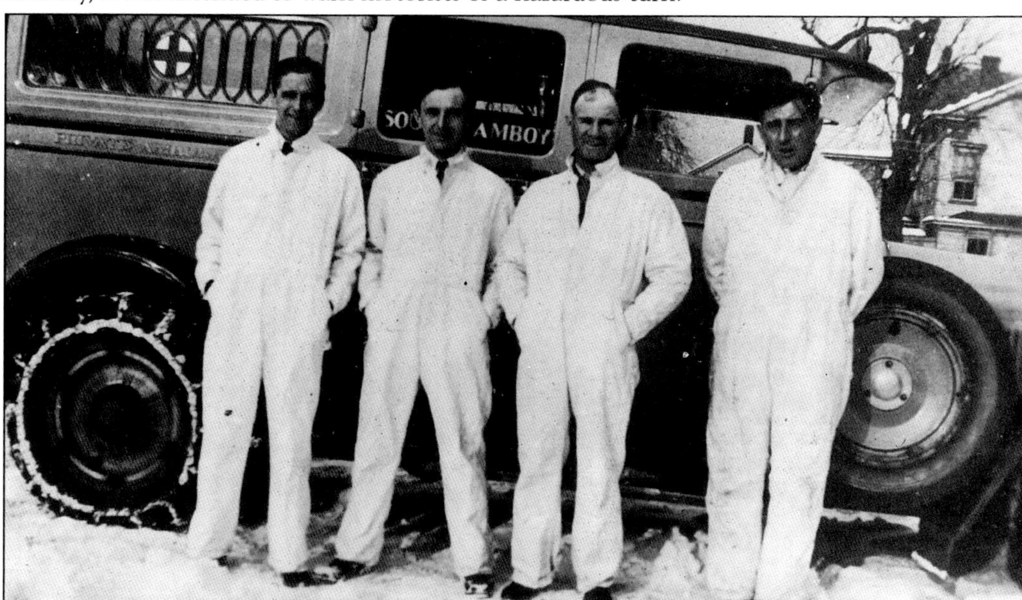

If there was an accident in the 1930s, these guys might be coming to help. This may be the first photo taken of the South Amboy First Aid and Safety Squad, from 1933. The vehicle shown was definitely their first ambulance. It was somewhat ominous, as it was a converted hearse (and supposedly contained a working sink). In front of the ambulance are John Grimley, Mike Szraga, Leo Freeman, and George Kurtz.

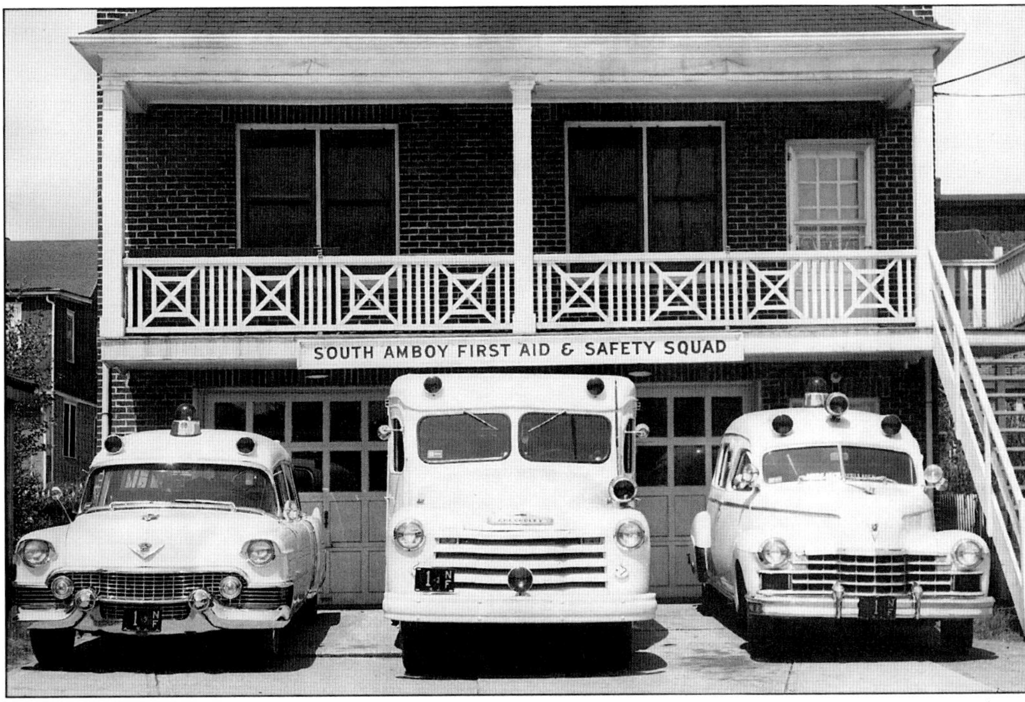

This is the second First Aid Squad headquarters, on First Street just a few doors from Broadway. The original First Aid Squad headquarters is pictured on the top of p. 53. There is conflicting information about whether the squad was formed in 1930 or 1931. It is still standing and bears some resemblance to this appearance.

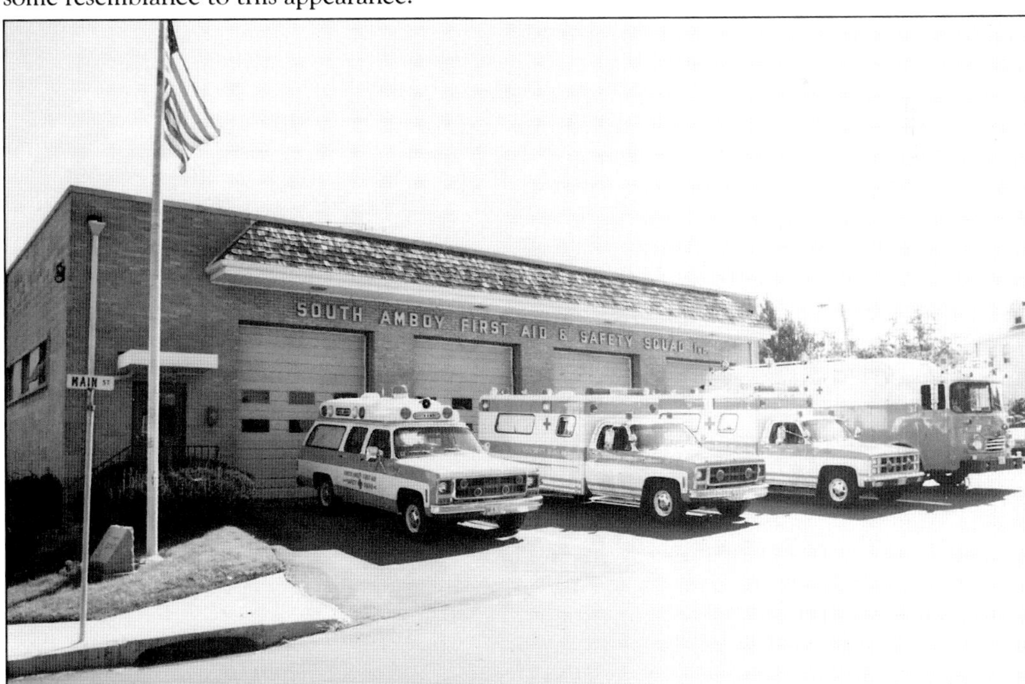

The current First Aid Squad building, on Main Street, is shown here in the 1970s.

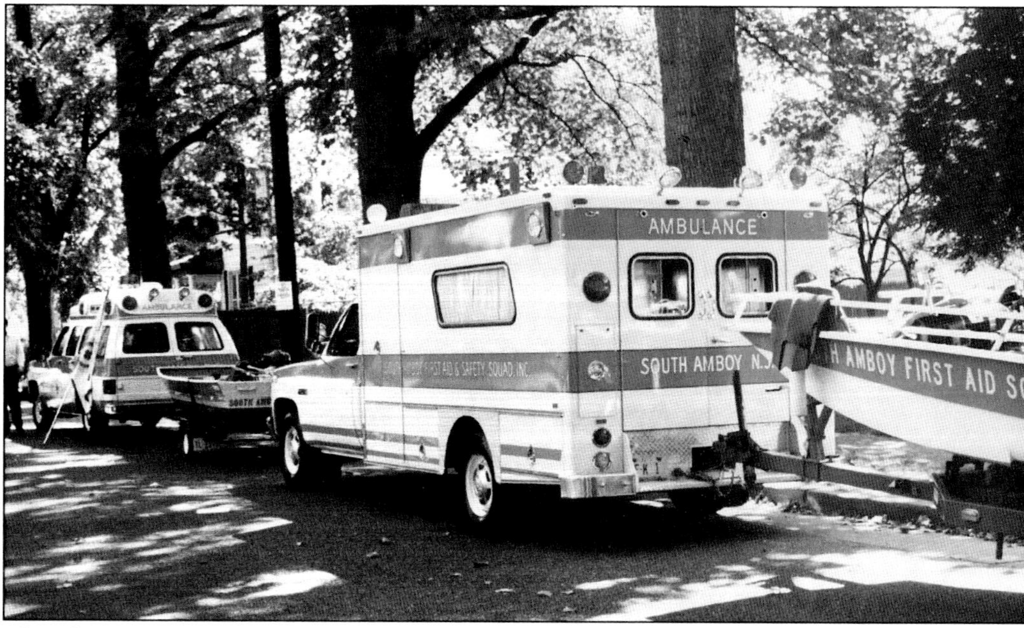

This photo was actually taken at a parade in Freehold, but it shows one of the challenges to the squad of being on a bay—boats were required for the occasional water rescue.

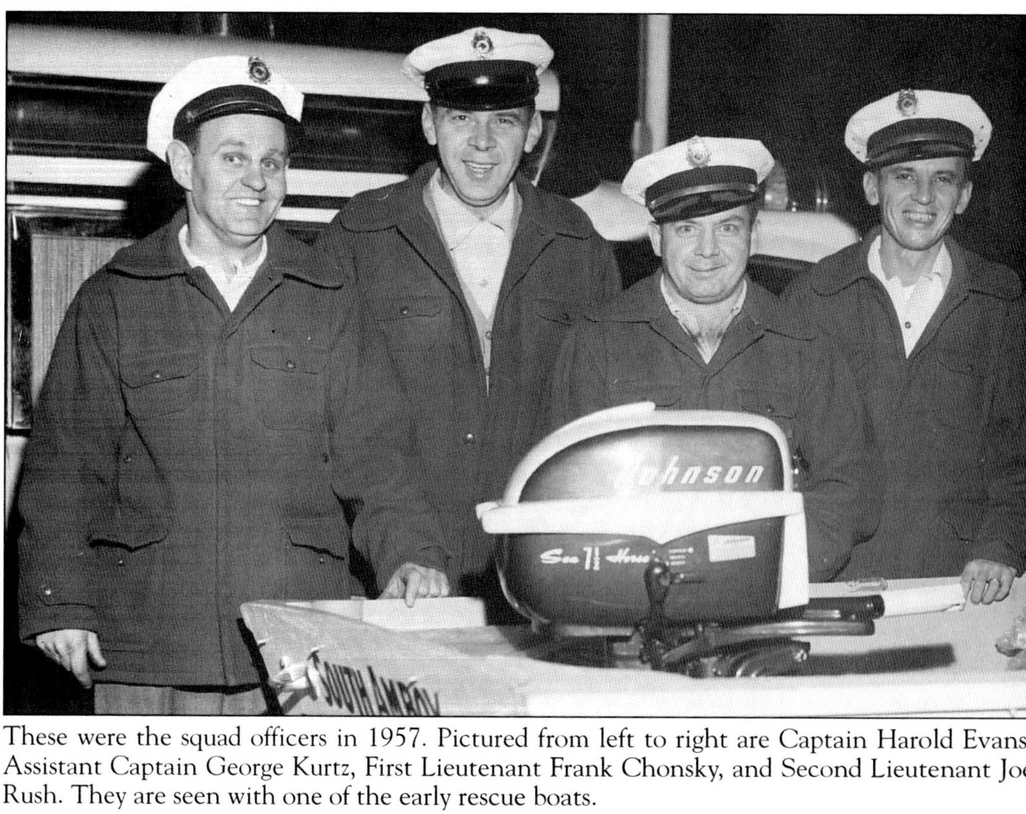

These were the squad officers in 1957. Pictured from left to right are Captain Harold Evans, Assistant Captain George Kurtz, First Lieutenant Frank Chonsky, and Second Lieutenant Joe Rush. They are seen with one of the early rescue boats.

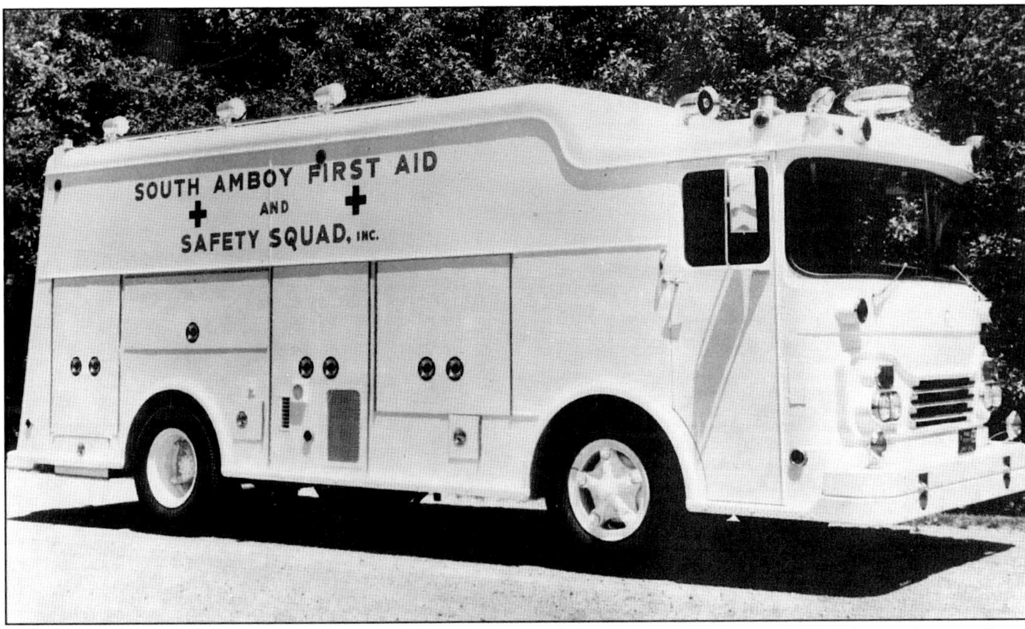

A 1963 Gertenslager, the squad's "crash rig," carried emergency equipment and supplies and was in service until 1982.

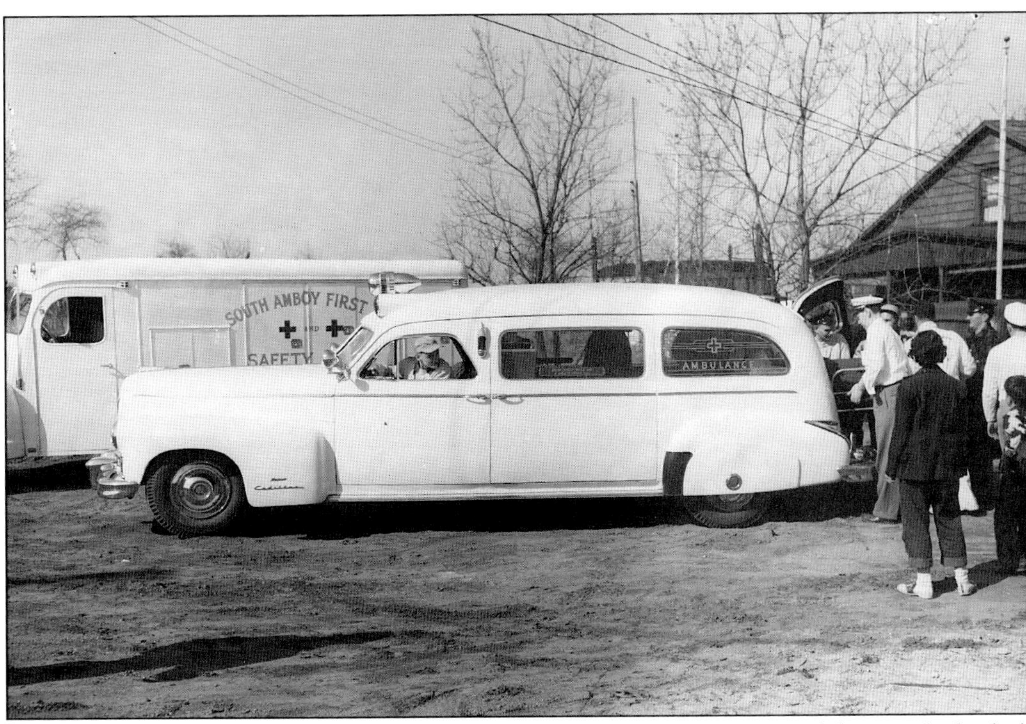

The Cadillac shown here was remembered by Betty Leveille, a mainstay of the squad who held just about every office in the organization, as a very proud acquisition. This is believed to be the first call on which it was used, on April 7, 1951, near the waterfront.

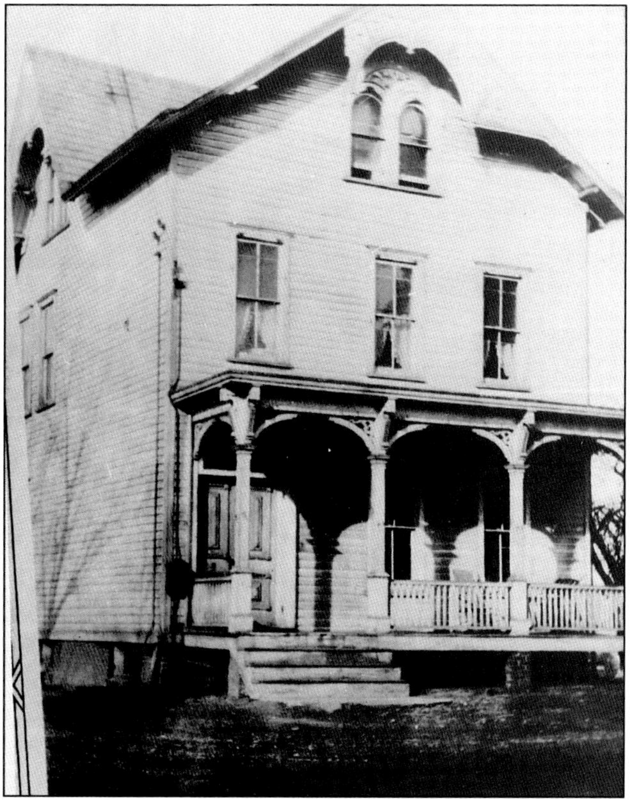

This was an early South Amboy hospital that later became a home for nurses. It was used from about 1919. Now demolished, it was located off what is today Route 35, at Catherine Street.

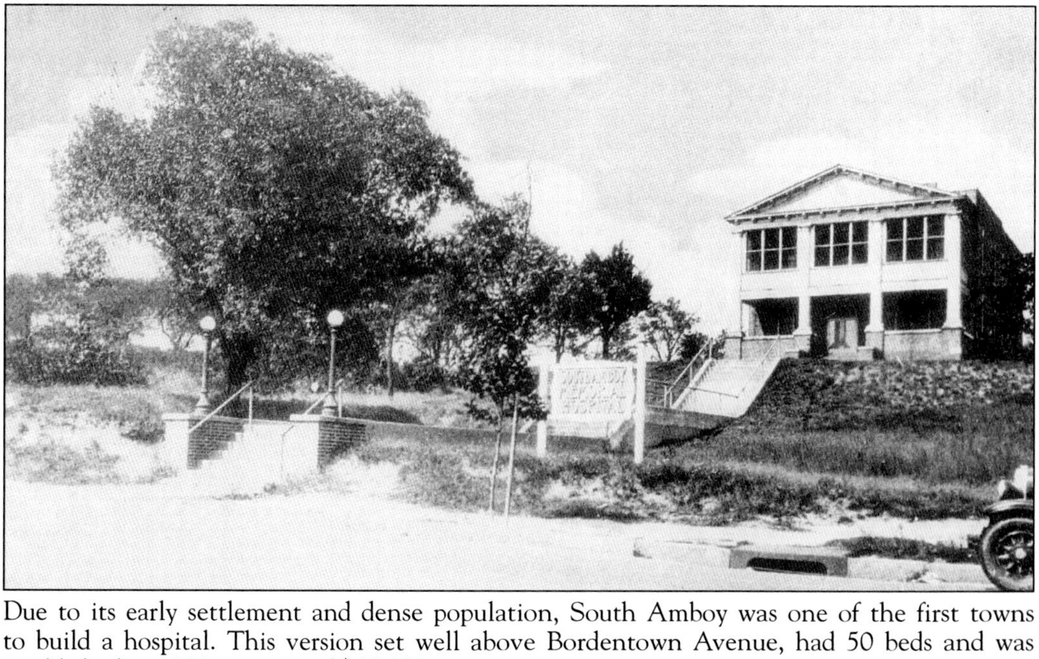

Due to its early settlement and dense population, South Amboy was one of the first towns to build a hospital. This version set well above Bordentown Avenue, had 50 beds and was established in 1924 at a cost of $66,000.

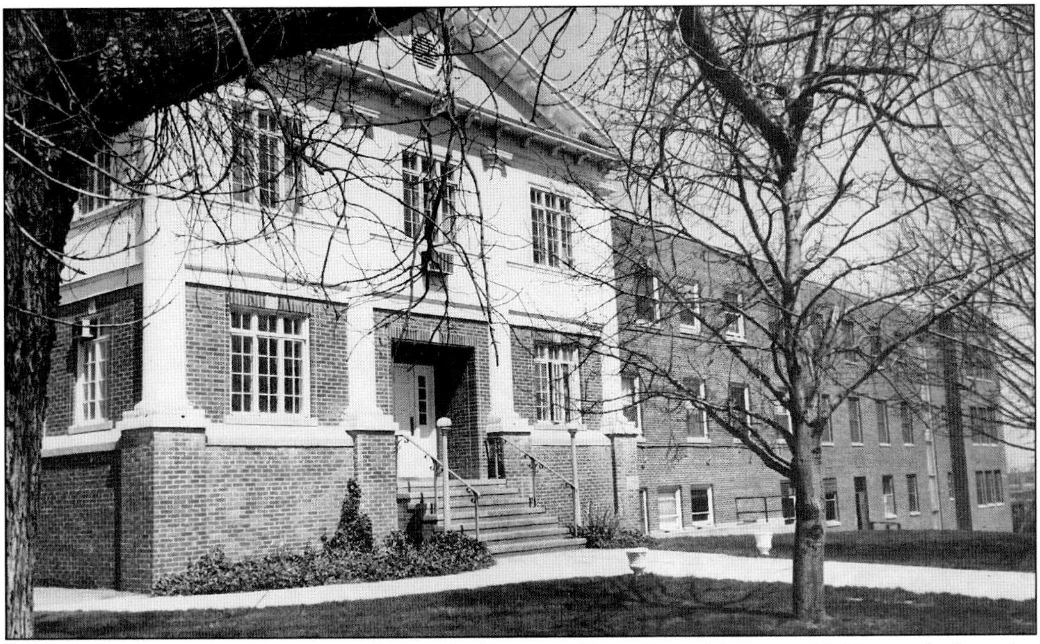

An already-grown South Amboy Memorial Hospital is pictured here in 1969, just before the new building was started. It remains the city's largest employer.

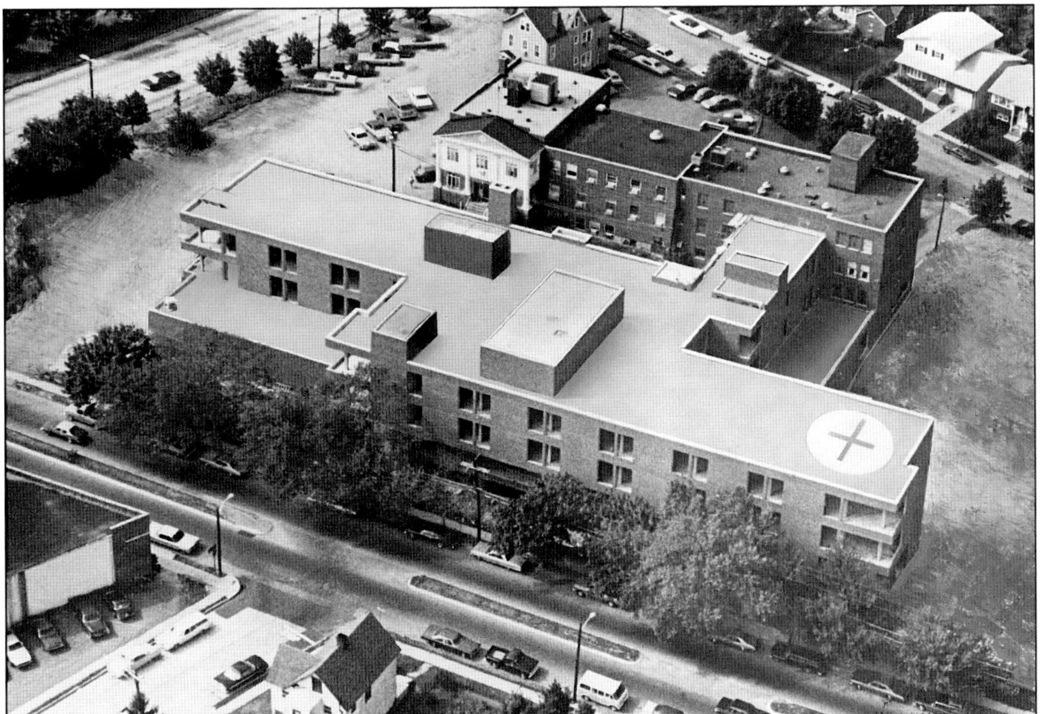

This shows the construction, in 1973, of the greatly expanded hospital, still recognizable today. It would go from 65 to 130 beds at a cost of some $4.2 million. Note the helipad on the roof, which was used until the early 1980s.

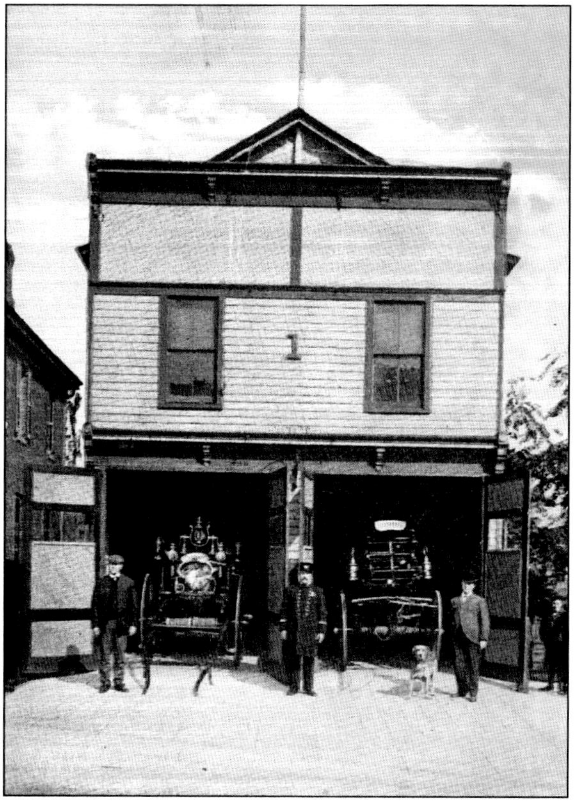

The early home of the Independence and Enterprise Fire Companies was on Broadway just north of Augusta Street. Both fire companies were formed after a group of concerned citizens banded together in 1890 following a devastating fire that took out an entire block on Broadway. This started the long and proud tradition of firefighting in the city.

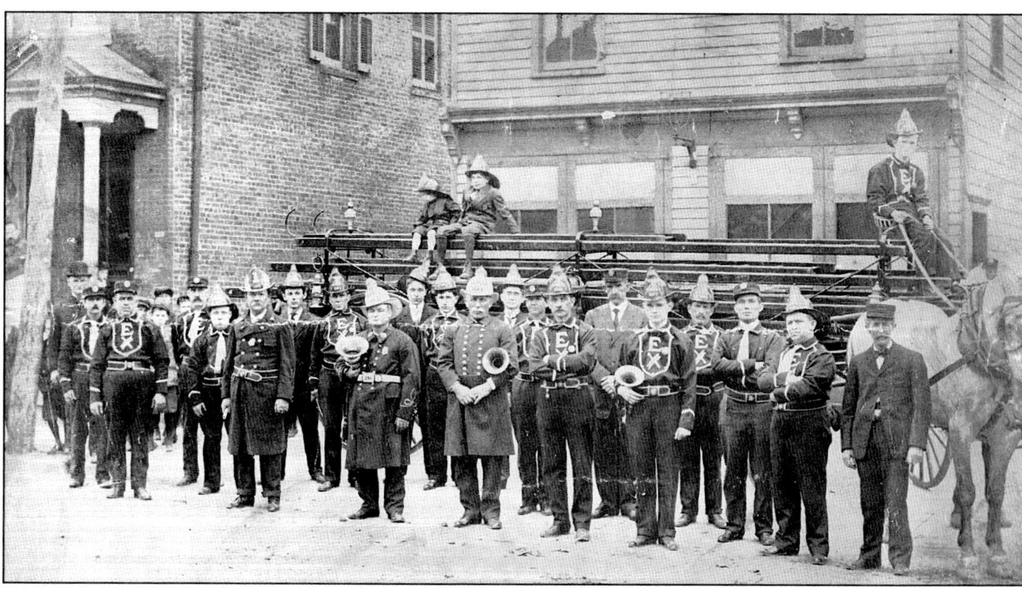

The Enterprise Hook and Ladder Company is pictured here in front of their firehouse. It is one of five fire companies, a large number for a town of a mile square with a peak population of about 8,000.

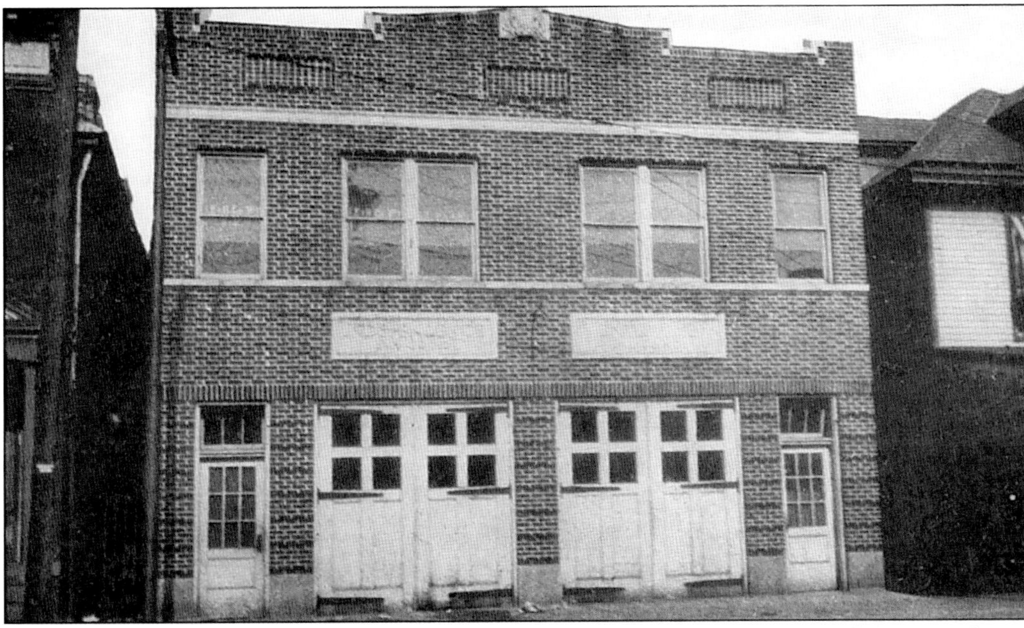

Here is the second version of the Independence and Enterprise Firehouse, still in use today on Broadway, just north of Augusta Street.

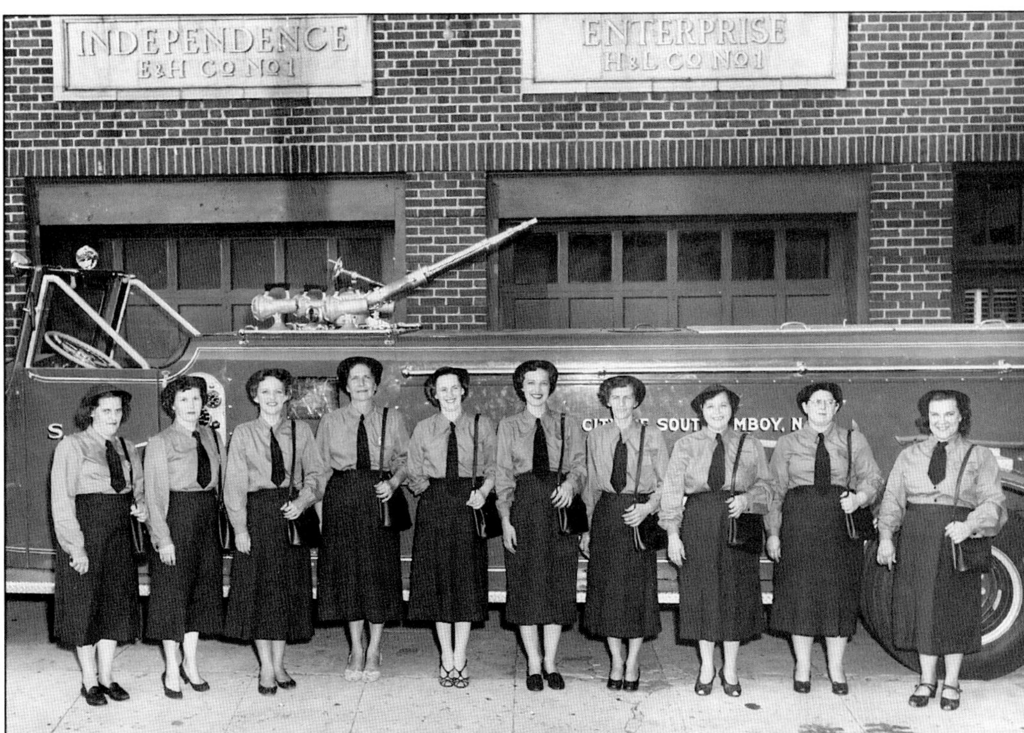

The ladies auxiliary was an important support for most fire companies. This is the Enterprise's Ladies Auxiliary.

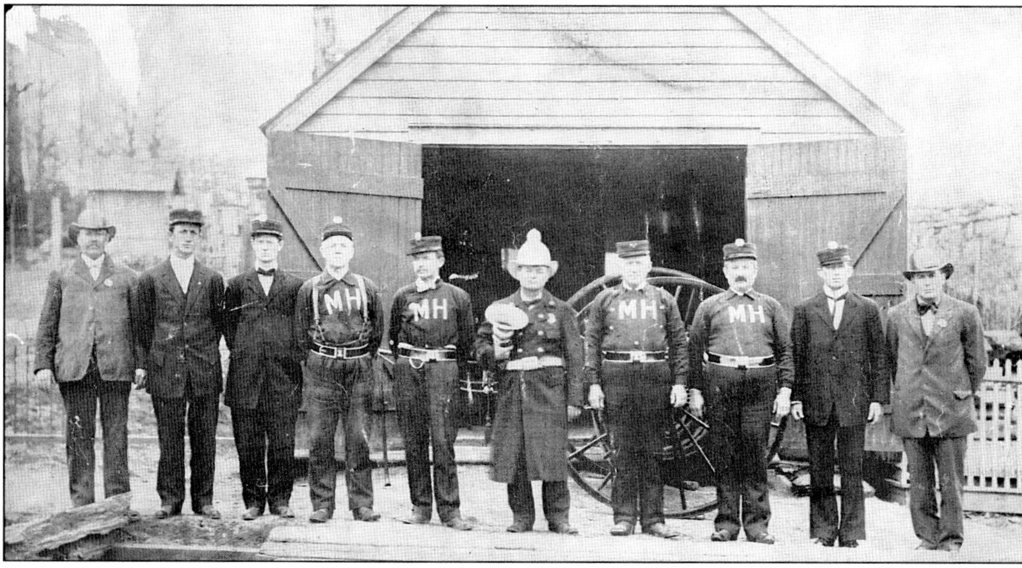

Pictured here in 1904 is an early Mechanicsville Hose Company. From left to right are Andrew Slover, Frank Guerin, John Salmon, Maurice Lucitt, Foreman Eugene Dooling, Chief Thomas Lovely, Andrew Wyler, Richard Neiltopp, William Lyons, and Charles Freeman.

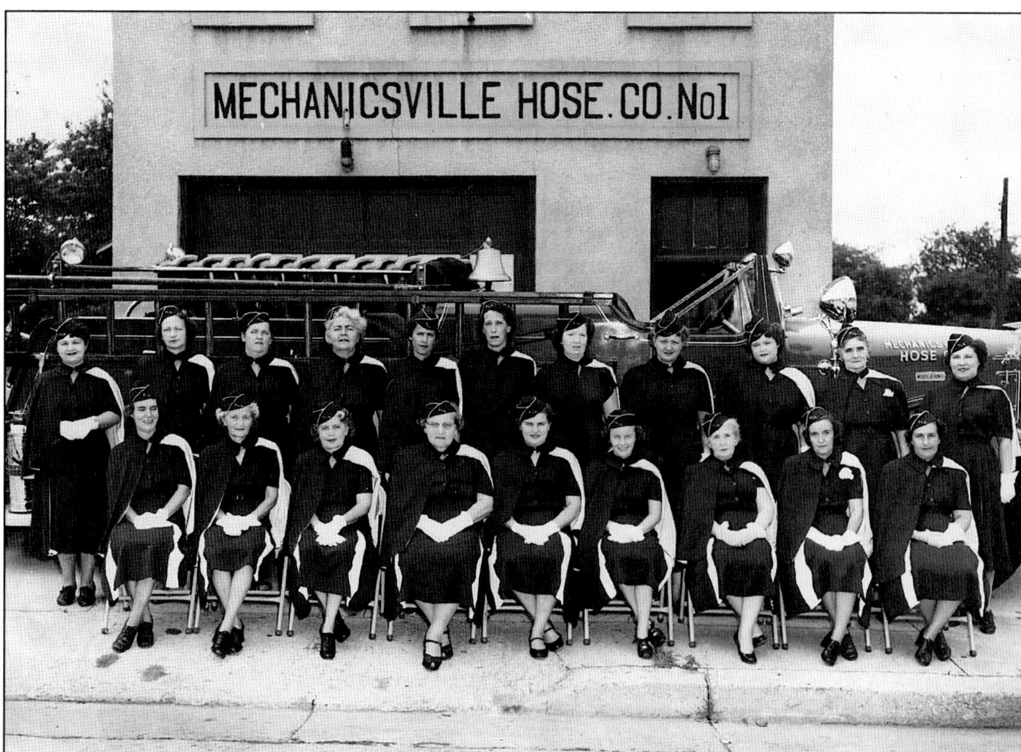

Mechanicsville's Ladies Auxiliary is pictured here in 1955, in front of their house on Raritan Street, which has since been renovated.

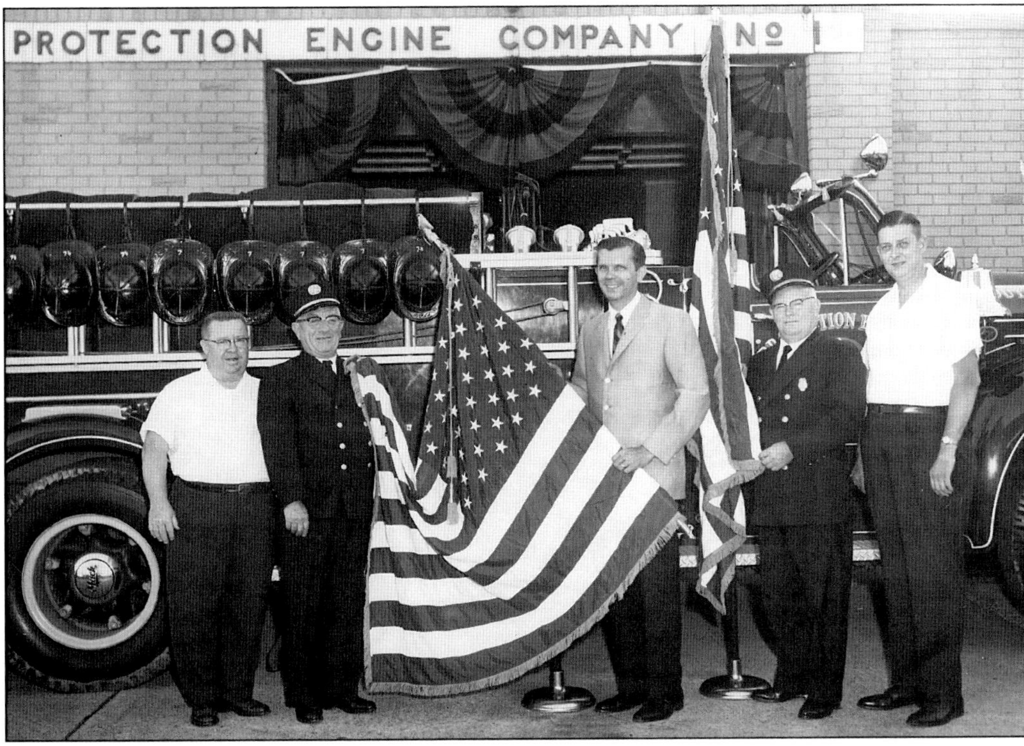

The second and current Protection Firehouse is located on Feltus Street. The occasion for this photo is not known. Second from right in this photo is Thomas Adamecs, the city's first firefighter to die in the course of duty; in 1966 he suffering a heart attack after a television exploded while fighting a house fire. To the left of the flag are John D. Leonard and Ed Snover, while to the right of the flag are Daniel Zack, Adamecs, and John Howley.

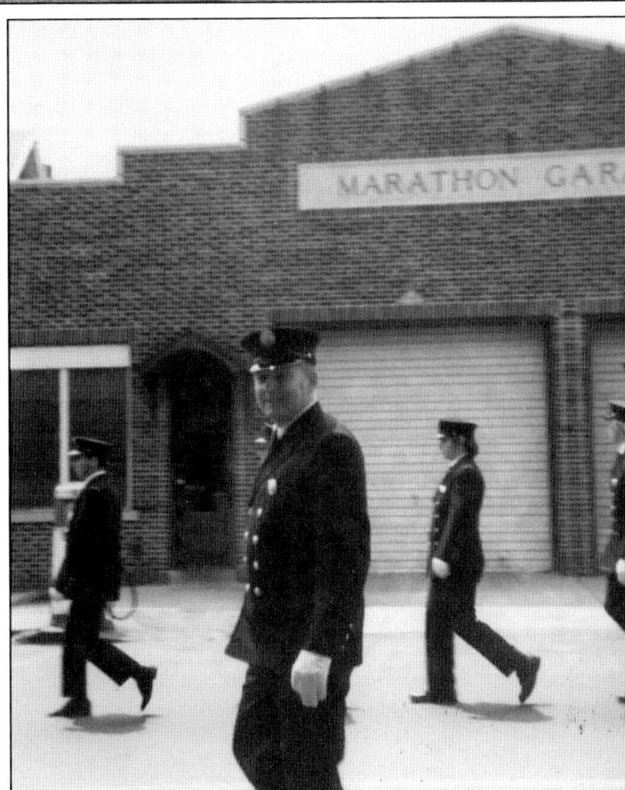

Here, marching in the center in a parade, looking at the camera, is Bob McGowan. This is the only shot found of the former Marathon Garage, a bus depot on Stevens Avenue, now the Dr. Charles W. Hoffman Senior Citizens Resource Center.

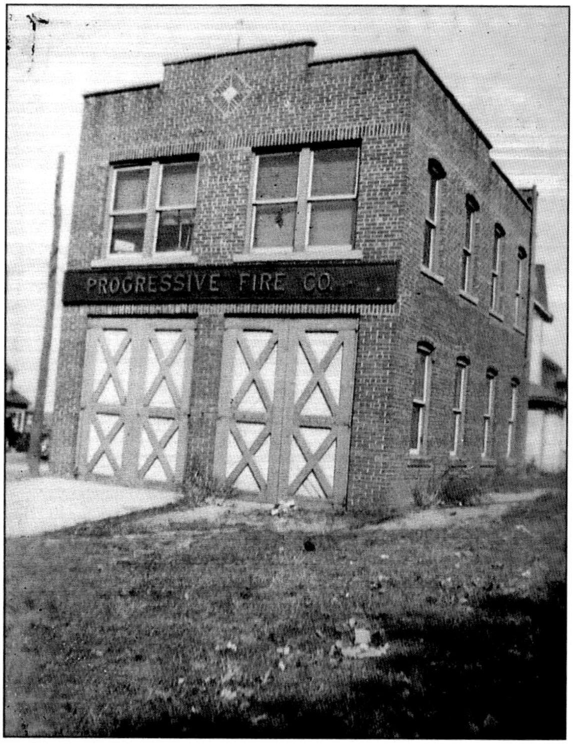

Progressive, the city's "youngest" fire company, formed in 1921 and is pictured here as it originally looked. This demonstrates how the firefighting apparatus expanded over the years—the double doors on this building would never accommodate today's trucks.

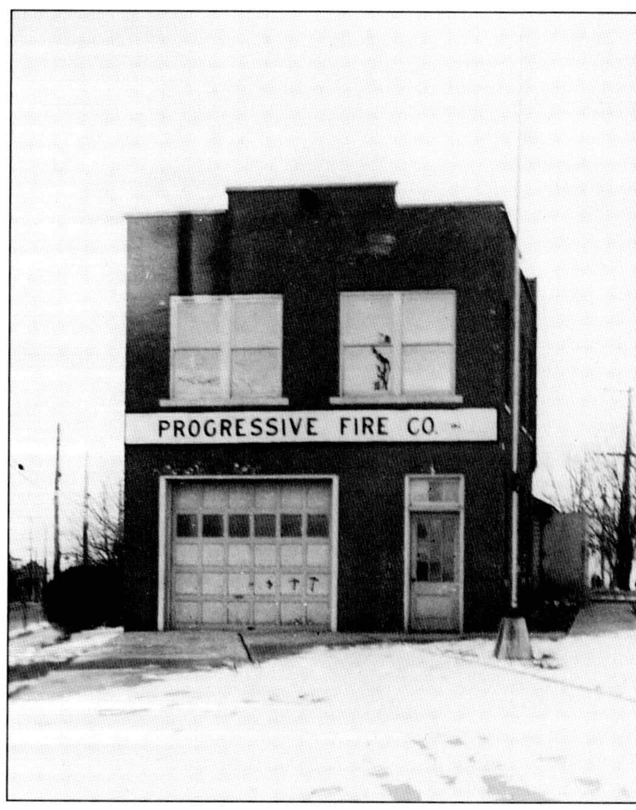

The Progressive Fire Company, on Bordentown Avenue, is pictured here in 1955. Aside from the color, it remains about the same in appearance to this day.

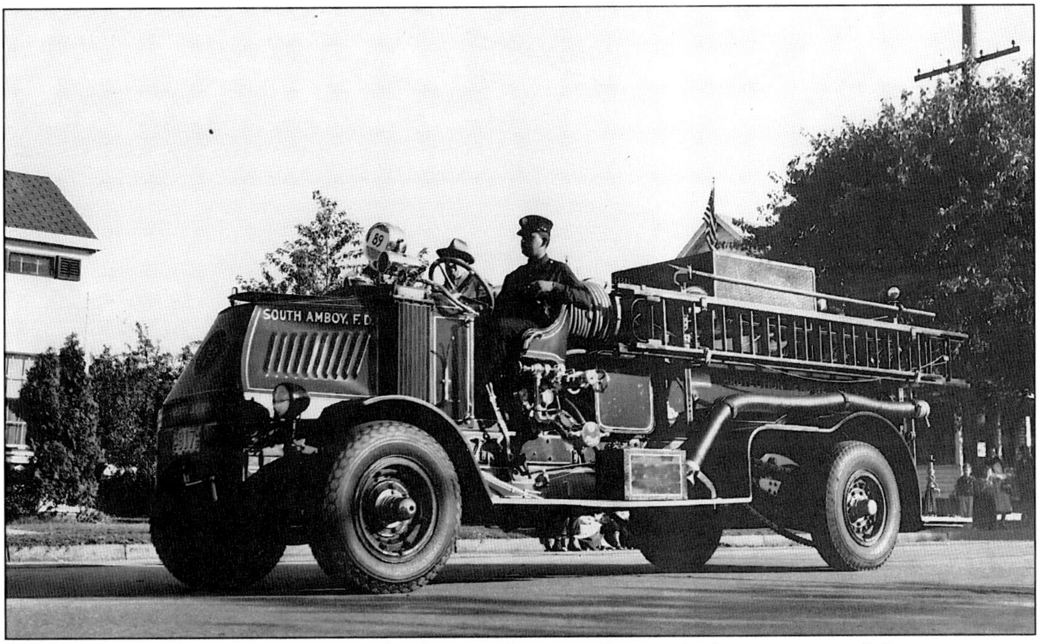

A 1924 Mack pumper, photographed in 1954, was the city's first motorized fire apparatus, according to Edward Szatkowski, who assembled a history of the fire companies for their centennial in 1990.

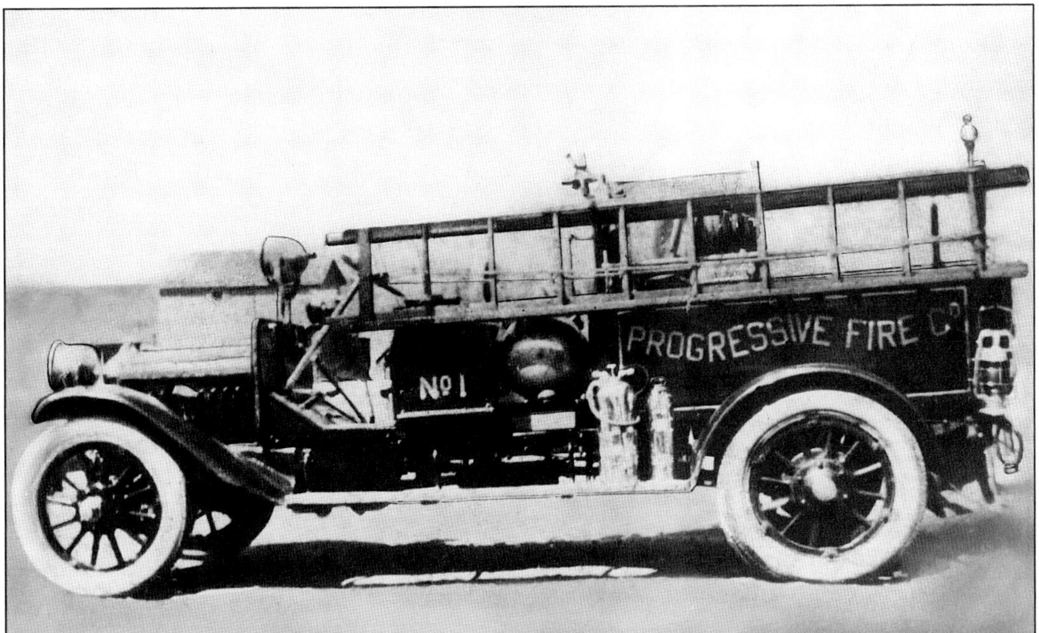

This is probably the first motorized truck that Progressive ever had.

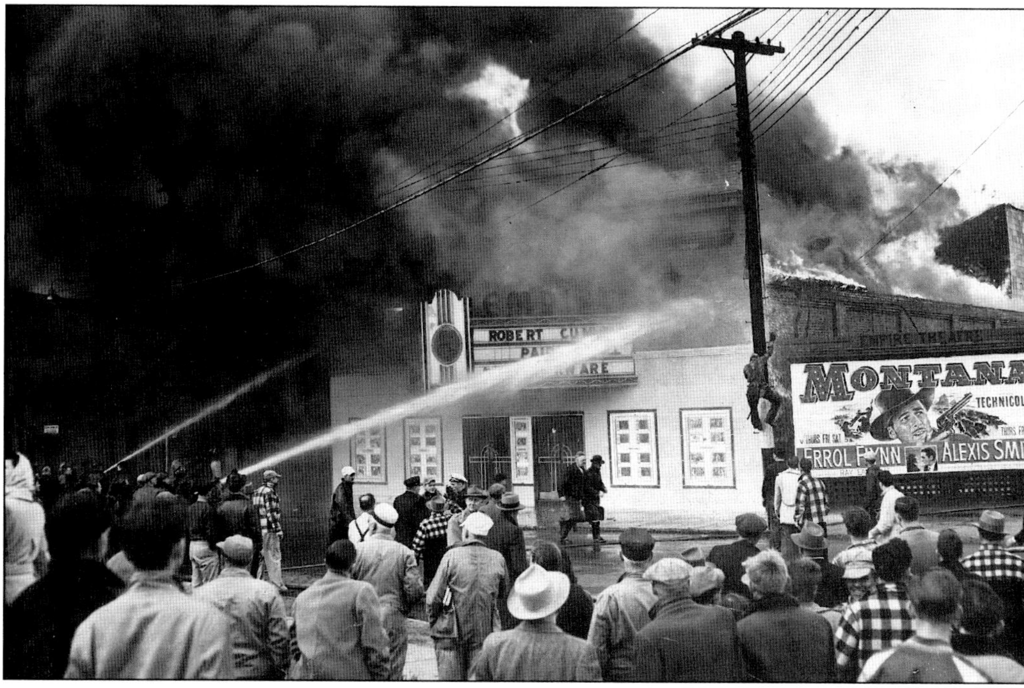

The Empire Theater, on Broadway, caught fire in April 1950. It would not be replaced, and apartments currently stand in its place. The movie playing at the time of the fire was *Paid in Full*, with Robert Cummings.

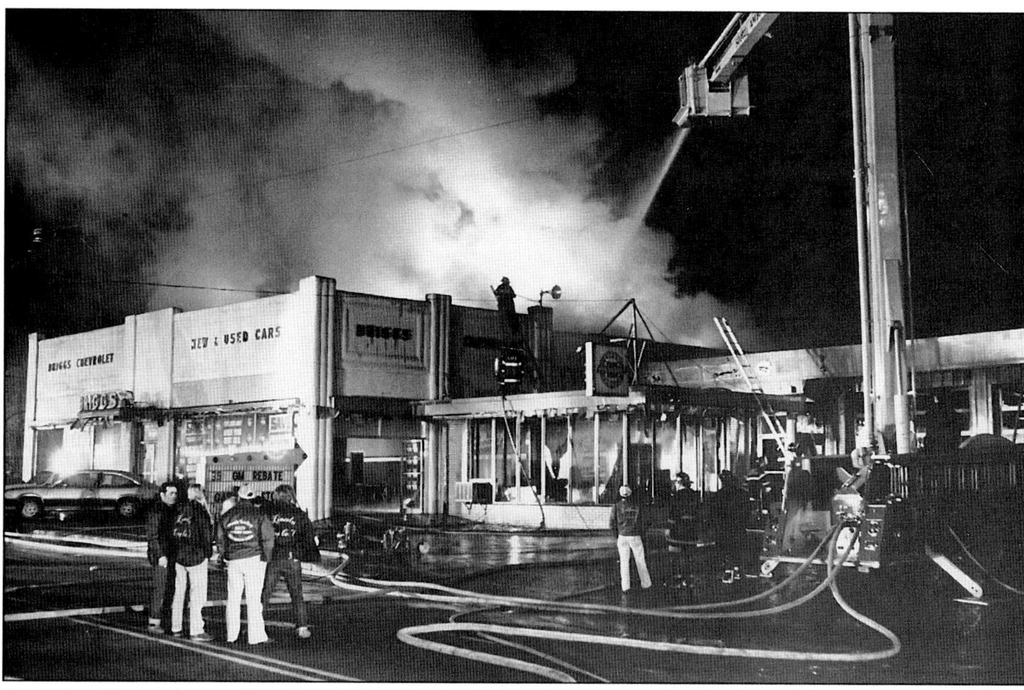

Briggs's Chevrolet suffered a fire in 1980. In the mid-1990s it became home to a private ambulance service.

This 1950s photo shows one of two fires that St. Mary's Elementary School suffered. St. Mary's was across Stevens Avenue from the church, where the high school is located today.

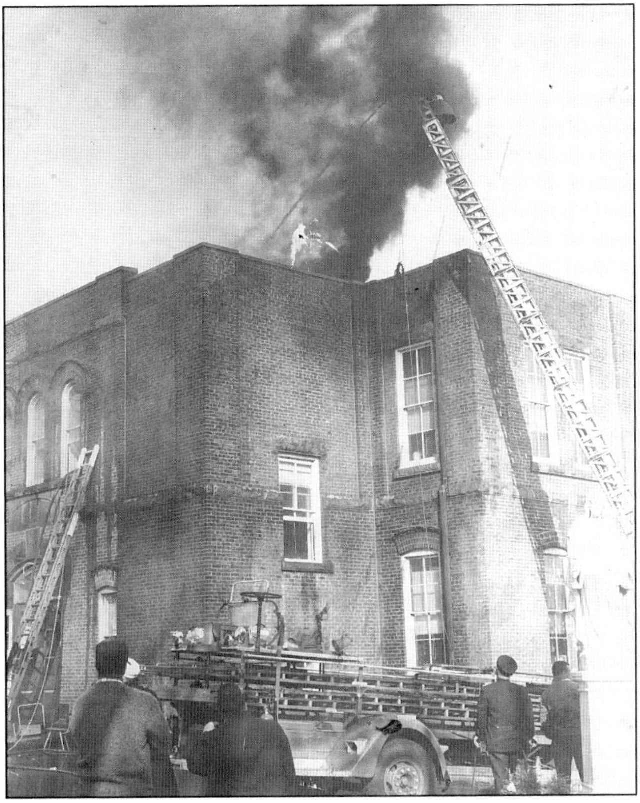

This is another of the fires at St. Mary's. The church steeple is visible on the left.

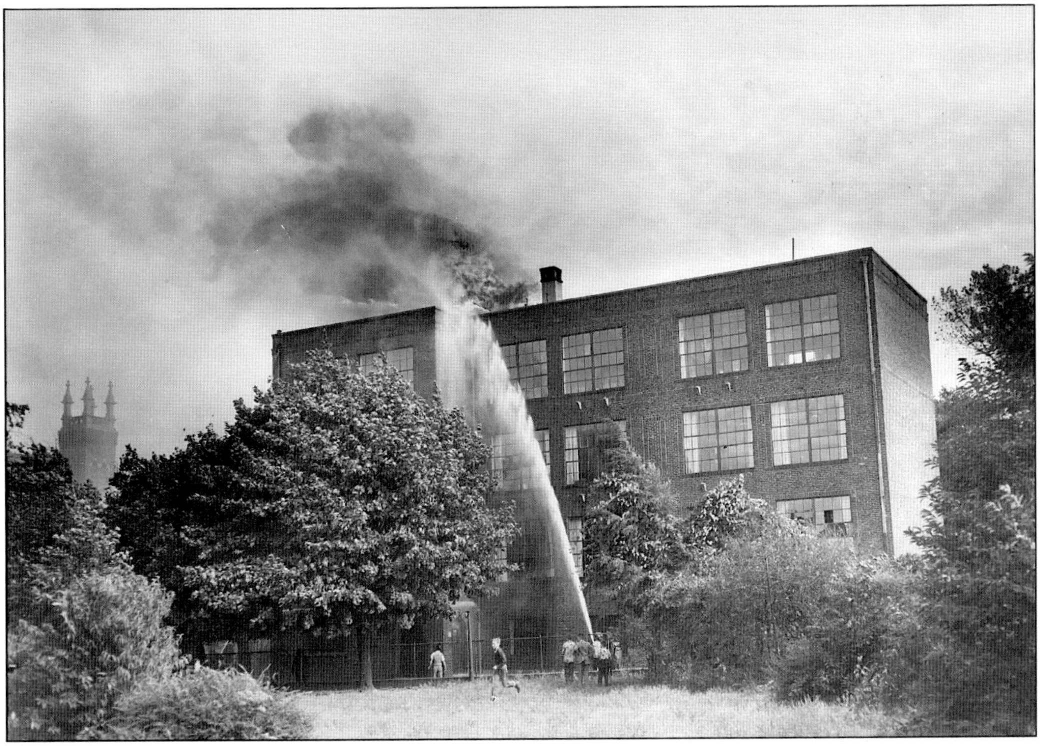

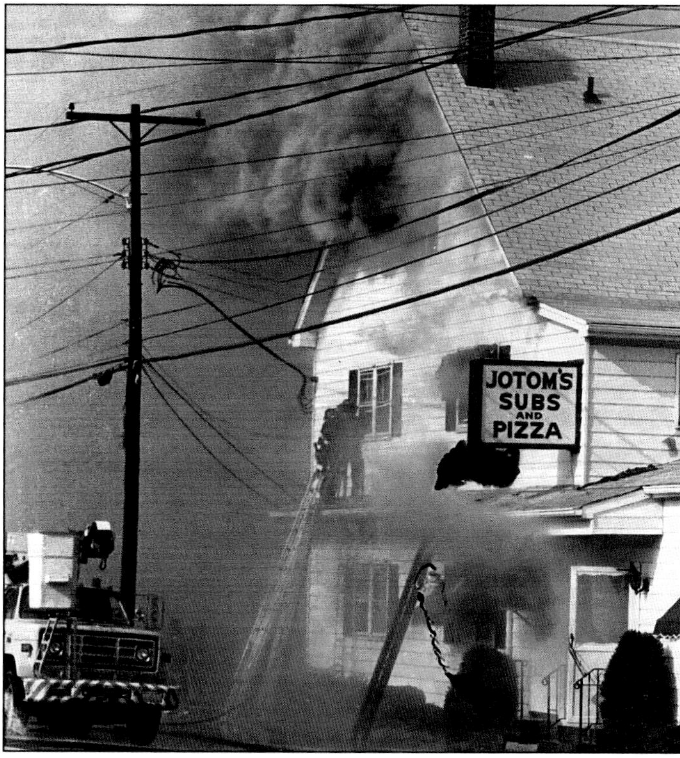

Jotom's, a popular pizza place, was located on Pine Avenue at the corner of John Street. It caught fire in 1982, and is now a private residence.

This is the Thunderbird Lounge, on Route 35, or what is left of it after a fire in February 1966. It would be rebuilt as "Mingles" only to burn down again in 1987 In the mid-1990s it became the site of the Music Box dance club.

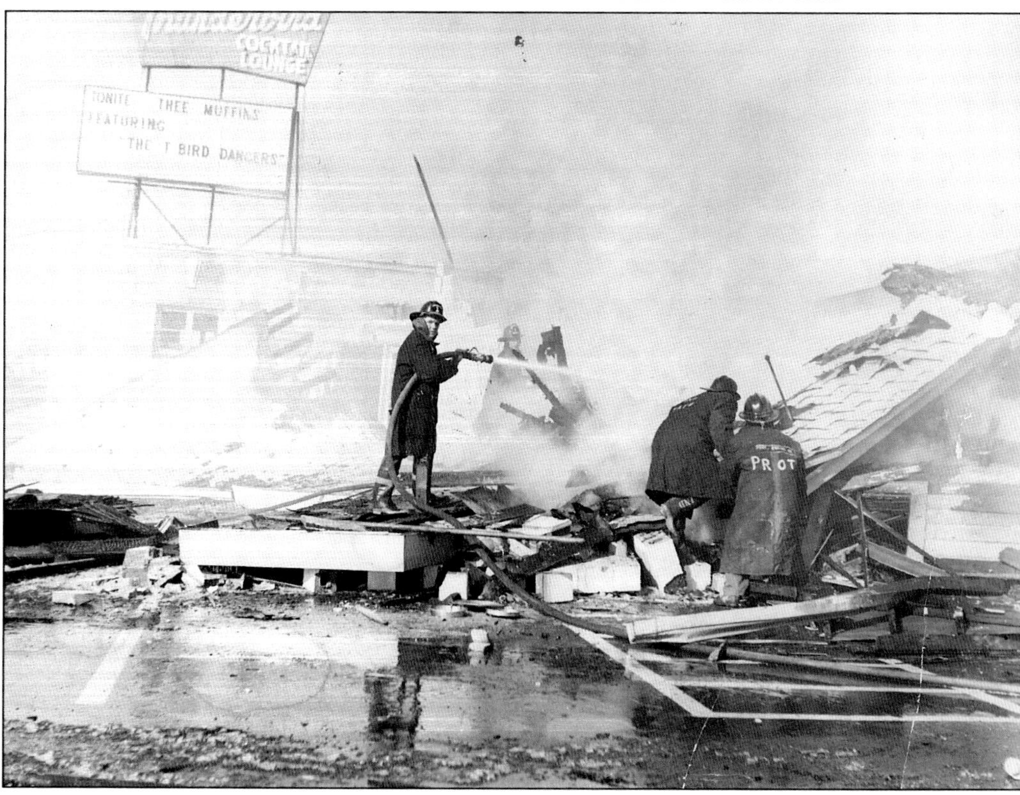

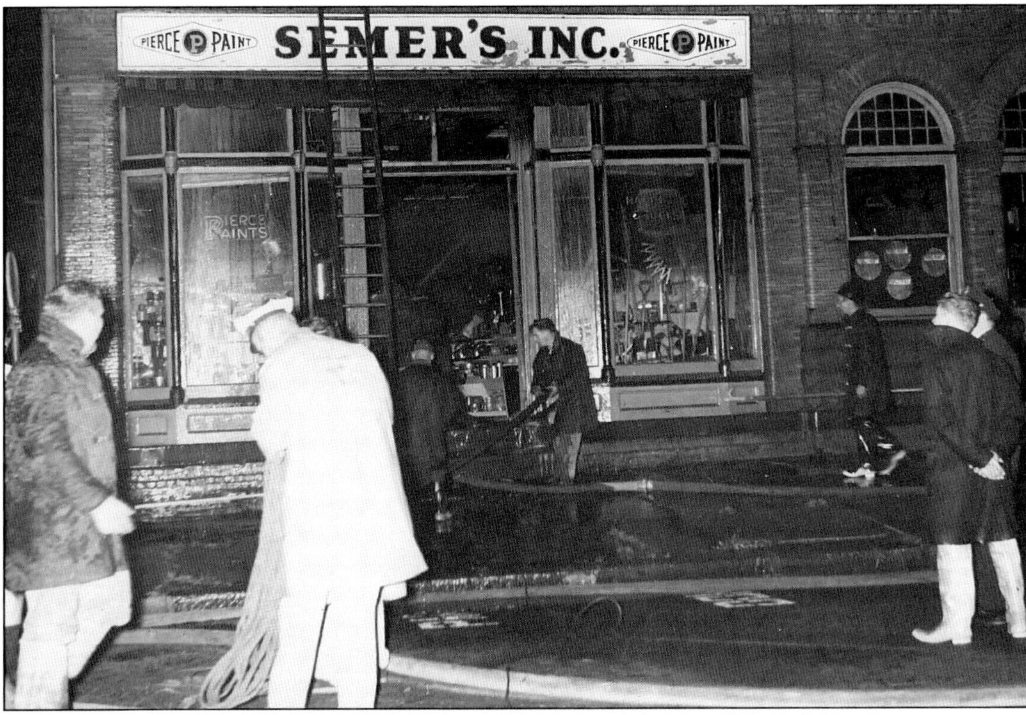

This was a fire at Semer's hardware, on the corner of Broadway and David Street.

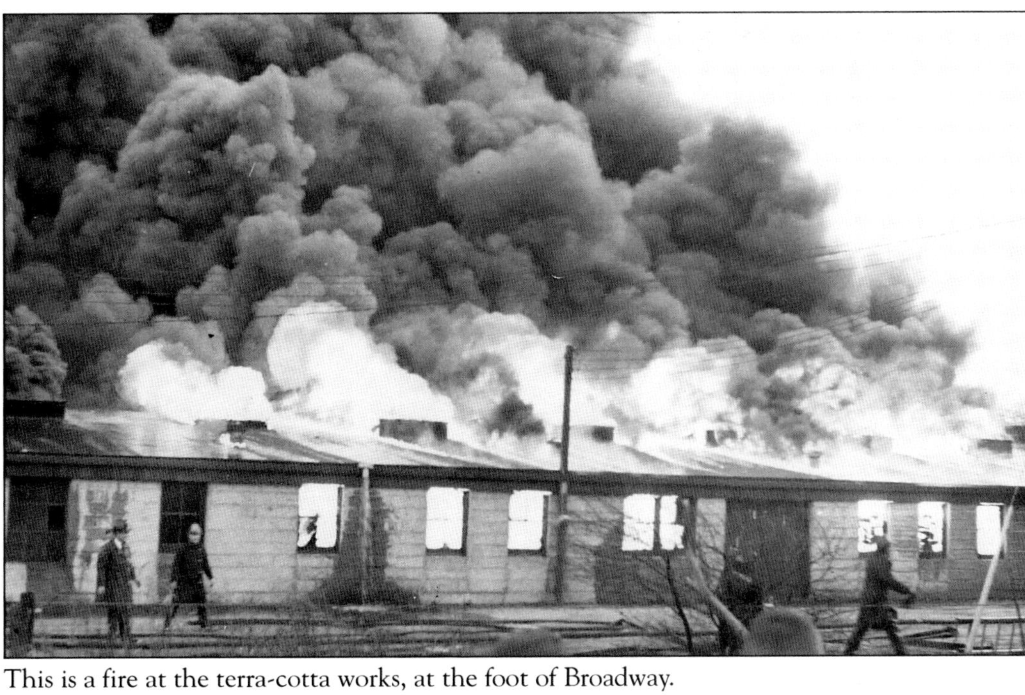

This is a fire at the terra-cotta works, at the foot of Broadway.

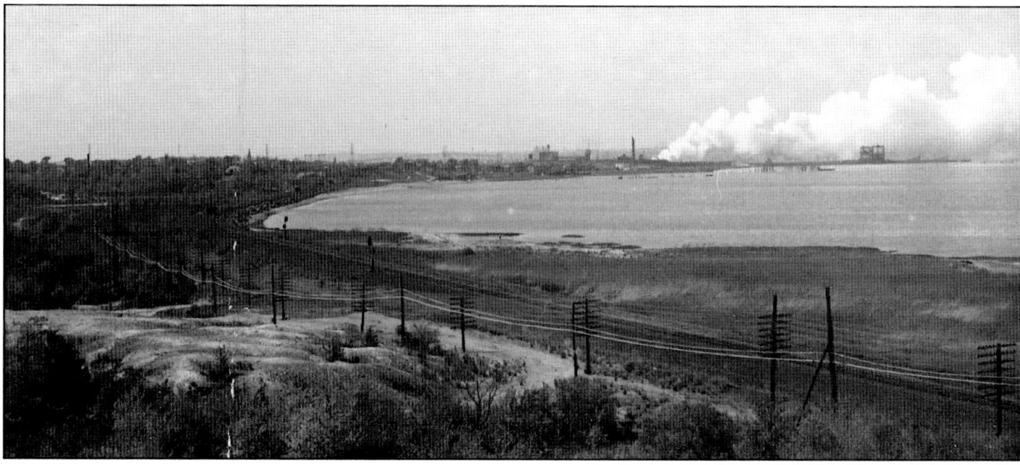

The smoke is pluming from the explosion at the "T" docks, and it is the day after what was truly one of the most shattering events ever to rock the city. On May 19, 1950, 420 tons of ordnance that was being loaded onto barges blew up, killing 31 and injuring 300. Unfortunately, this was not the first ordnance explosion to rock the city—the first was in 1918 in Morgan, which is actually located within Sayreville.

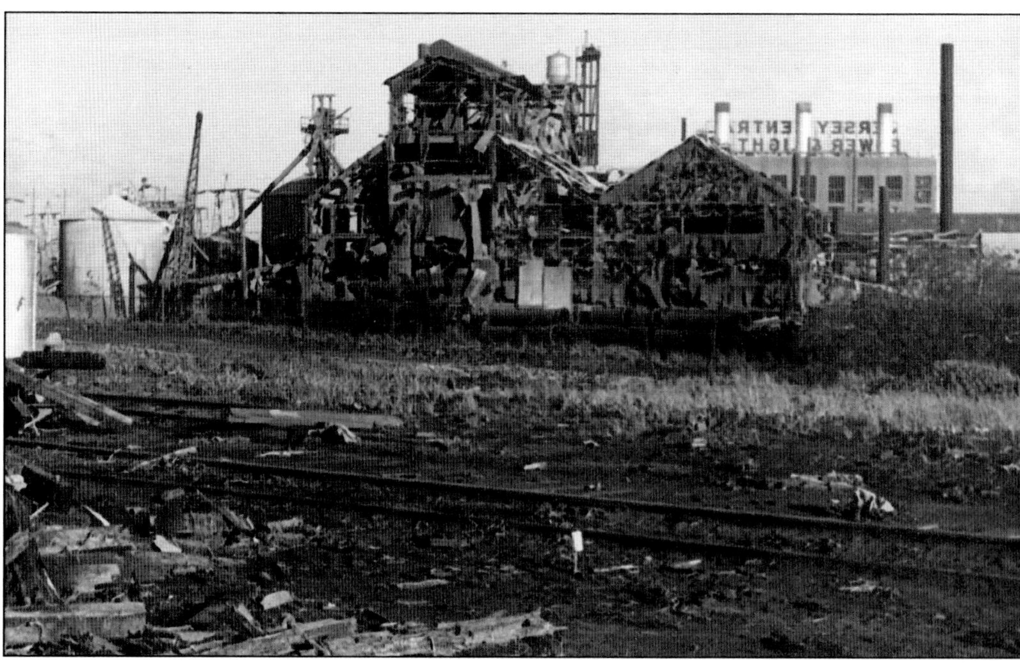

Seen here is the damage to neighboring industries from the 1950 explosion. This is American Agriculture, which made phosphorous, and Jersey Central Power and Light can be seen in background. Supposedly every window in town was broken.

This is Red's Package Store on Broadway near Henry Street, with the windows blown out by the explosion.

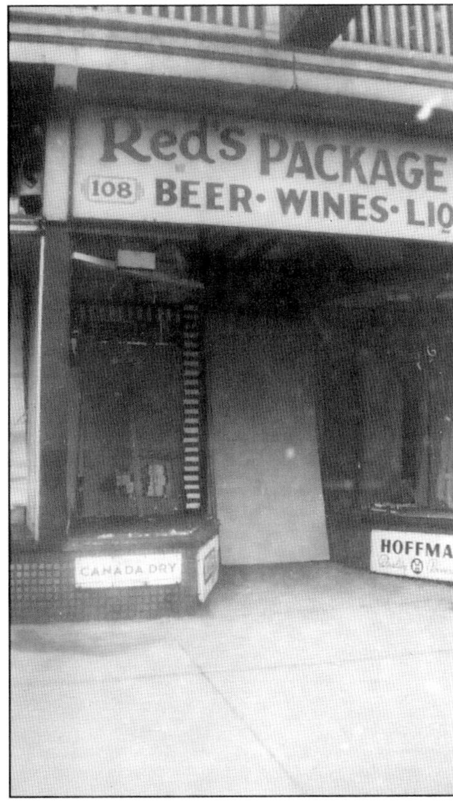

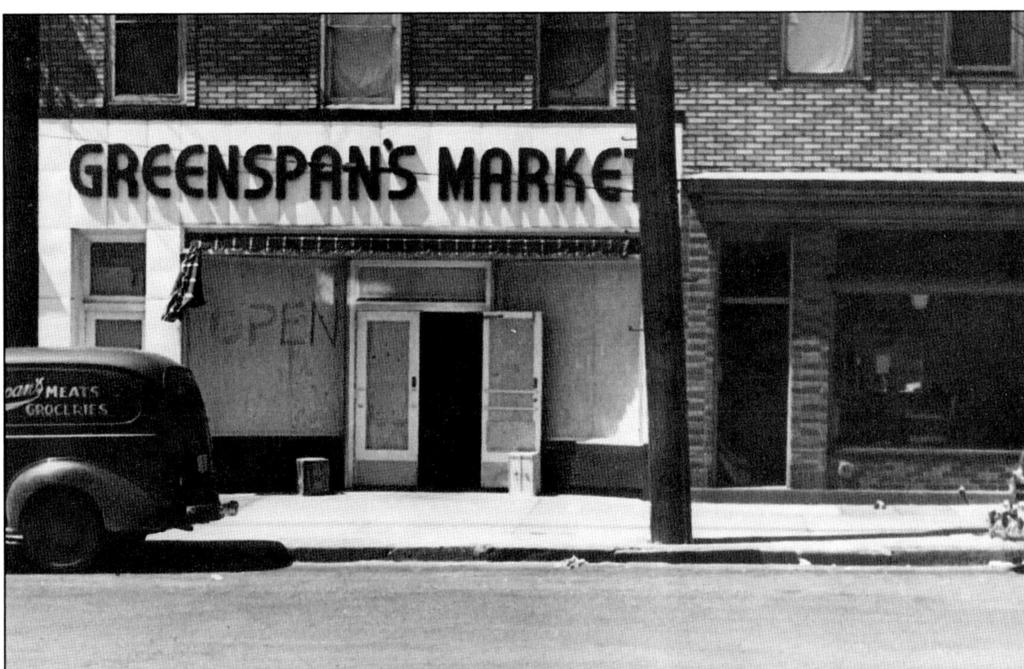

Greenspan's Market, on Broadway about midway between Augusta and Church Streets, was boarded up, but reopened soon after the explosion.

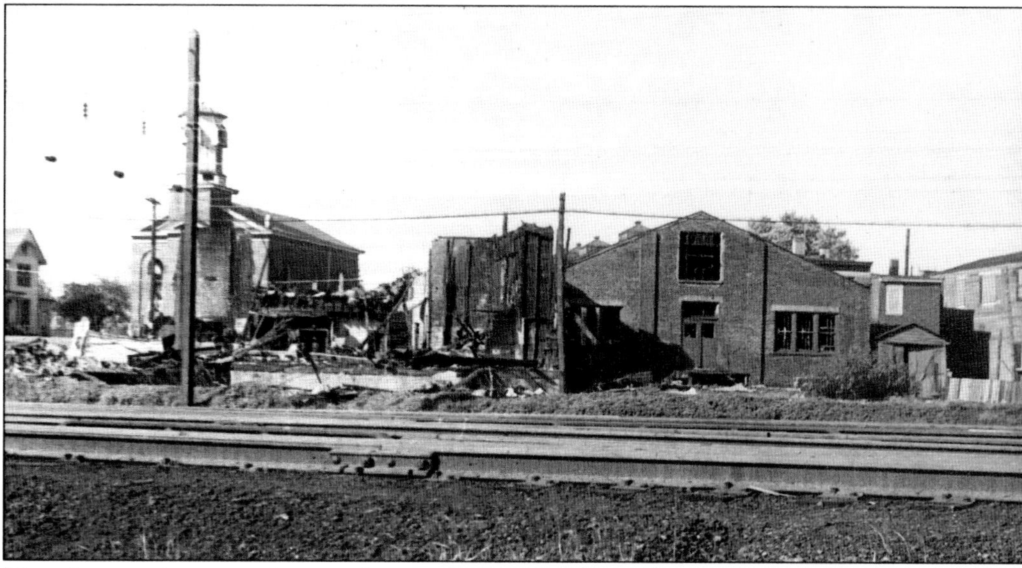

This photo is deceptive. It was taken at the time of the explosion, but the devastated building nearly in front of the Presbyterian church is the Empire Theater, which had burned just a month before. It was a rough spring that year in South Amboy.

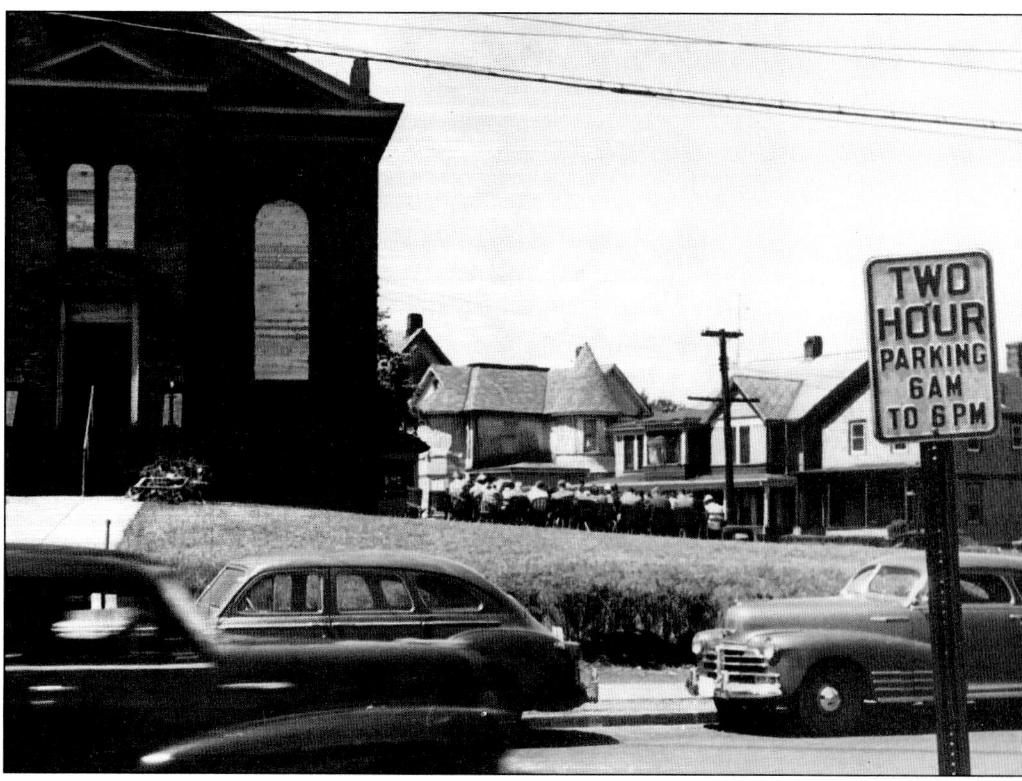

Service was conducted outside on May 21, 1950, due to the damage to the Presbyterian church. Note the boards over the stained-glass windows. St. Mary's Monsignor Francis Sullivan also had to resort to outdoor Mass because of damage at his church, which is over a long block away.

Four

FAITH AND YOUTH

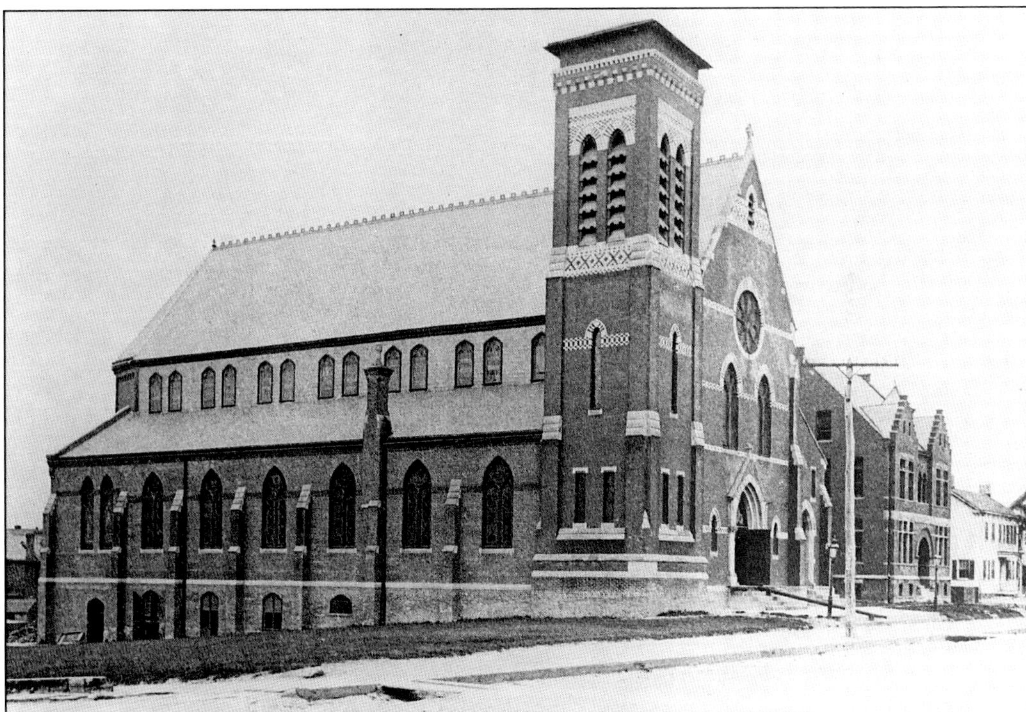

This chapter looks at South Amboy's religious organizations and schools. St. Mary's Roman Catholic Church (above), located on Augusta Street and Stevens Avenue, was the largest congregation in town and one of the oldest, along with Christ Episcopal Church. It started forming before 1849, with Mass officially said in a chapel on what is today the parish's cemetery. It is pictured here upon its completion in 1876. The entrance has been altered, and trees and shrubs have yet to grow, but otherwise it looks much the same here as it does today.

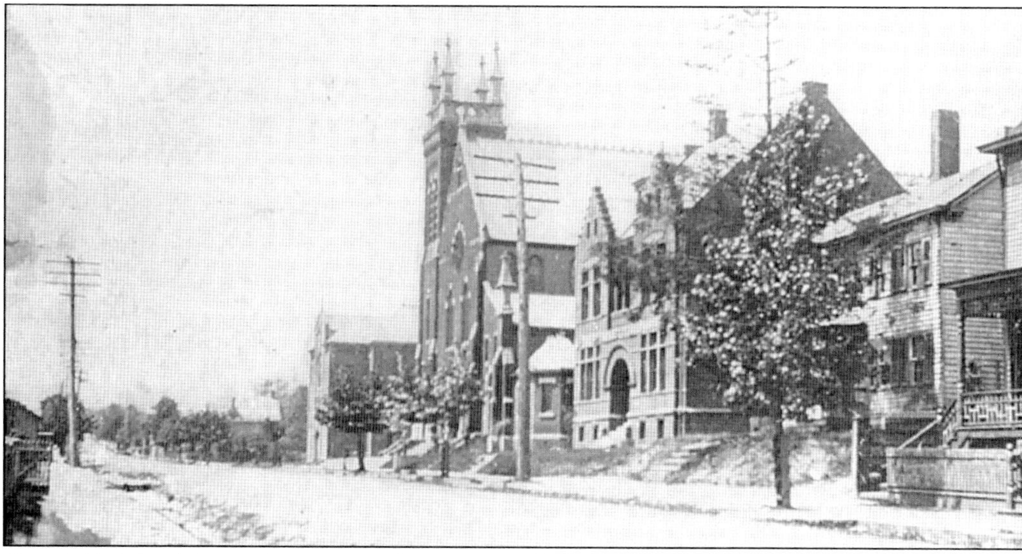

Here is St. Mary's from the opposite direction, with the rectory visible to the right of the church and the school to its left. The city's largest congregation, St. Mary's has traditionally been the church for the Irish population, one of the two main ethnicities in town, while Sacred Heart is commonly known as the "Polish church."

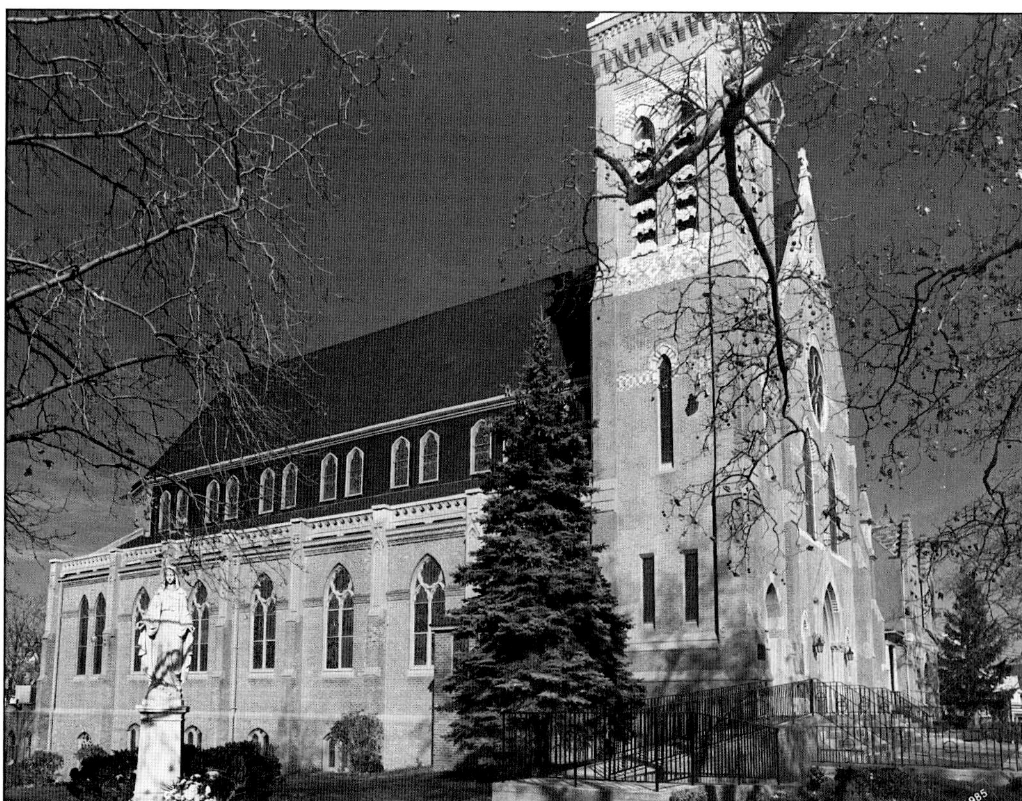

St. Mary's is pictured here in 1985, with some changes.

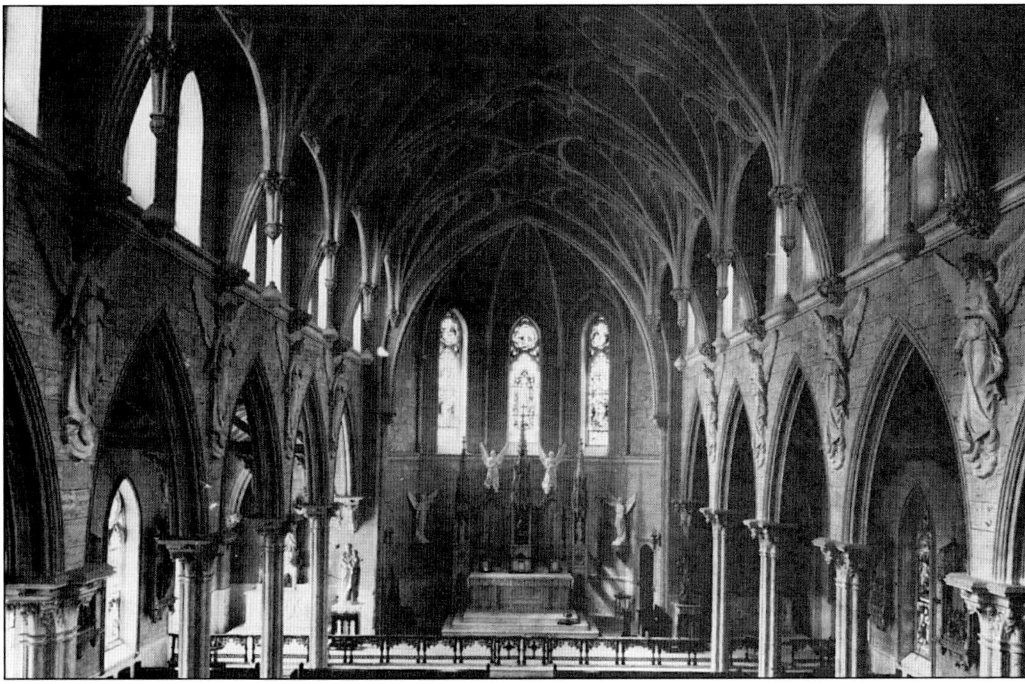

This is the interior of St. Mary's before a massive renovation that took place in the 1970s. Gone now are the angels that hang from the walls and behind the altar, as well as the rail in front of the altar.

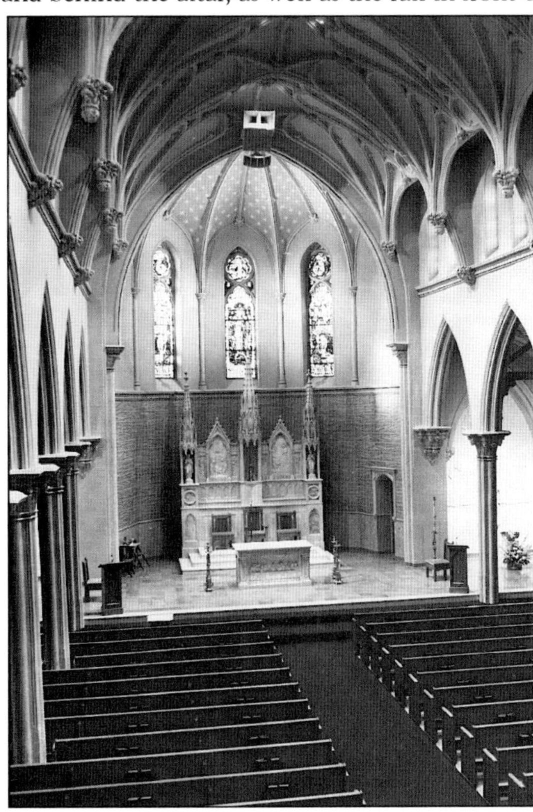

This view is inside St. Mary's today, with the rail and angels gone and the altar moved out so that the priest could stand behind it while facing the congregation.

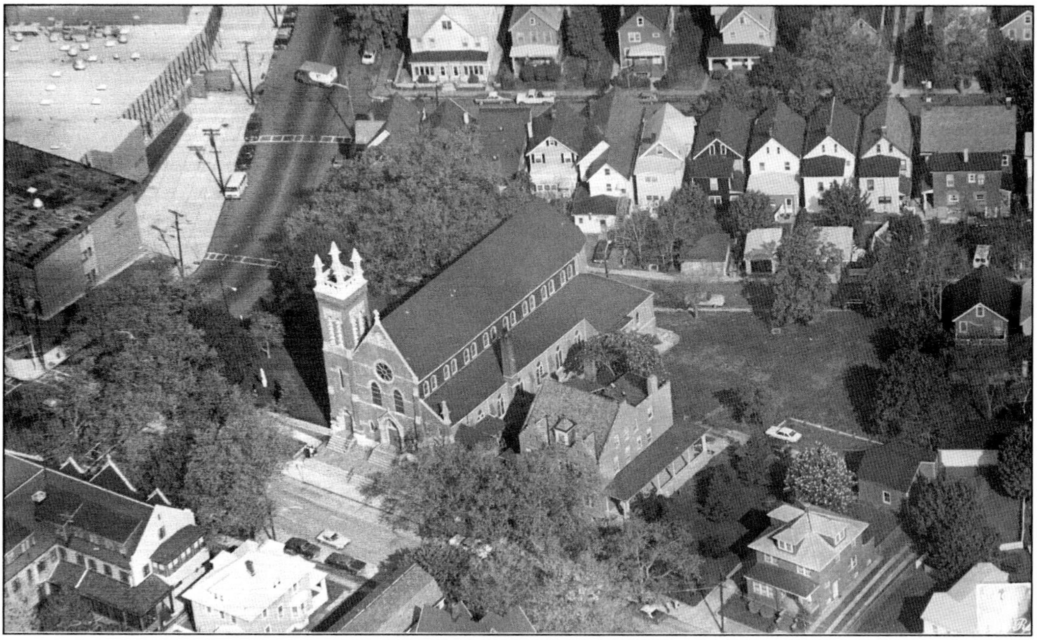

This aerial photo shows the impressive size of St. Mary's. There is a catwalk that runs just under the peak of the roof which is used for working on lighting and amplification.

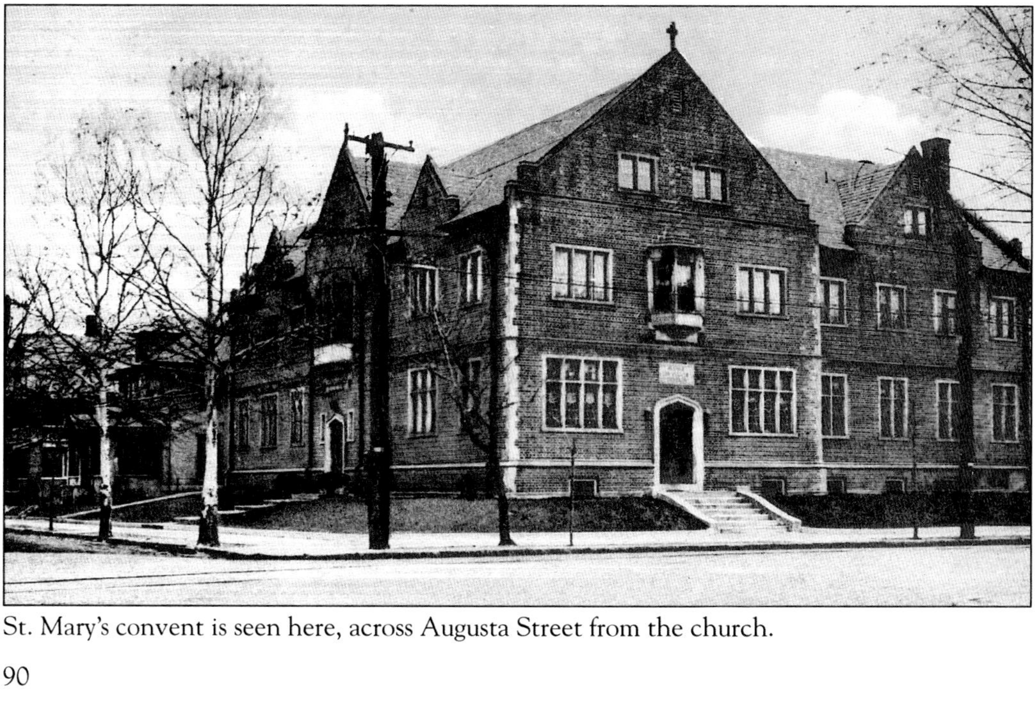

St. Mary's convent is seen here, across Augusta Street from the church.

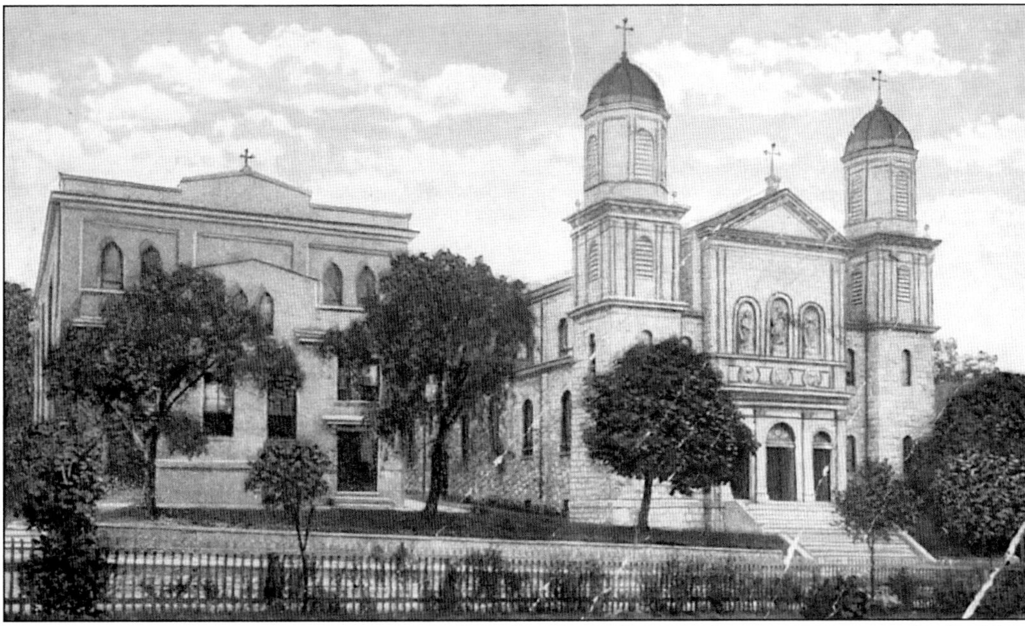

This is Sacred Heart Church, the "Polish Church," located on Washington Avenue. The building to the right was the first church, which held a school after the new sanctuary was built.

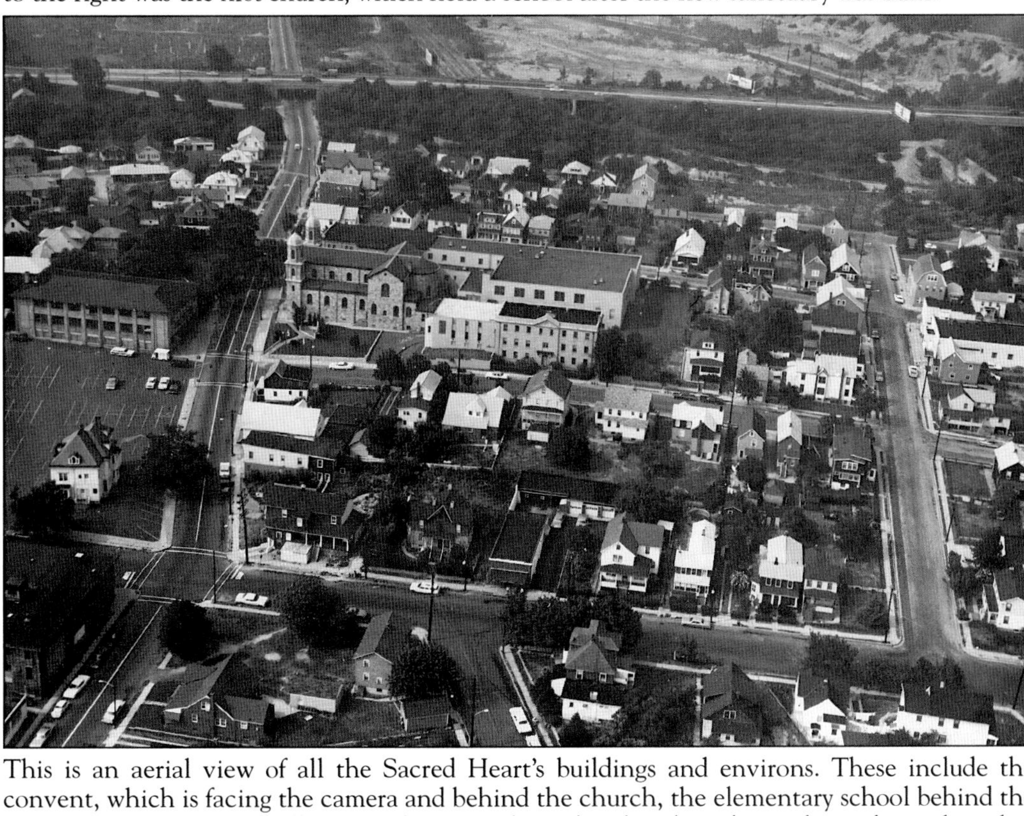

This is an aerial view of all the Sacred Heart's buildings and environs. These include the convent, which is facing the camera and behind the church, the elementary school behind the church, and the parish hall, across the street from the church and just above the parking lot. Route 9 and 35 run across the photo at the top.

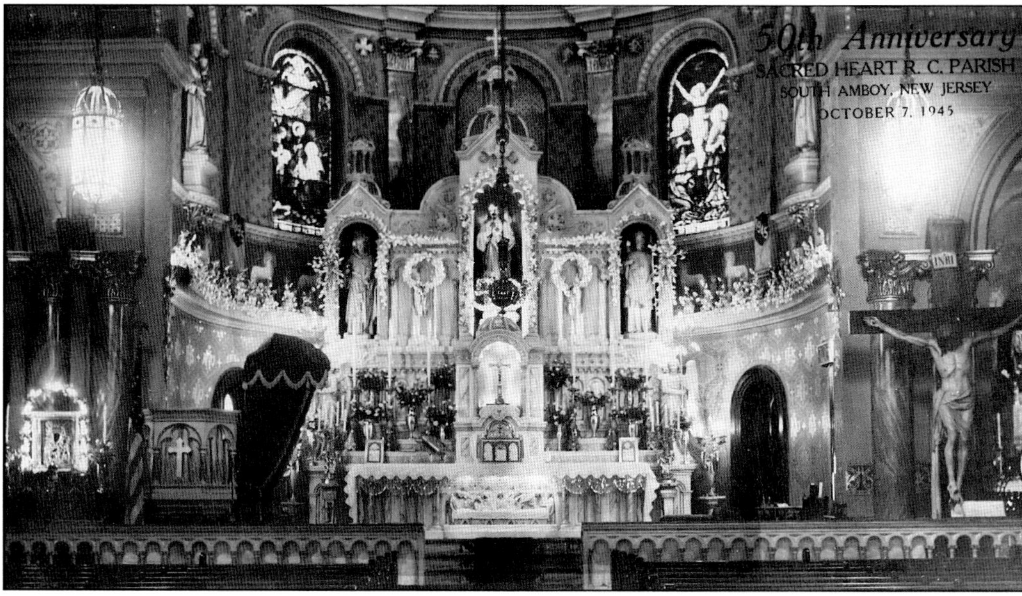

The interior of Sacred Heart Church is pictured here.

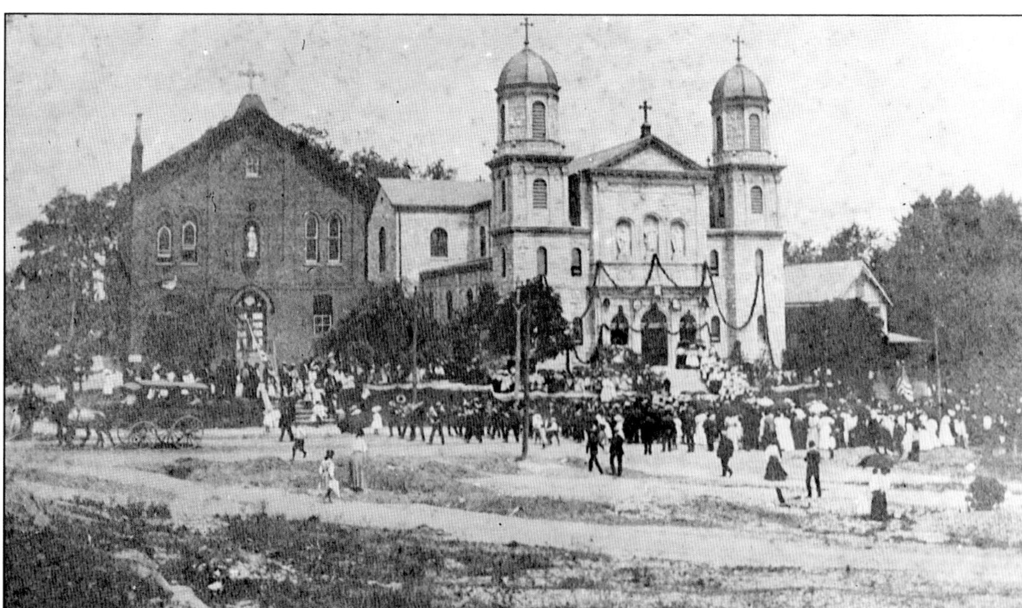

This is Sacred Heart at the dedication of the church building in 1907.

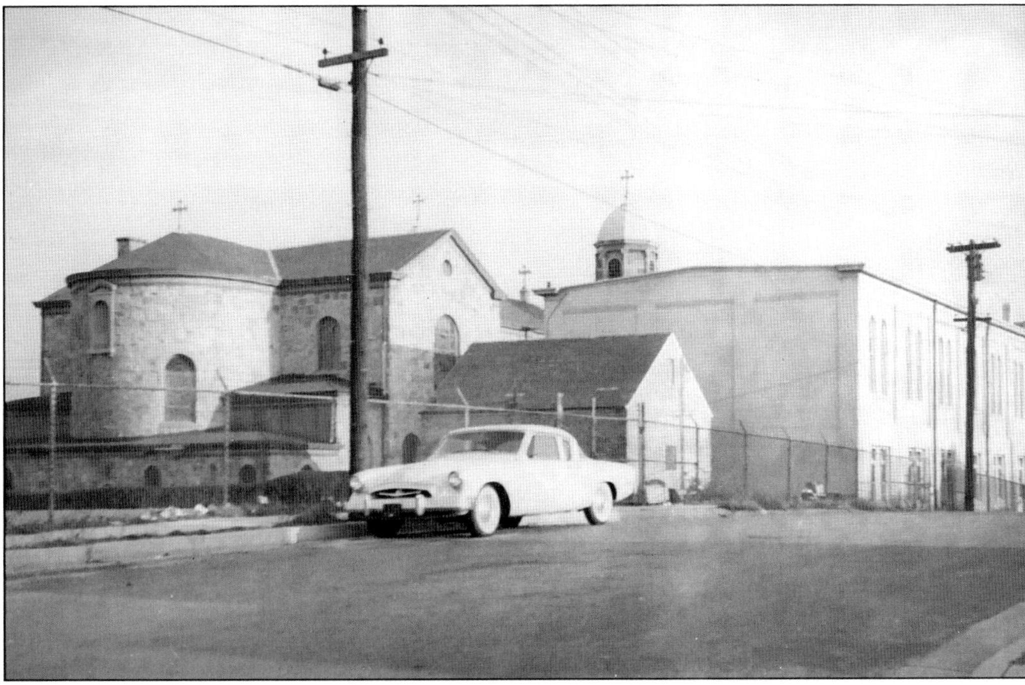

Pictured here is Sacred Heart from the rear, on Cedar Street, before the current elementary school was built.

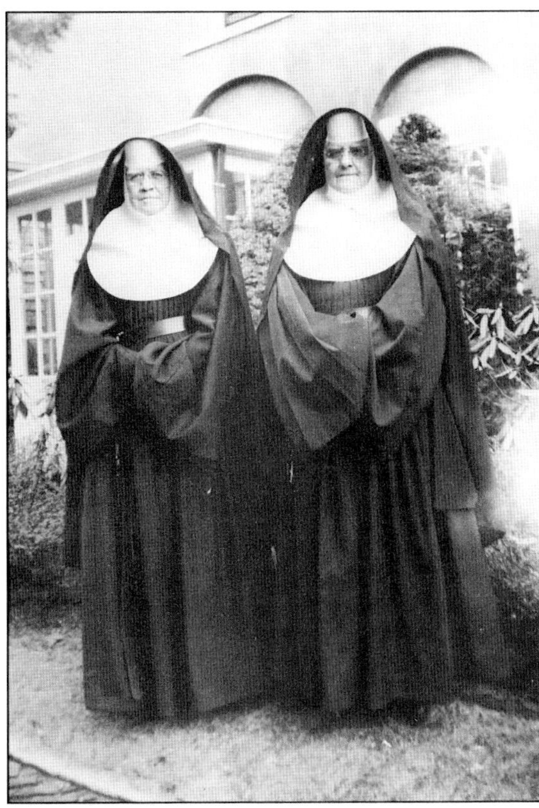

Anyone who had a parochial school education in South Amboy saw nuns dressed like this, or in similar robes. These two women, literally sisters, are Sister Carmelita Scully (left) and Sister Mary Cecelia Scully, both of South Amboy. They were the siblings of Congressman Thomas Scully. Sister Mary Cecelia was one of the founders of Georgian Court College in Lakewood, and its president from 1924 to 1940. She was also one of the founders of Mount St. Mary Academy in North Plainfield.

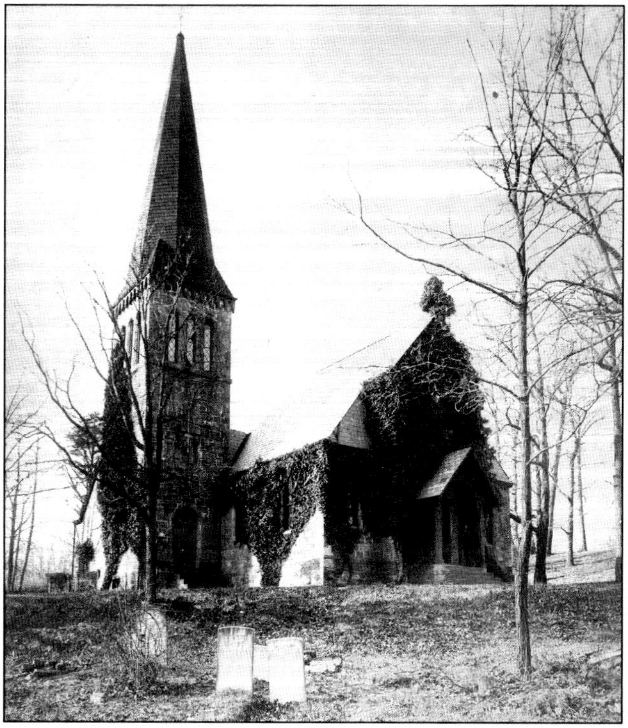

Christ Episcopal Church, high above Main Street, is one of the city's oldest congregations, and is seen here with gravestones in the foreground. There are several crypts below the church where its founding members rest in peace.

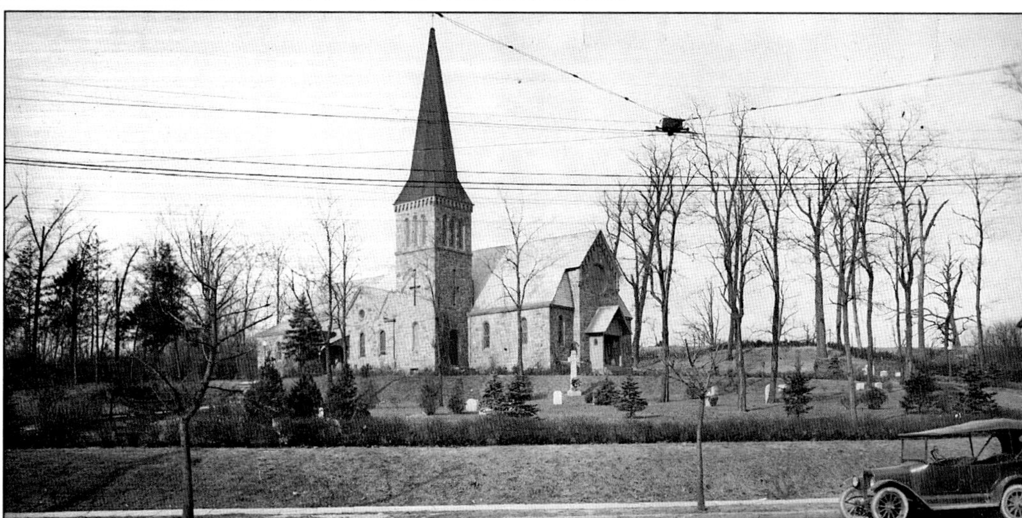

Christ Church was formed in 1852 by Esther Stevens of the Stevens family of railroad fame (also the namesake for the Stevens Institute of Technology in Hoboken). The present church was built in 1858, making it the oldest church, and possibly the oldest building, in South Amboy. It was originally called St. Stephen's (for the saint, not the family), which was also the name of an offshoot organization, the local Free and Accepted Masons Lodge. The lodge is still strong today, making it the oldest surviving fraternal organization in South Amboy. The church's roots stretch back even further, however, possibly to 1833, when a pastor from St. Peter's in Spotswood would occasionally visit and celebrate Mass in a small wooden building in the front of the present church yard.

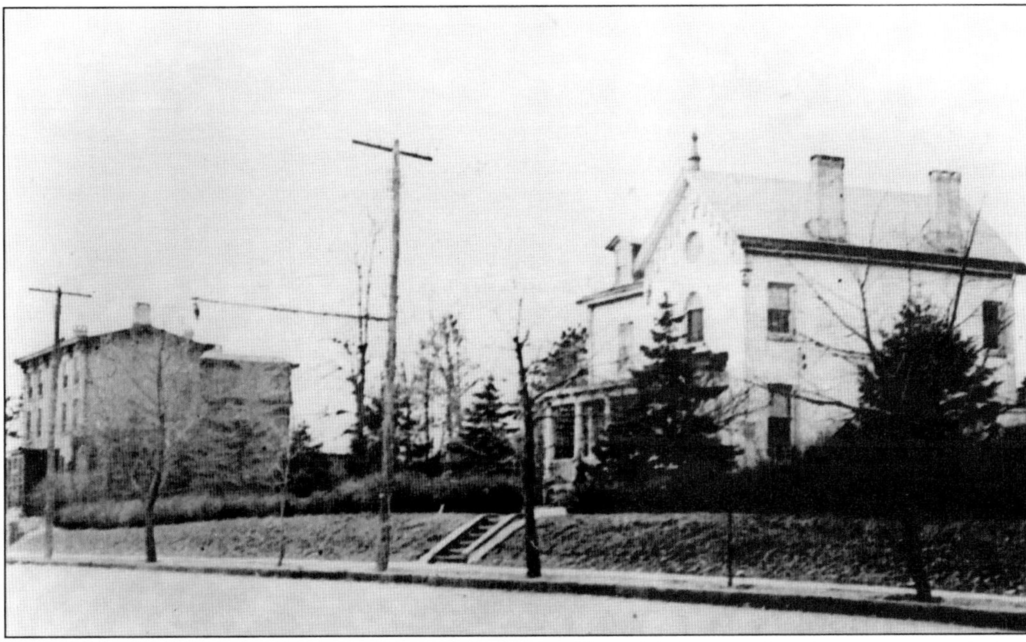

This is apparently one of the few photos of Christ Church's home school, seen on the left. It was also known as the church home, and was an orphanage. This was later the site of Dr. Elias Younes's offices. The home moved to Helmetta (where there is also a strong Episcopal parish, St. George's) in the 1930s and was torn down soon after. To its right is the parish house, where the pastor lived. Both buildings were constructed in 1856.

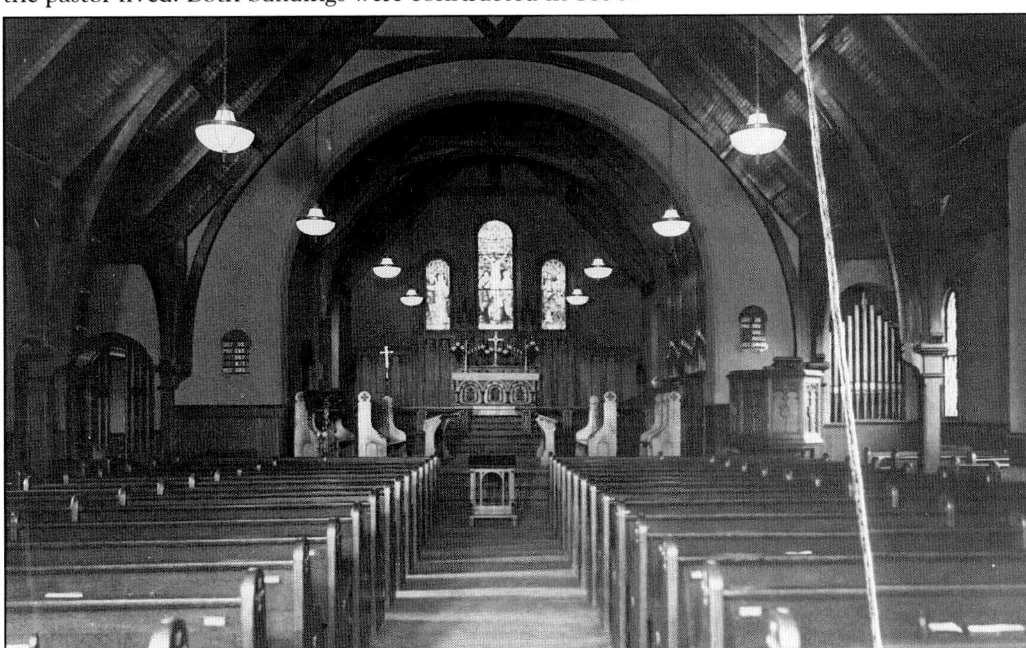

This is the interior of Christ Church in the 1950s. The pulpit has now been moved to the left side and the choir pews removed from the altar. Recordings of the choir were made on 33 and 1/3 rpm records.

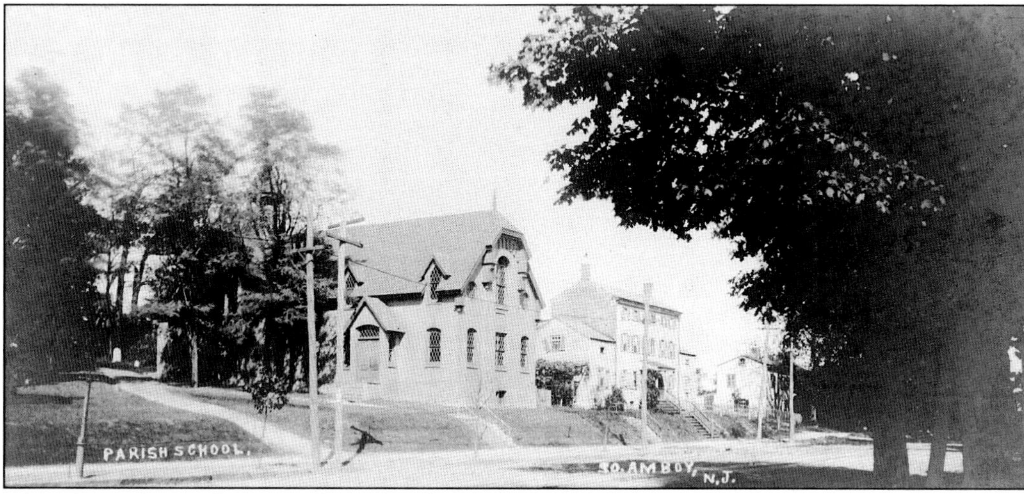

This photo shows the second parish school, which, through the 1990s, has been the church's thrift shop. The house next to it is now gone, and its site, once occupied by Briggs' Chevrolet, has been occupied by a private ambulance service in the 1990s.

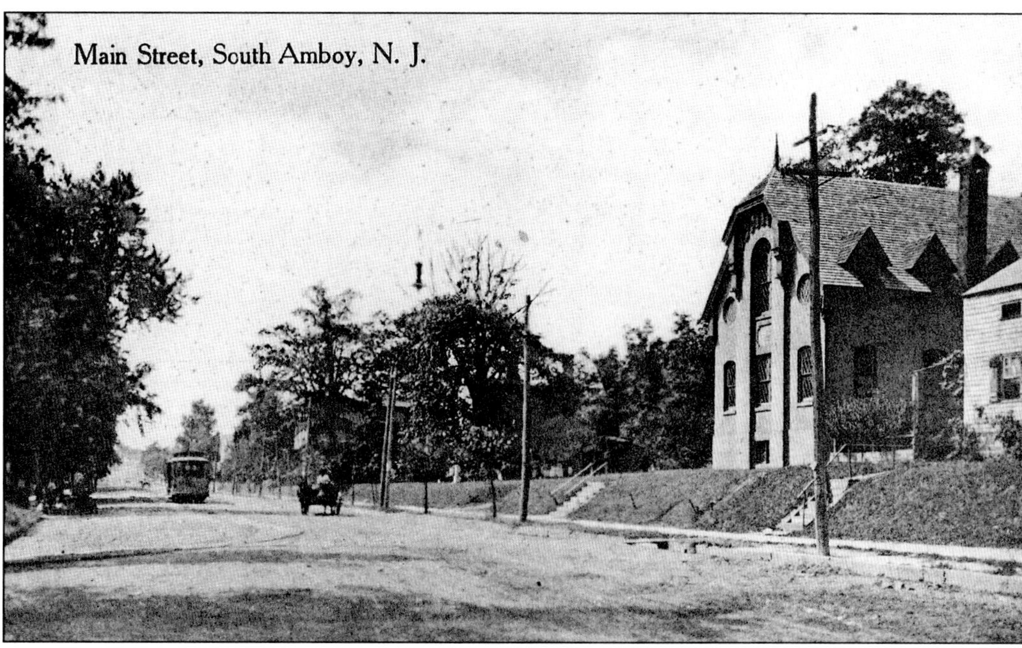

The Christ Church parish school is shown here again, with a trolley car approaching on Main Street.

This is a rare find. The city's only Jewish Temple, the United Brothers, also referred to as Beth Israel Mordecaí, was an Orthodox congregation located on the 500 block of Henry Street, where today there is an apartment building. It formed in 1917 and reportedly burned in the 1950s and was not replaced due to the small Jewish population.

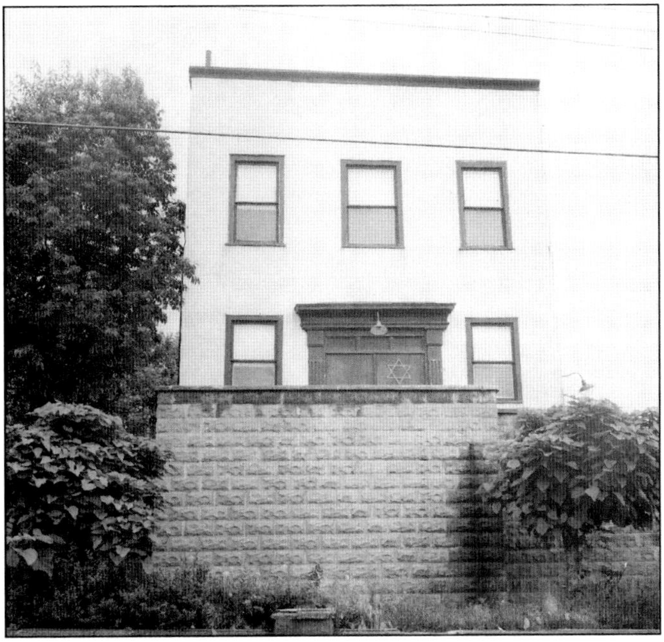

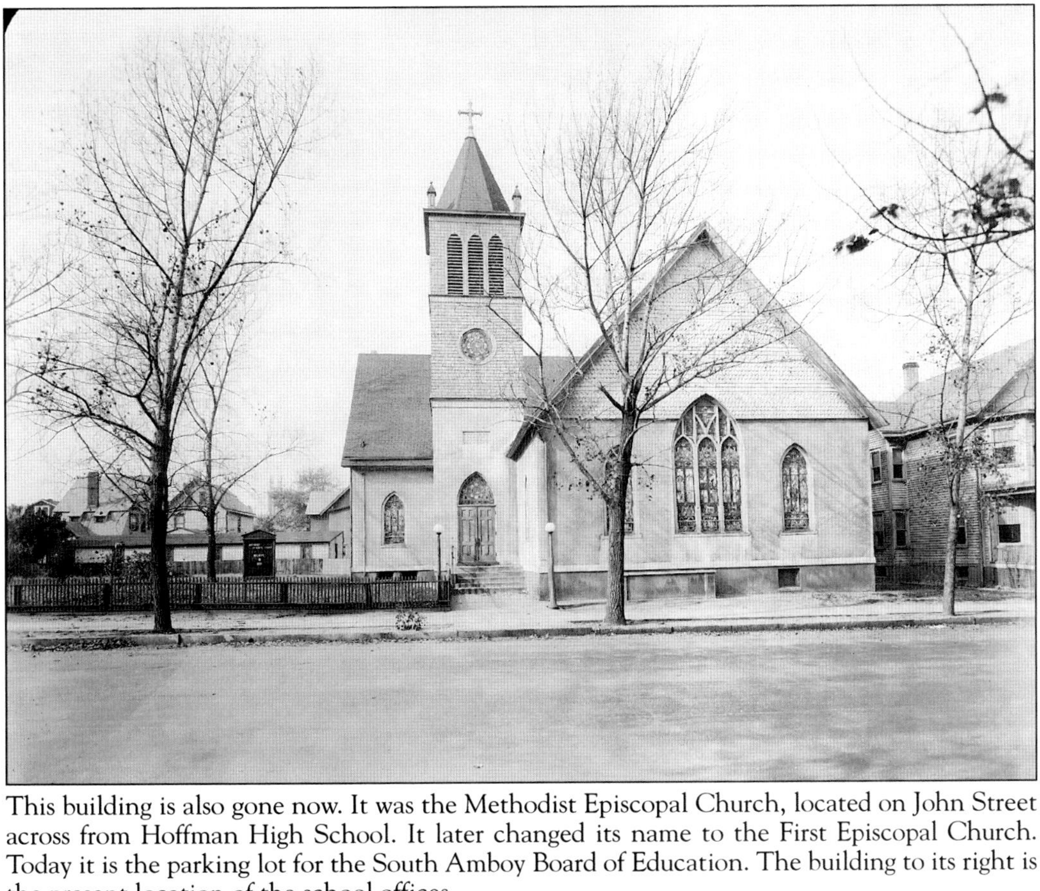

This building is also gone now. It was the Methodist Episcopal Church, located on John Street across from Hoffman High School. It later changed its name to the First Episcopal Church. Today it is the parking lot for the South Amboy Board of Education. The building to its right is the present location of the school offices.

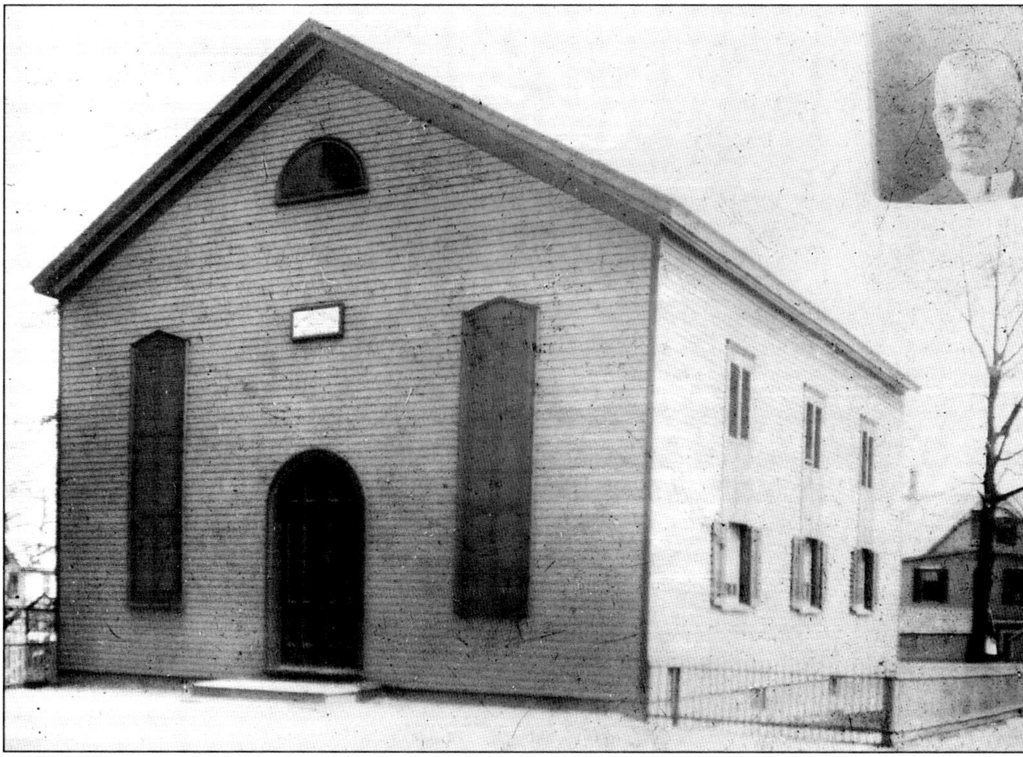

This building is located on Second Street. Watch the progression in the next two pictures. In this photo it is the Methodist Protestant Church, established in 1868, which would later change its name to Calvary Methodist Church.

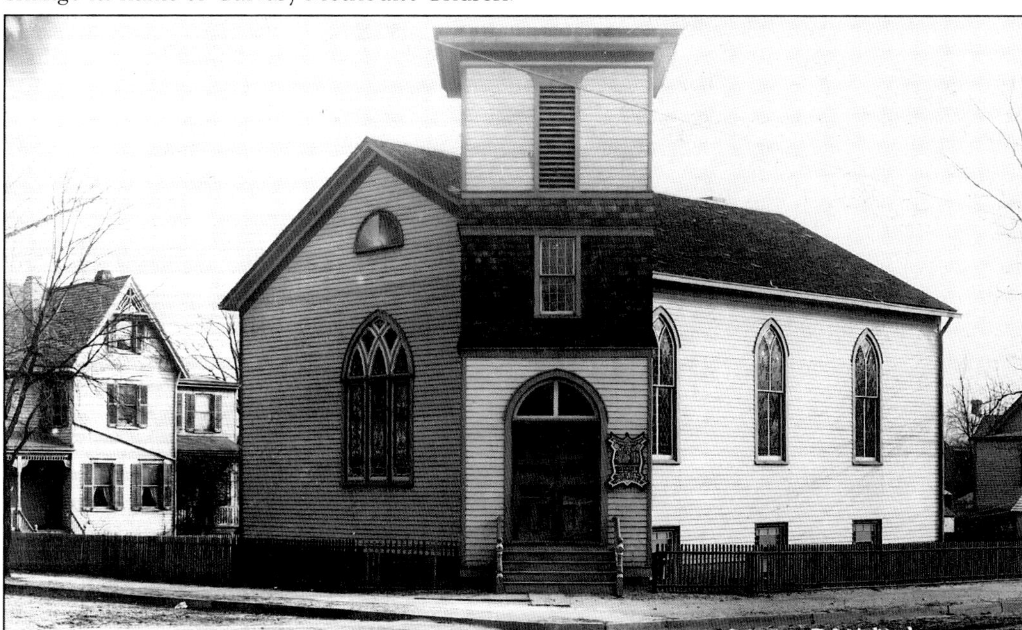

Yes, this is the same building as above, as evidenced by the roof line and small window in the center, but it is now starting to take on the look it retains to this day.

The building is still a Methodist church at this point, but it is looking much as it does today except for the dark paint, which is now white. In 1965 it became the Sadie Pope Dowdell Library, named for the woman who was its biggest booster and ran it for many years.

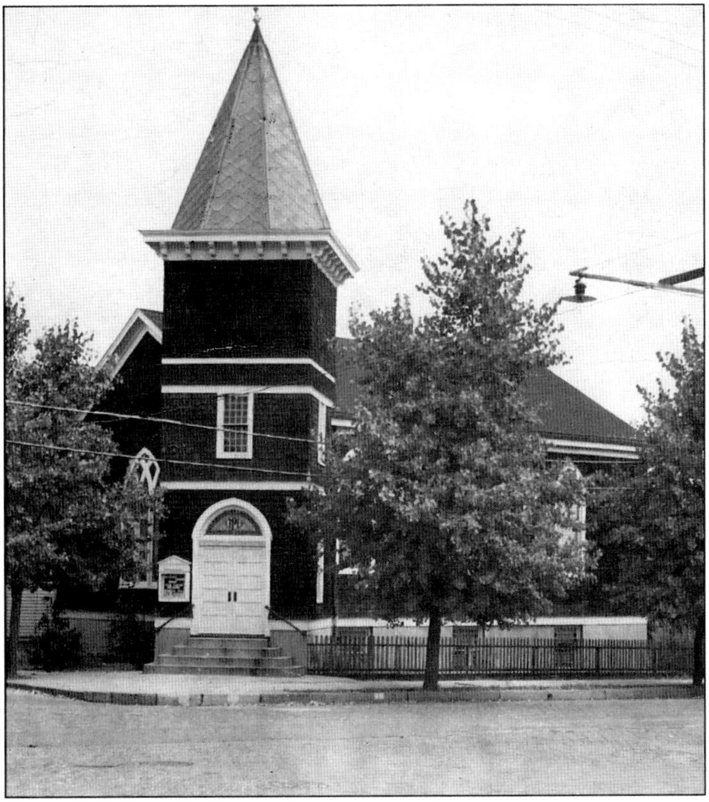

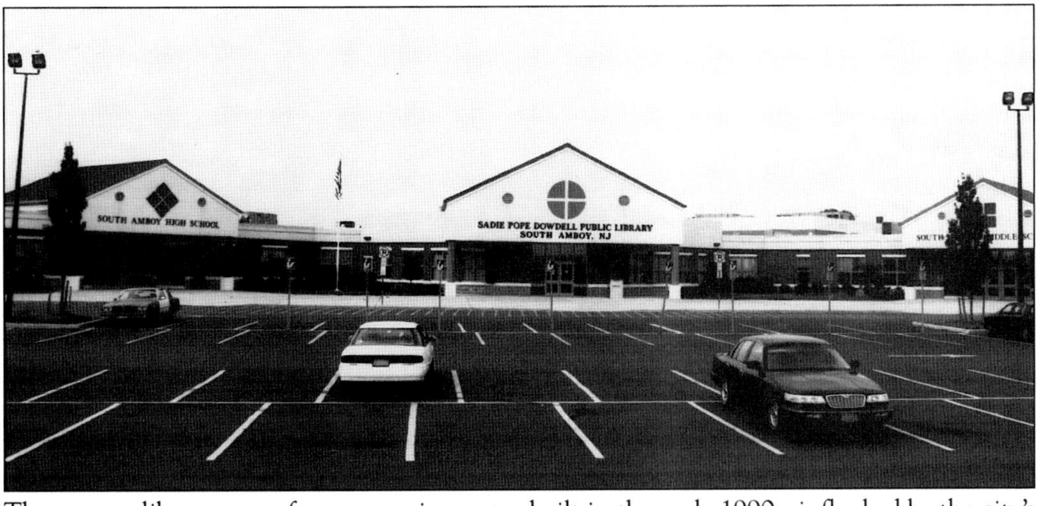

The present library, part of a community center built in the early 1990s, is flanked by the city's middle school on the right and high school on the left.

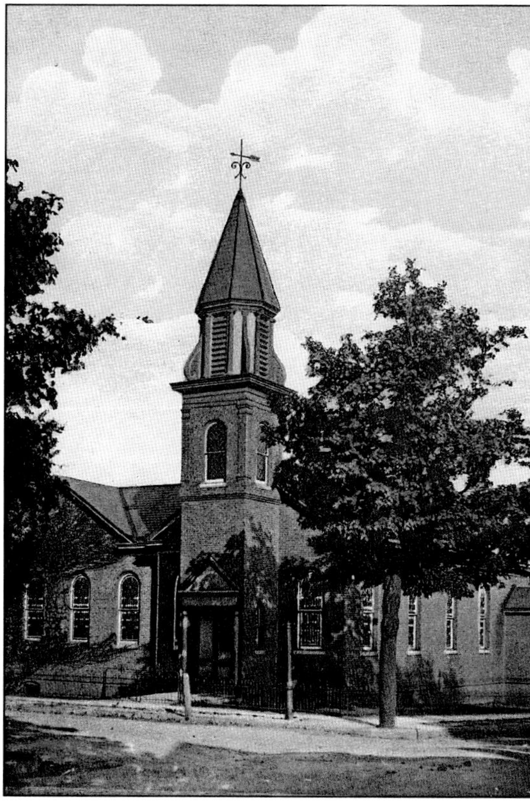

The First Baptist Church, on the corner of Stockton and Second Streets, was established in 1873.

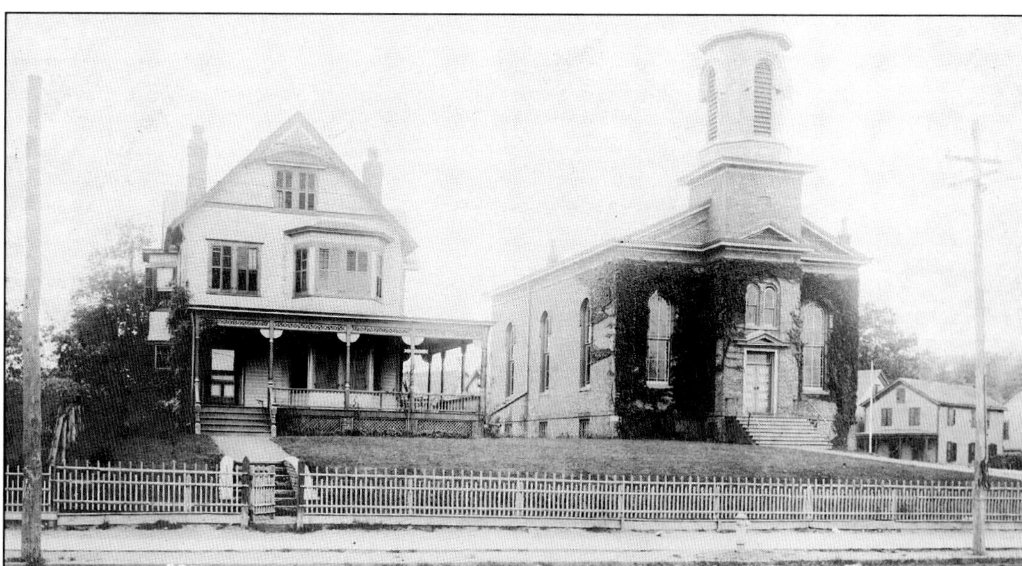

The First Presbyterian Church and parsonage was located on Broadway at the corner of Church Street. The parsonage has been replaced by the church's hall, located next to city hall.

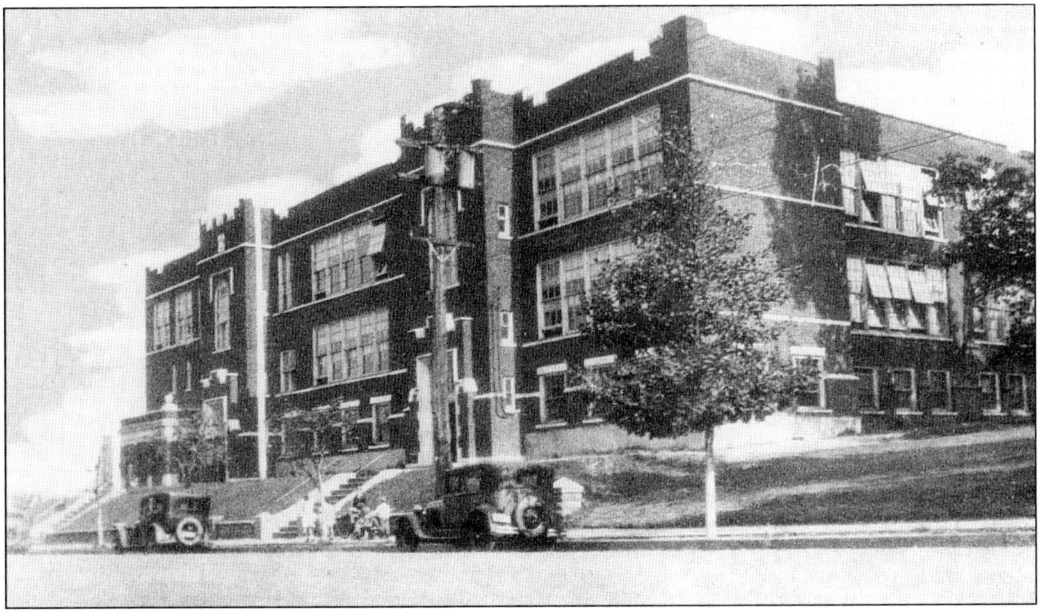

South Amboy High School, on John Street near Stevens Avenue, was built in the 1920s and named Hoffman High School for Governor Harold Hoffman in about 1937, when he was still in office. It looks largely the same today.

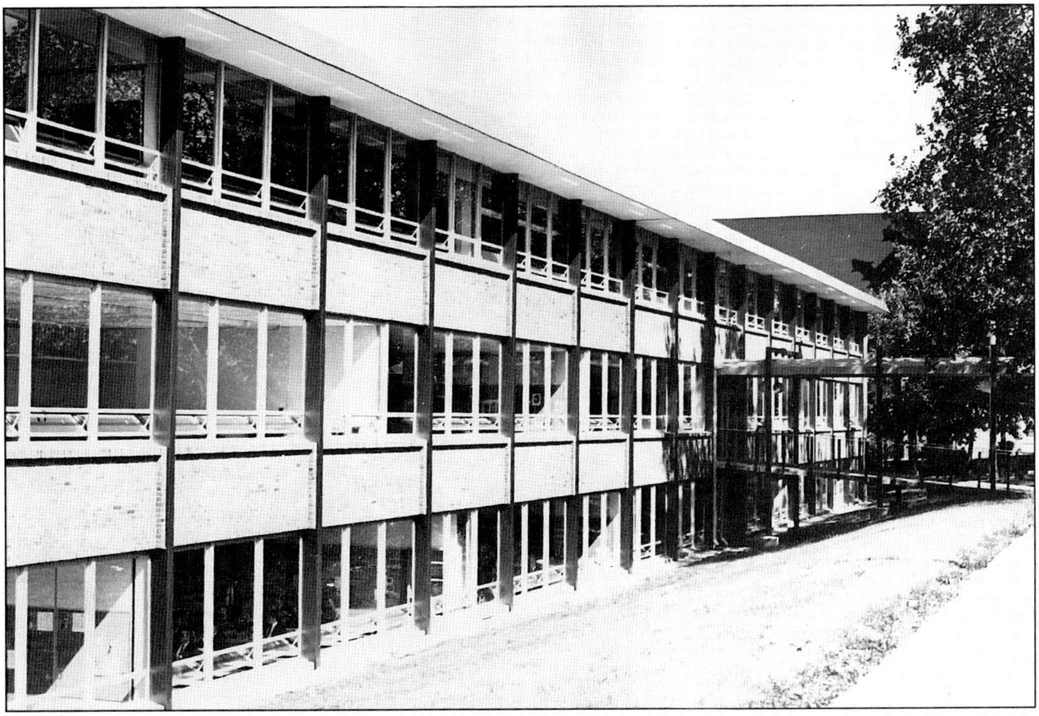

St. Mary Regional High School, located on Augusta Street at Stevens Avenue, opened in 1968.

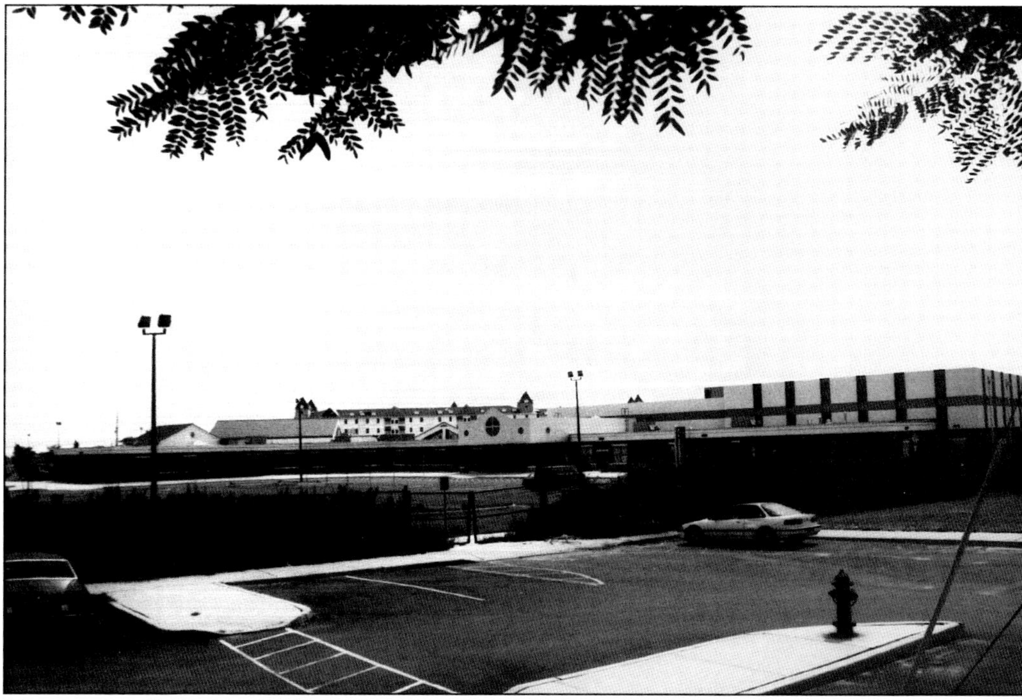

The new South Amboy High School is pictured here. In a very contentious debate, they dropped "Hoffman" as the name. It opened in 1996.

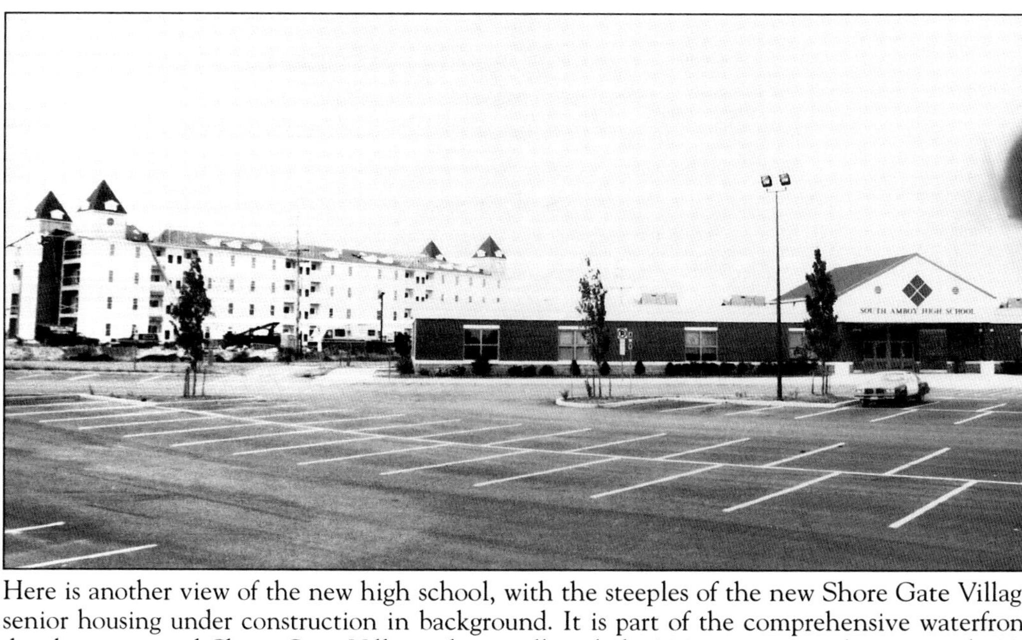

Here is another view of the new high school, with the steeples of the new Shore Gate Village senior housing under construction in background. It is part of the comprehensive waterfront development, and Shore Gate Village alone will include 114 age-restricted units, with 124 townhouses and 90 single-family homes.

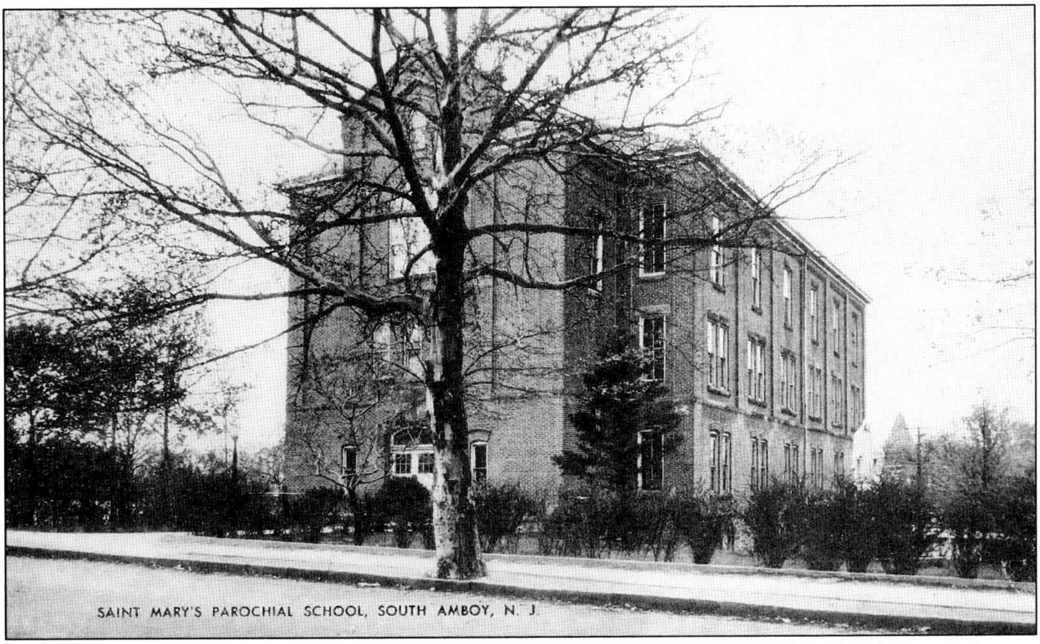

The first St. Mary school was located on Augusta Street, where the high school is now. It was dedicated in 1892, and burned in the 1950s. In 1966 it burned again, catastrophically, when it was being used as a high school.

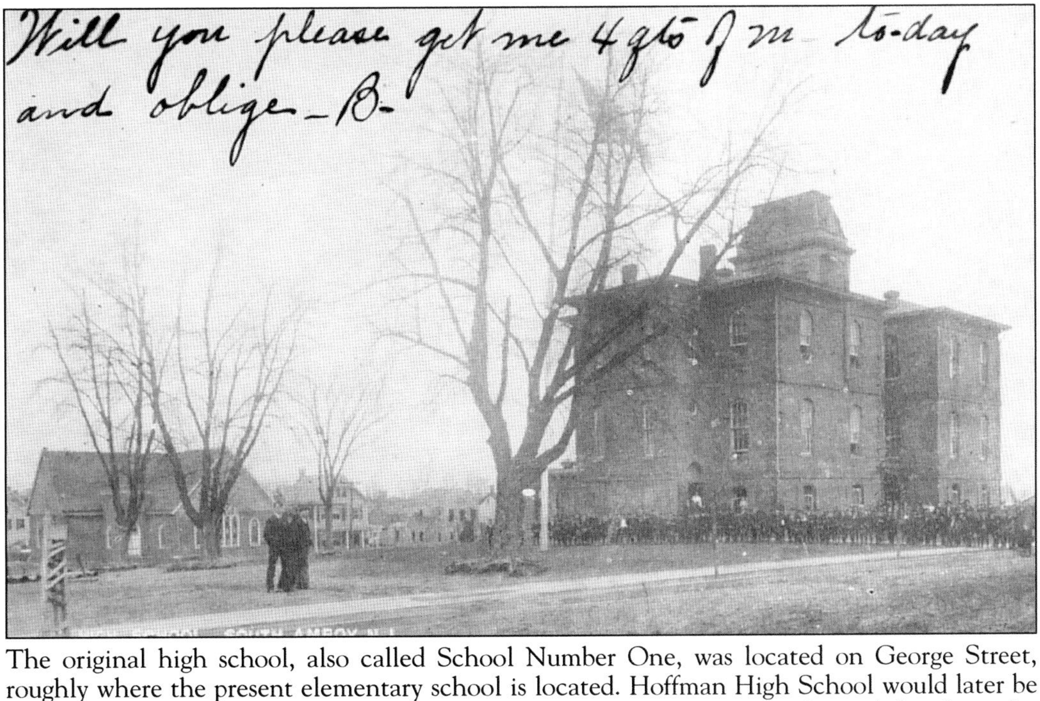

The original high school, also called School Number One, was located on George Street, roughly where the present elementary school is located. Hoffman High School would later be built to the left. The Methodist Episcopal Church can be seen to the lower left, where the present Board of Education offices are located.

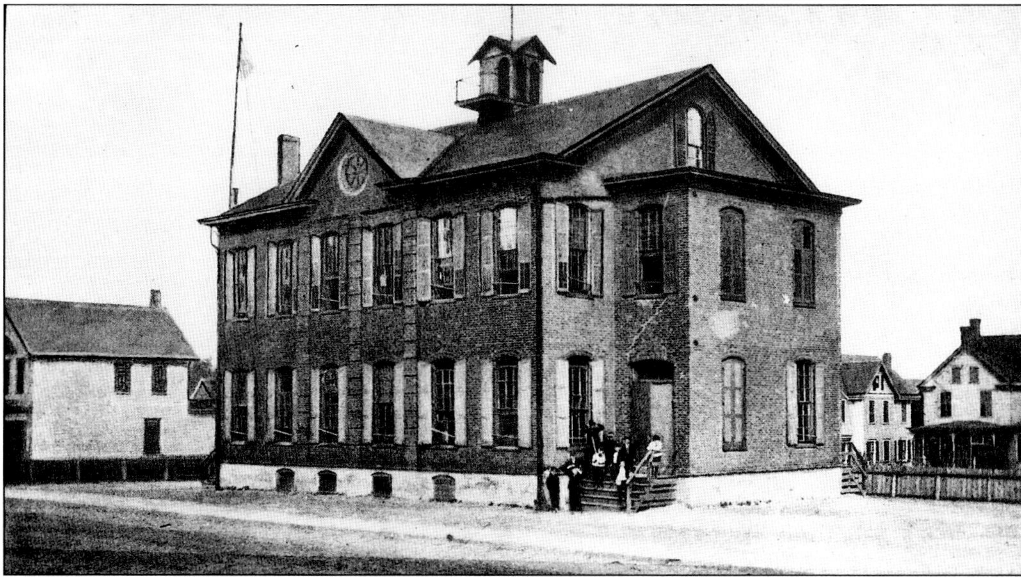

Public School Number Two was located on Fourth and Potter Streets.

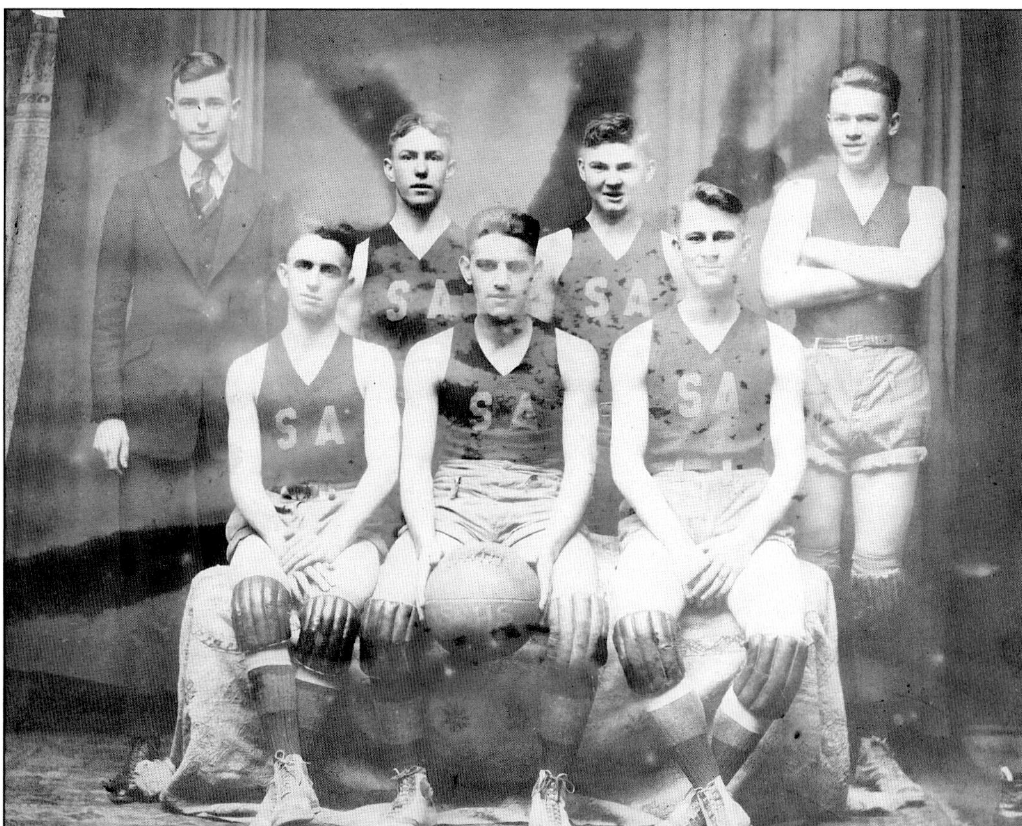

This is the South Amboy High School basketball team of 1919. The only person identified is the man in the suit, Raymond Dowdell, the team manager and brother of Sadie Pope Dawdell of the city's library.

Public School Number Two is pictured here, now with an addition in the foreground.

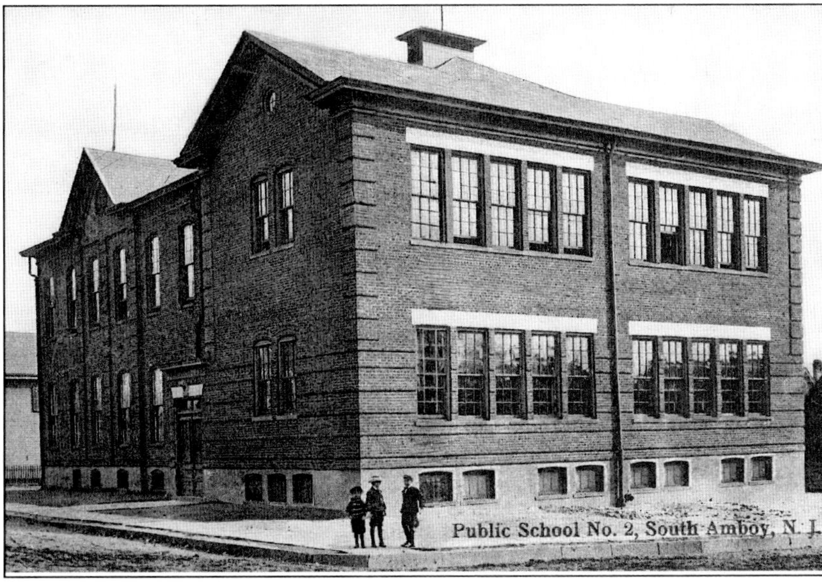

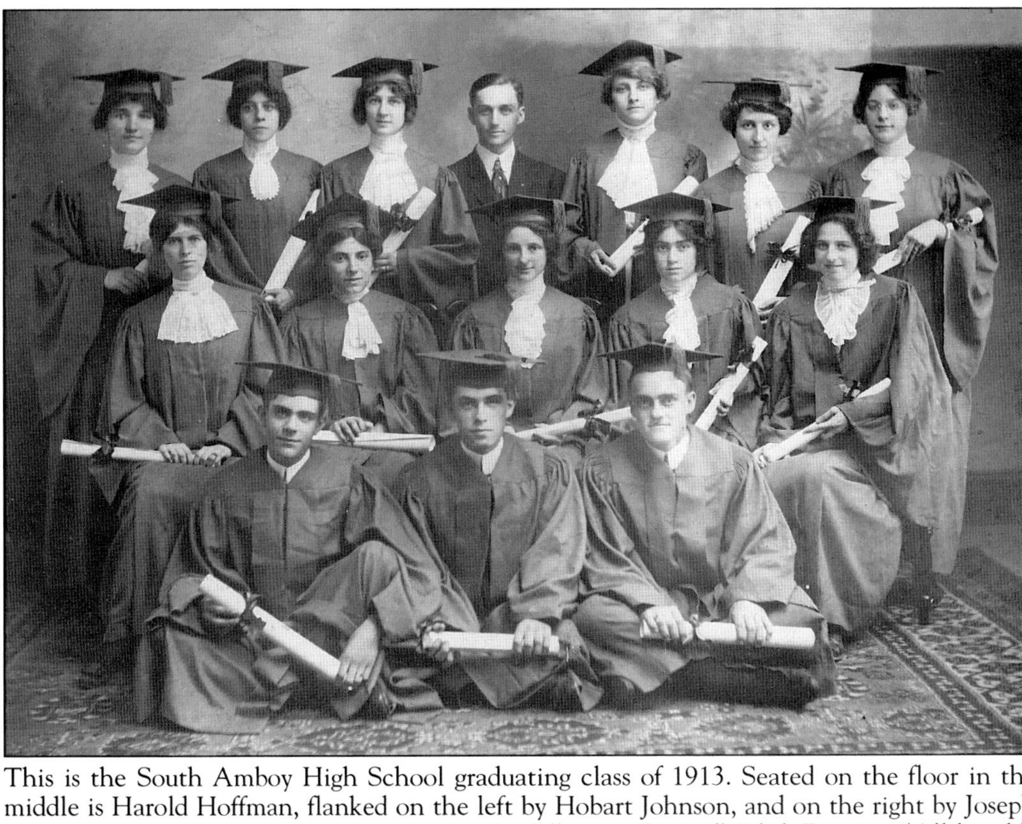

This is the South Amboy High School graduating class of 1913. Seated on the floor in the middle is Harold Hoffman, flanked on the left by Hobart Johnson, and on the right by Joseph Capner. Behind them, from left to right, are the following: (seated) Edith Freeman (Allsbrook), Gladys Johnson (Bennett), Elizabeth Douglas (Diefenbach), Myrtle Spangenberg, and Dorothy Bergen; (standing) Ellen R. Parisen (mother of city historian William Marshall), Gladys Walters, Florence Thompson, Paul Miller (the school principal), Mildred Deats (McCormick), Elsie McDowell (King), and Charlotte Rehfuss (Rivers).

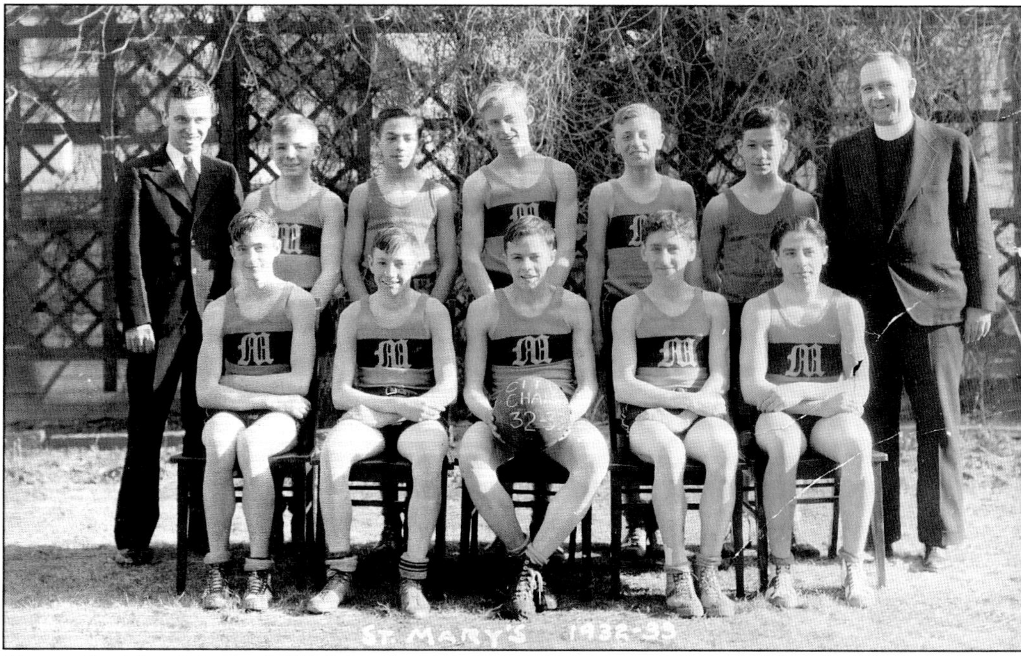

Here is St. Mary's basketball team of 1938–39.

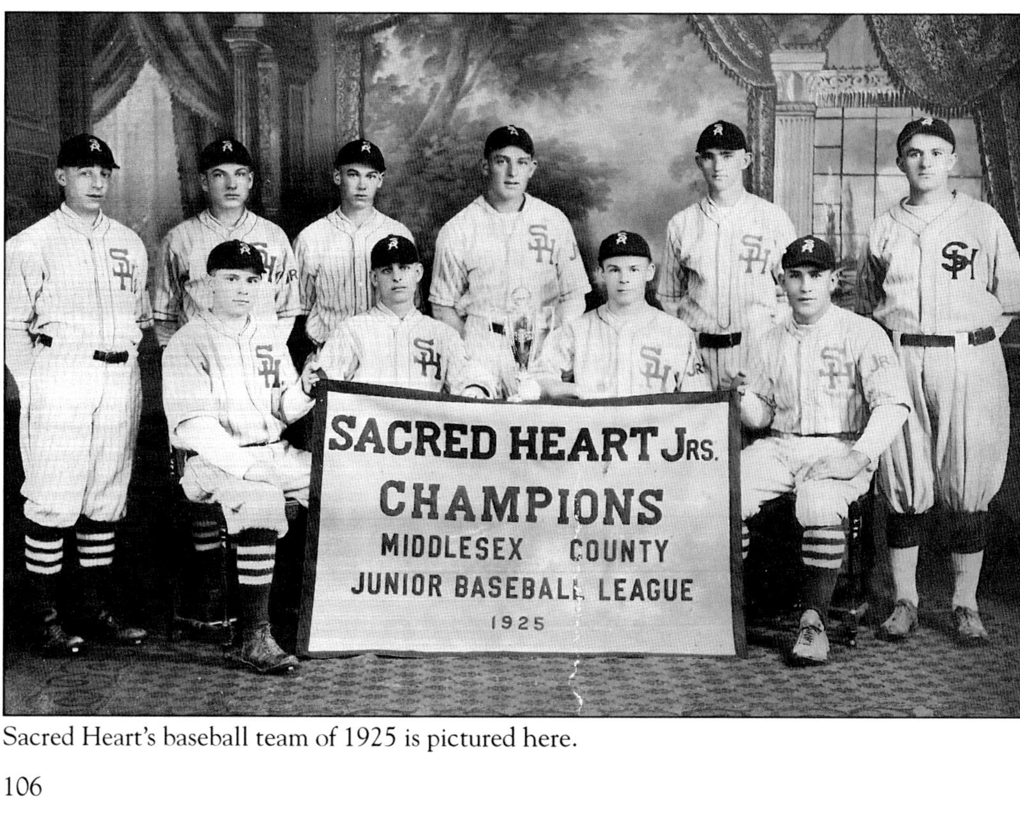

Sacred Heart's baseball team of 1925 is pictured here.

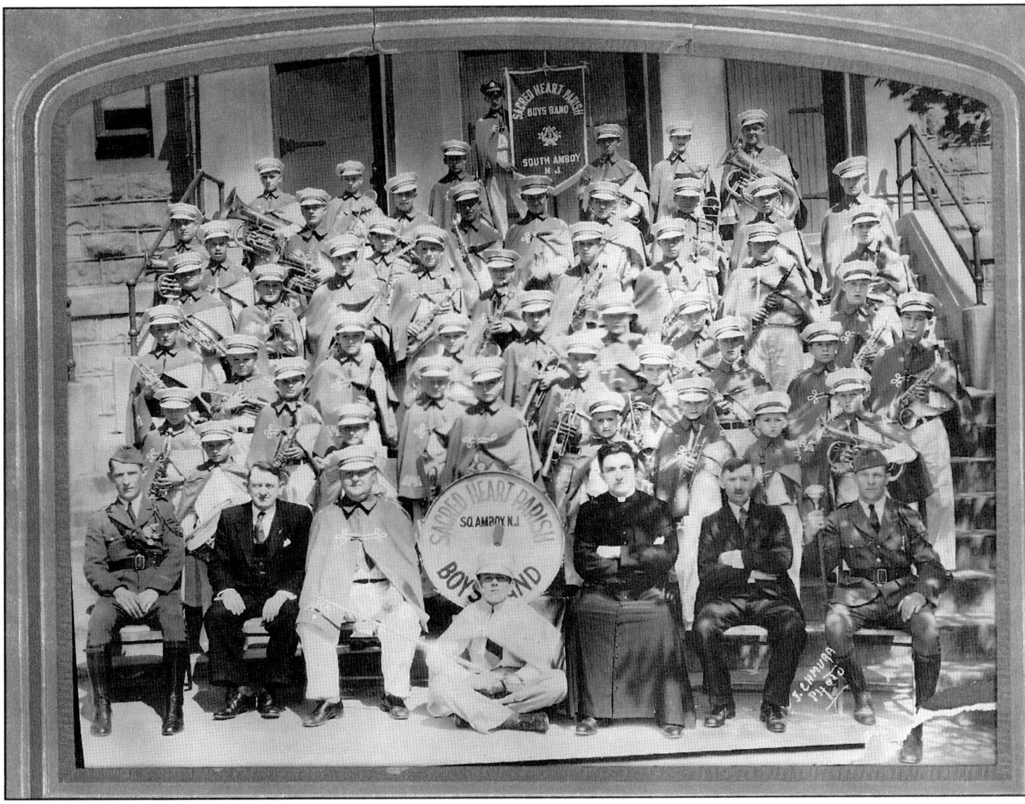

Sacred Heart's band is pictured here on the steps of the church.

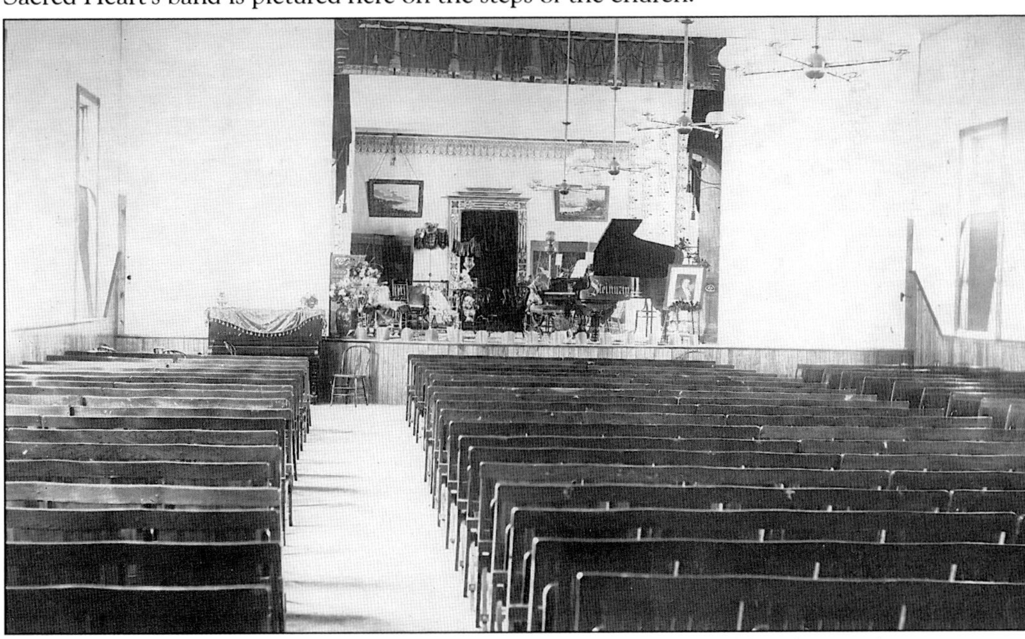

This view is inside the Knights of Pythias Lodge, one of the city's oldest fraternal organizations. Located on First Street and Stockton Street, it began around 1889. Here it is set up for a piano recital by Fannie Davis Parisen.

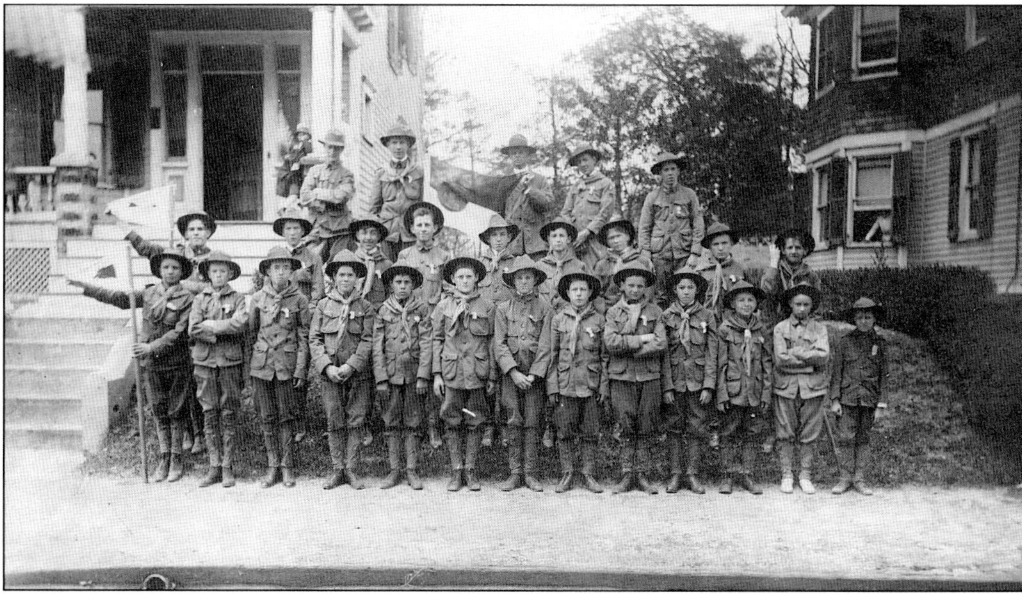

The city's first Boy Scout Troop, Troop 91, was organized in 1916 by the First Baptist Church. The scoutmaster was John Tracy Dill.

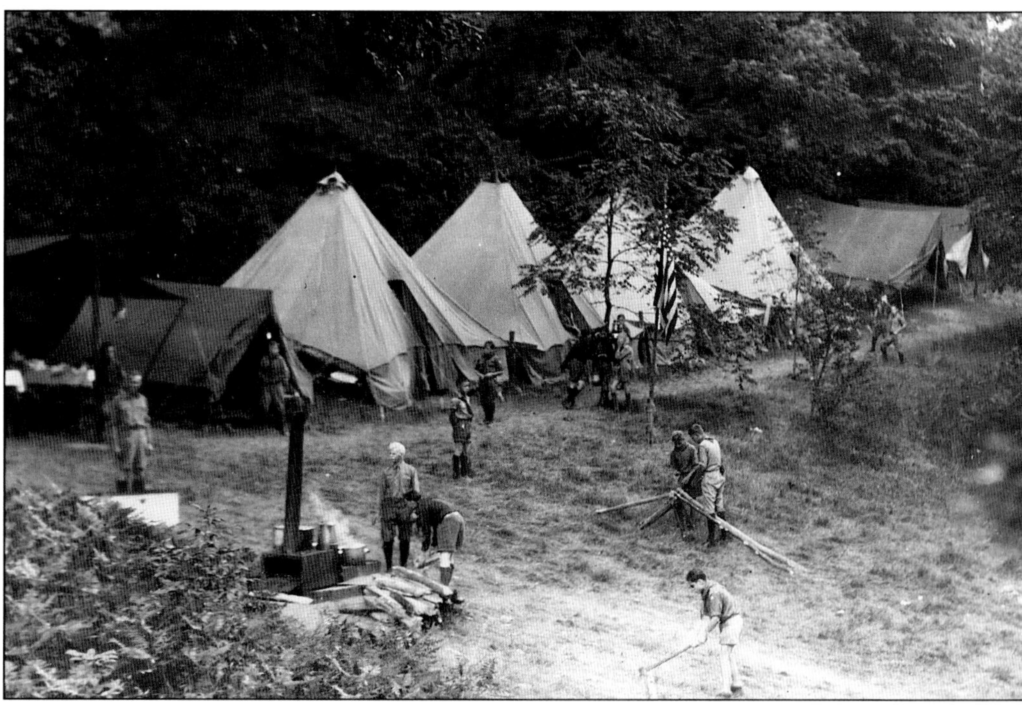

Camp Dill was named for the founder of Troop 91, John Tracy Dill, who is standing near the stove, with white hair. The camp is in High Bridge in Hunderdon County, on Lake Solitude. Many of the city's boys passed through, gradually building a cabin. This photo is believed to be from the 1930s.

Five

THE GOOD LIFE

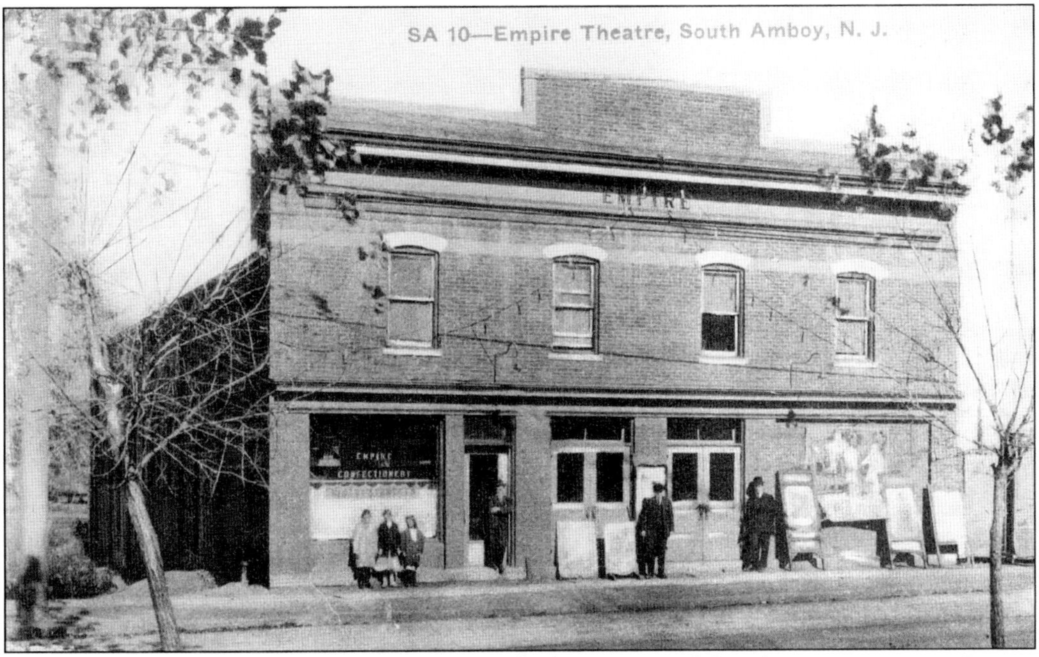

This title of this chapter has two meanings. It looks at some of the places to enjoy good times around South Amboy as well as looking at some of the noteworthy people who lived well. The Empire Theater, on Broadway across from Church Street, is pictured here before it added a marquee. This was the site of many fun nights on the town.

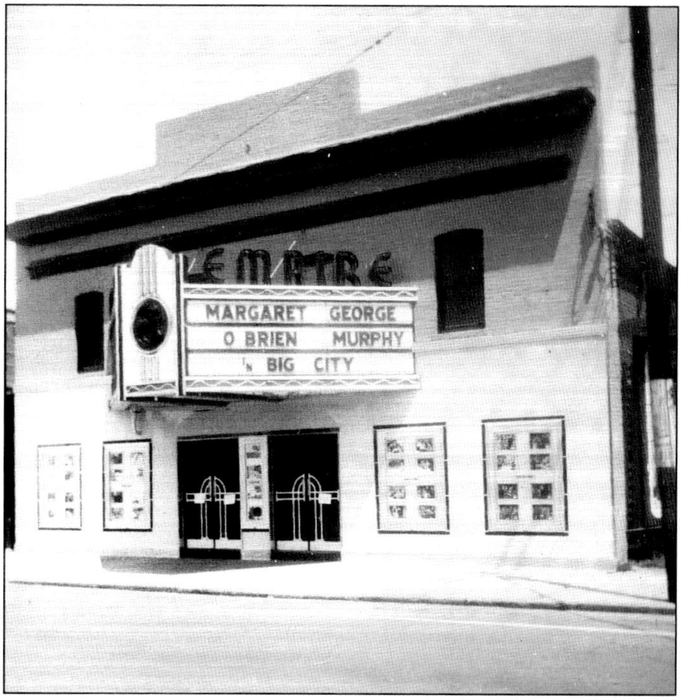

The Empire is seen here with its marquee and facelift. It was affectionately known as "the itch," for its permanent insect inhabitants.

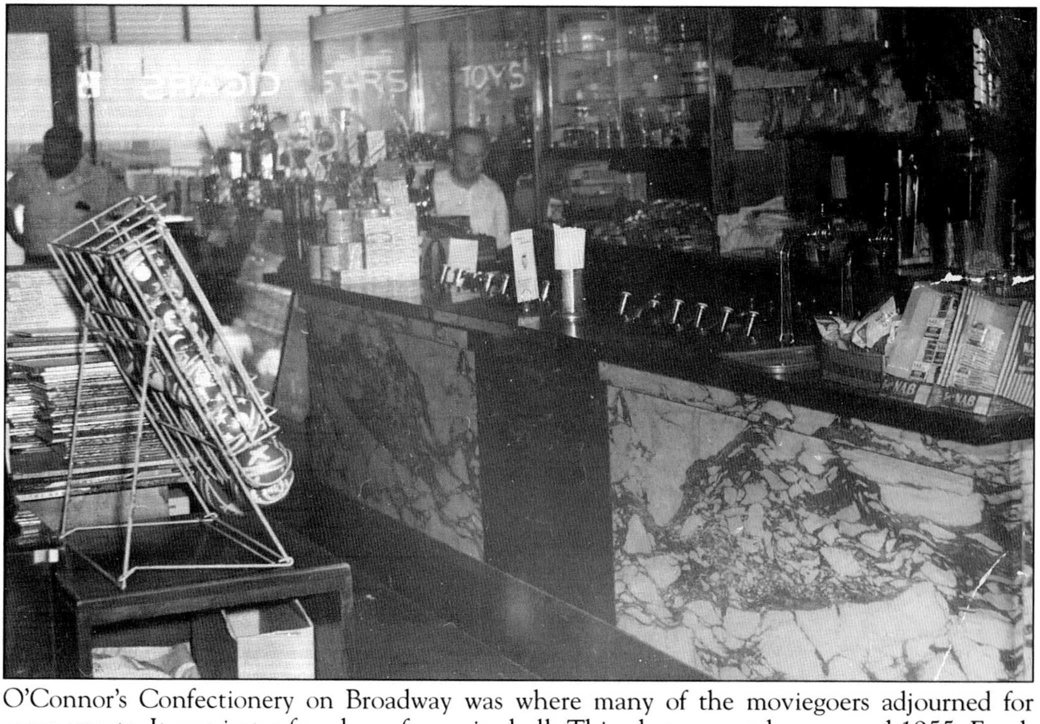

O'Connor's Confectionery on Broadway was where many of the moviegoers adjourned for some sweets. It was just a few doors from city hall. This photo was taken around 1955. Frank O'Connor is pictured on the right.

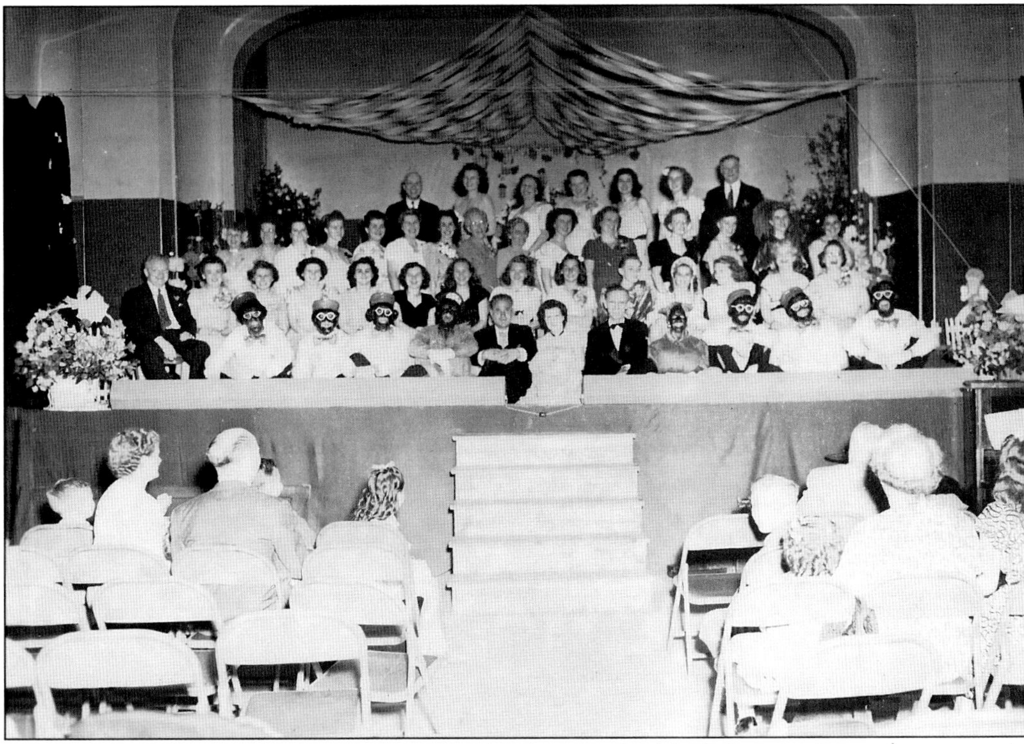

This is a minstrel show at Hoffman High School. Note the black face on the performers in the front row, which makes identifying those people almost impossible.

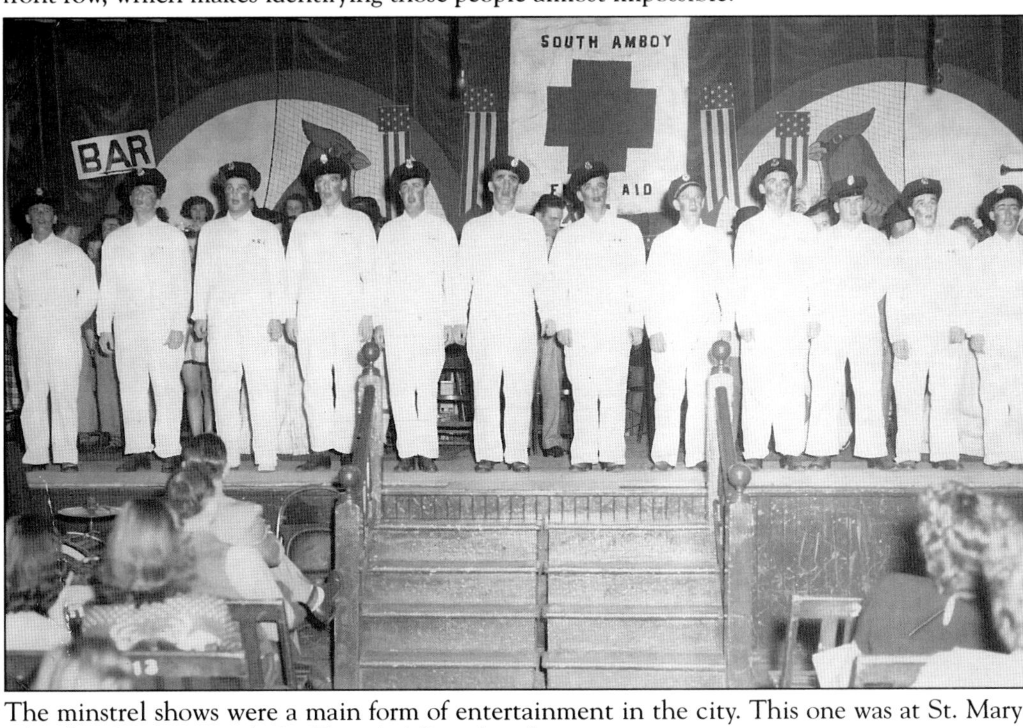

The minstrel shows were a main form of entertainment in the city. This one was at St. Mary's school auditorium, with the First Aid Squad performing.

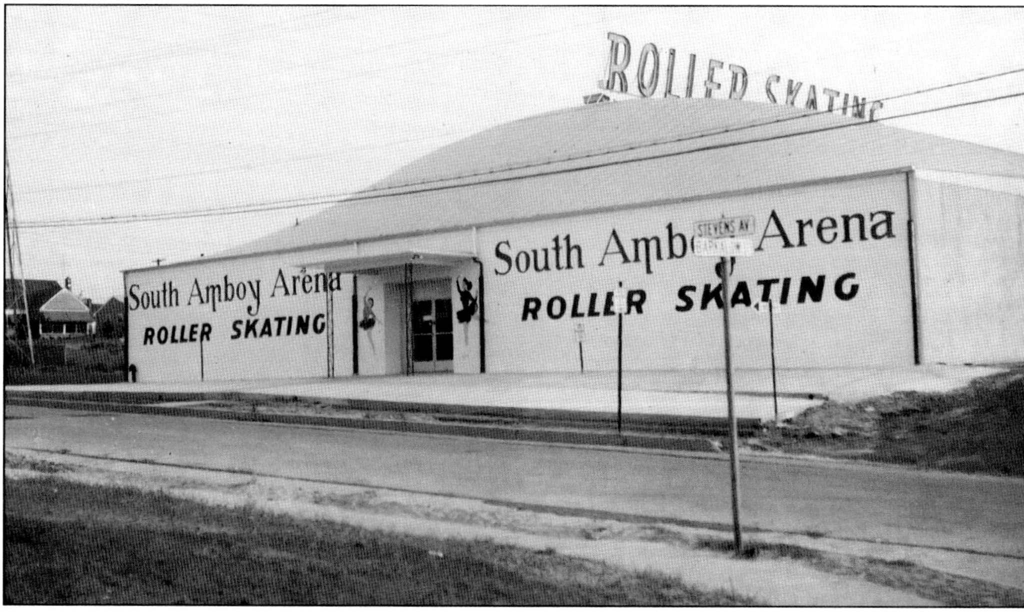

Another big night out, at least for the young, was at the roller skating rink on North Stevens Avenue. The South Amboy Arena was established in 1958 and is one of the few in the area. Although it looks somewhat different, it is still going strong today.

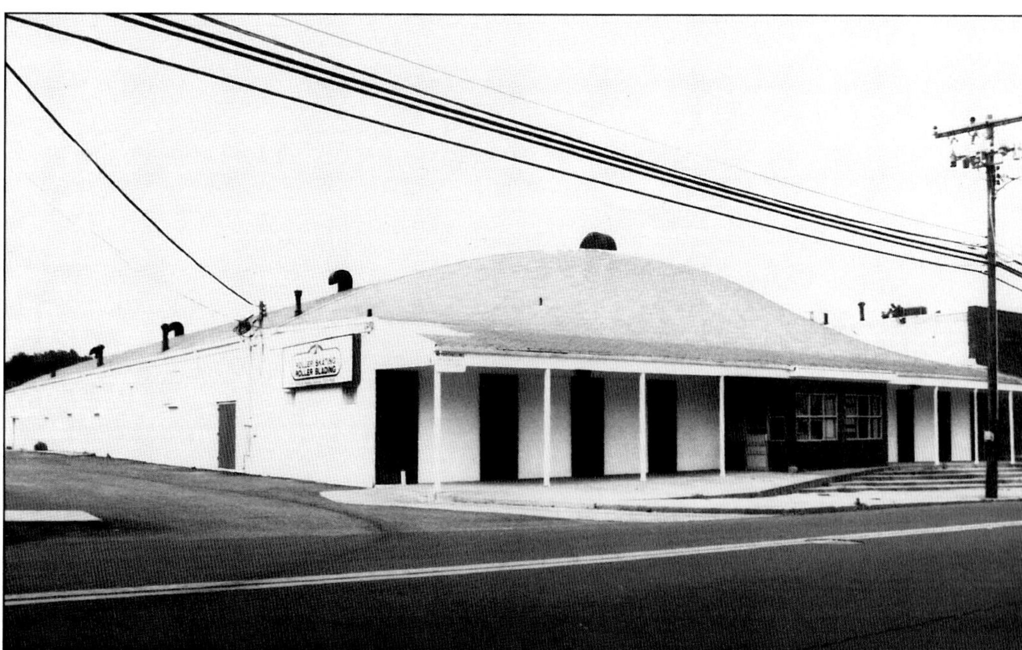

Here is the skating rink as it appears today.

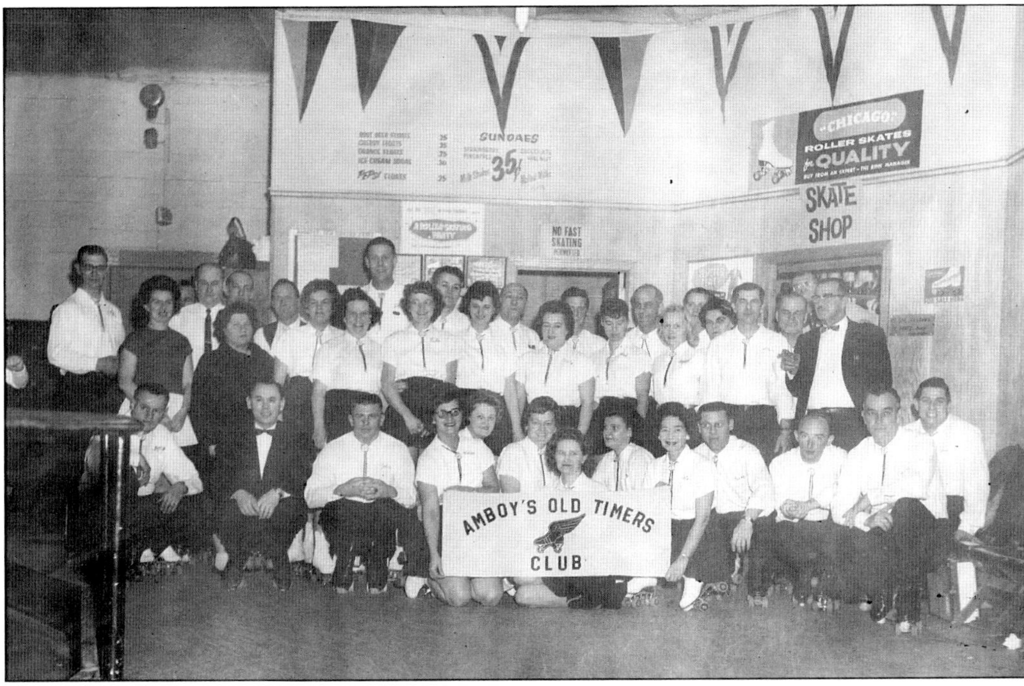

This is the "Old Timers Club," although that is a relative term, given that most of the patrons are teens or pre-teens. Owner John Durnye is squatting at the far left in a bowtie.

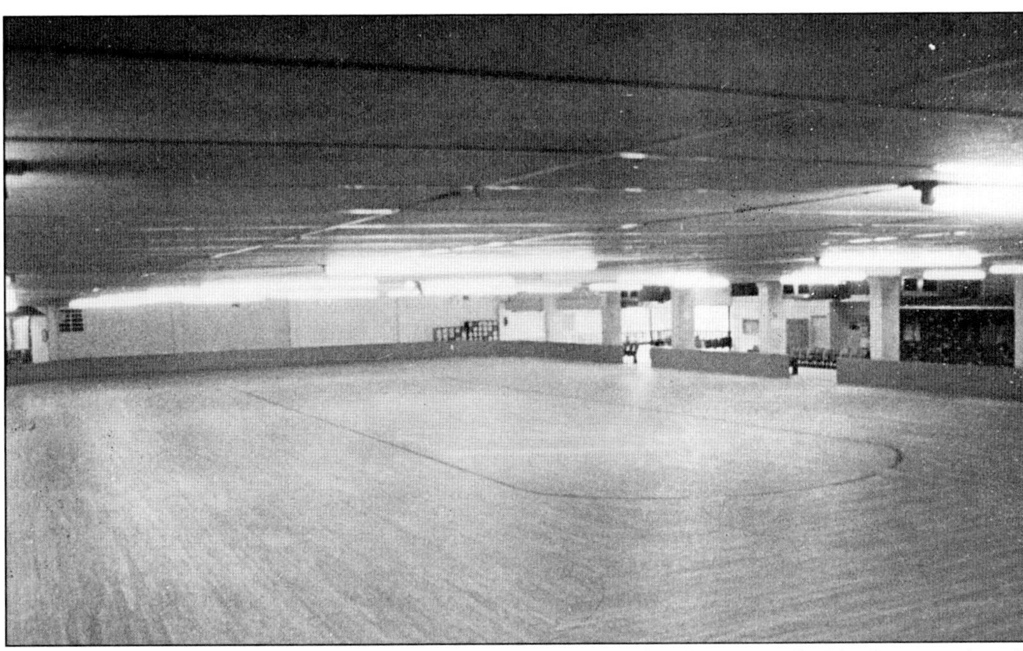

This was taken before the crowds were out on the floor at the skating rink. The beginner's rink, now replaced by another concession, is visible in the far corner.

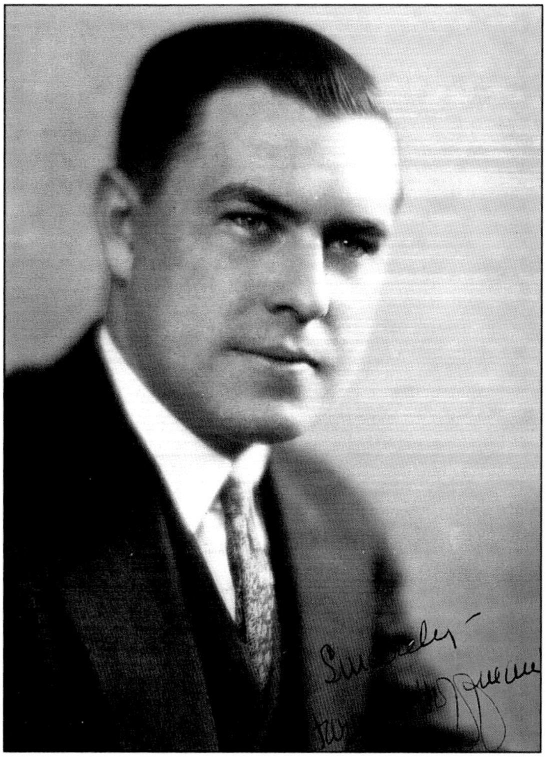

Governor Harold Hoffman (1896–1954) is pictured here. He served from 1935 to 1938. New Jersey has had only 39 governors, and South Amboy supplied one. He presided during the infamous trial of Bruno Hauptman for kidnapping Charles Lindbergh's baby. He also served as mayor of South Amboy and as a congressman in the 1920s.

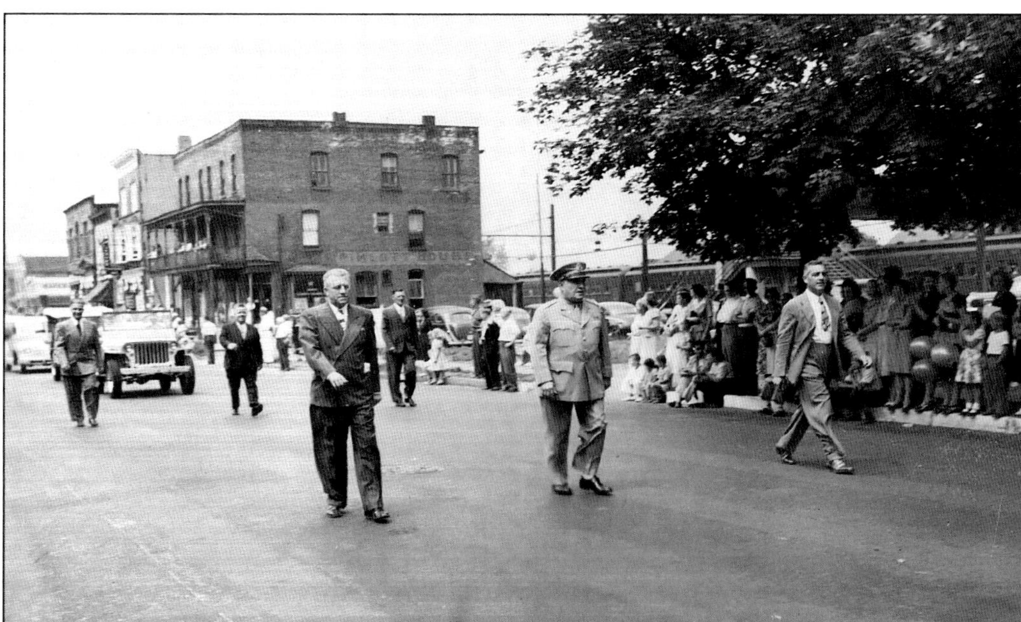

Hoffman is shown here marching on Broadway shortly after returning from World War II.

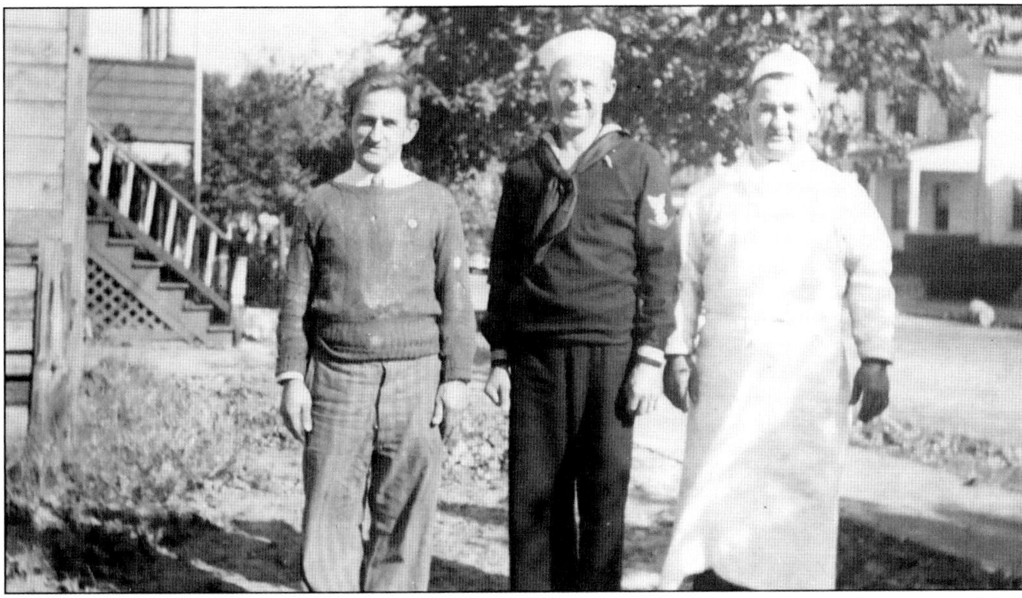

Another respected member of the community, Adam Isaac Rzepka, is pictured here in a Navy uniform between his brothers, Joseph "Chappy" and Michael, in 1942. Adam ran Air Electric, named using his initials, into his 90s, and died in 1998 at age 96.

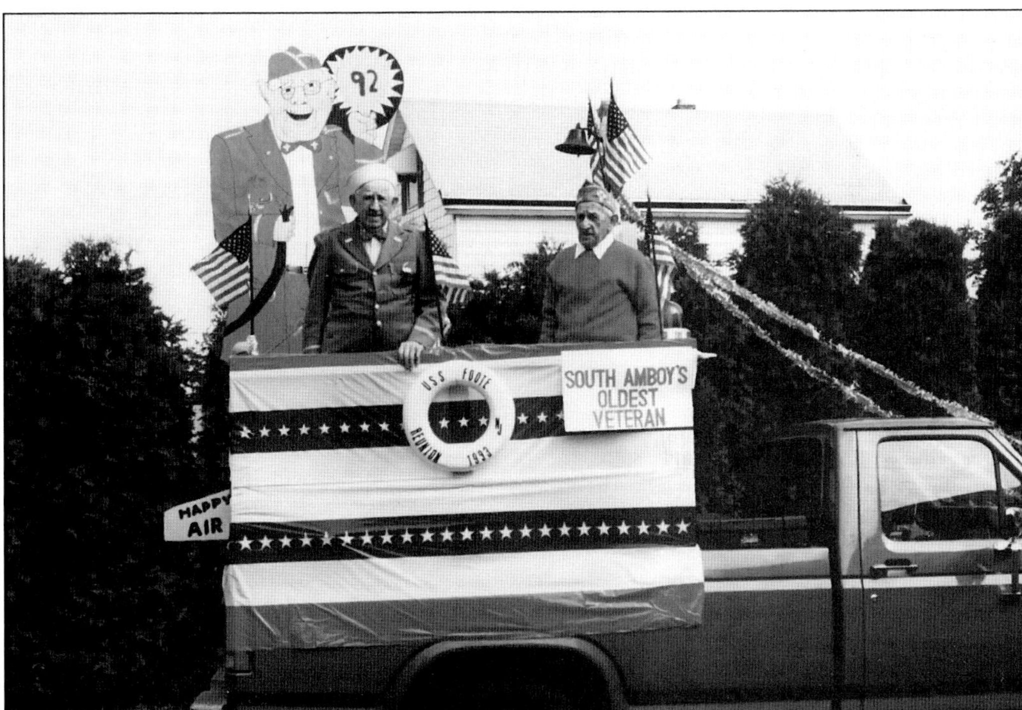

Adam Rzepka was deservedly recognized for his military service, but many other city men risked their lives for their country. One who gave all was Luke A. Lovely, who was the first New Jersey man killed in World War I. The local American Legion post is named for Lovely.

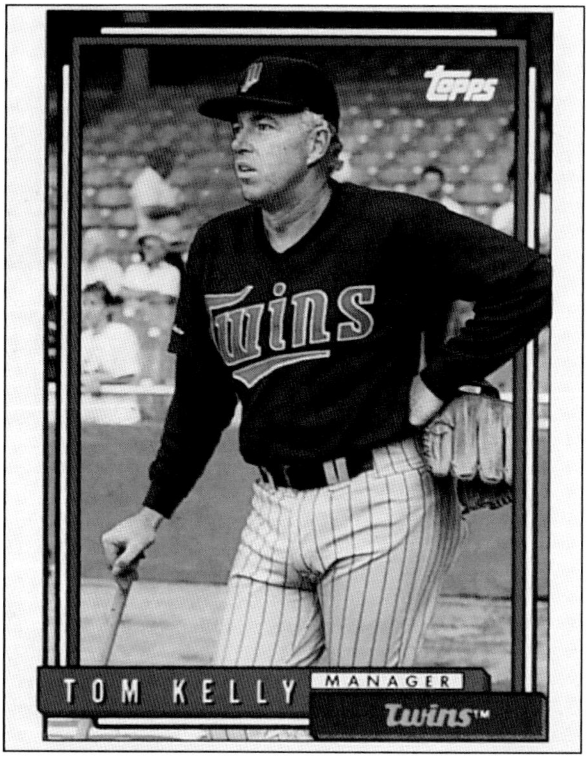

South Amboy has sent five men to Major League Baseball, a point of pride in a city of 8,000 people. Two are managers and three were players. Tom Kelly really used to live in Parlin, but he attended St. Mary's, so South Amboyans lay a claim to him. He has managed the Minnesota Twins from 1986 through 1998, leading the team to two World Series wins, in 1989 and 1991.

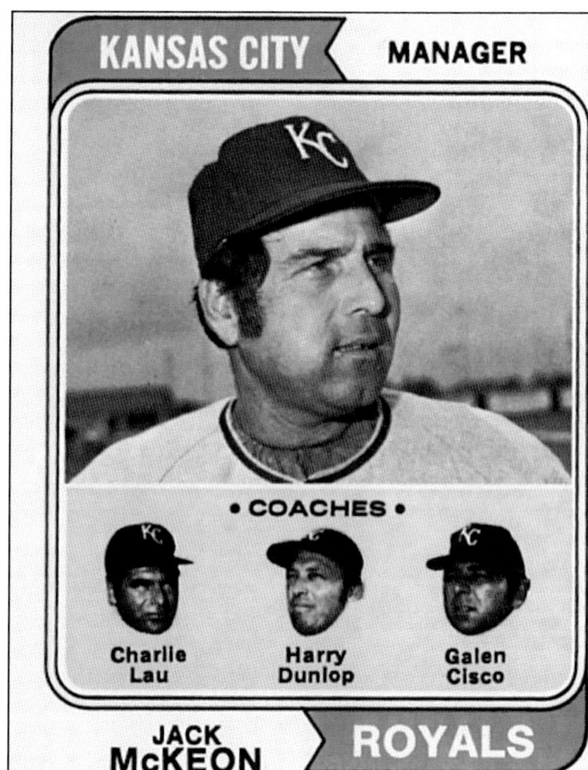

The other manager is Jack McKeon, who managed the Kansas City Royals from 1973 to 1975, the Oakland A's in 1977–78, and the San Diego Padres from 1988 through 1990. After years as a senior advisor of player personnel for the Cincinnati Reds, he took the reins as manager in 1997, and is scheduled to continue in that role.

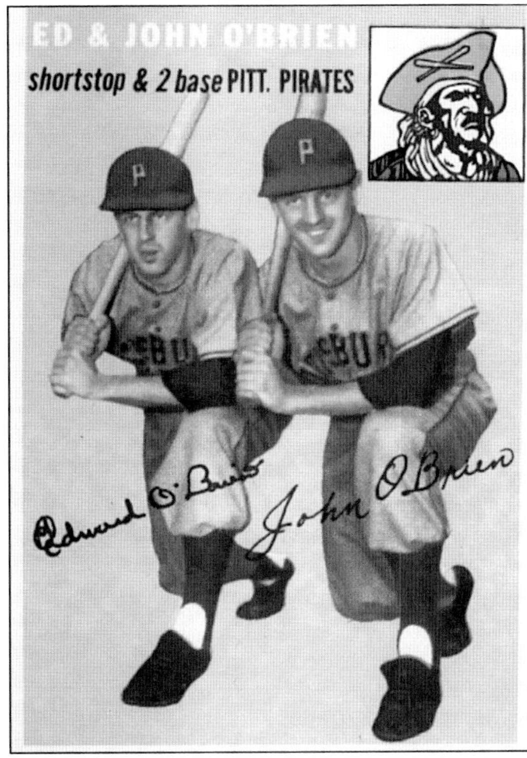

The O'Brien twins, Ed and Johnny, played on the same team, the Pittsburgh Pirates, the only set of twins ever to do that. They played from 1953 to 1958, with Johnny going on an extra year and being traded, first to the St. Louis Cardinals and then to the Milwaukee Braves. Today they live in the Seattle area.

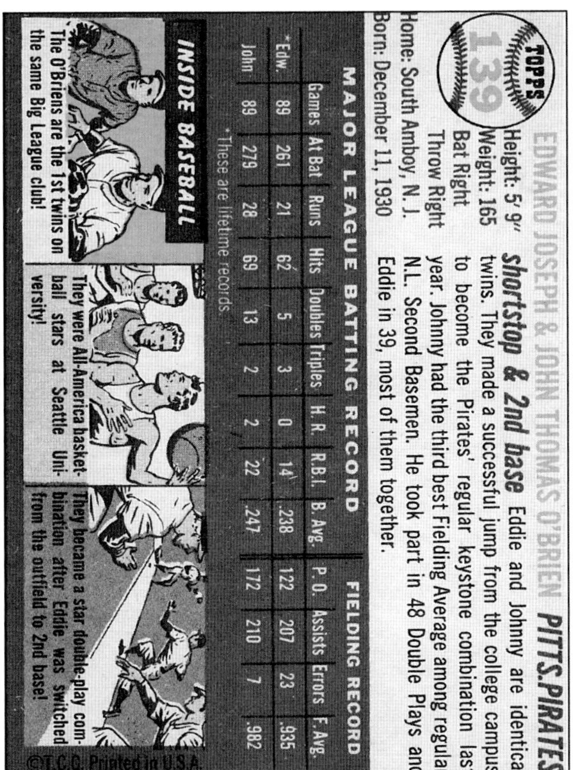

EDWARD JOSEPH & JOHN THOMAS O'BRIEN **PITTS.PIRATES**

TOPPS 139

Height: 5' 9"
Weight: 165
Bat Right
Throw Right
Home: South Amboy, N.J.
Born: December 11, 1930

Shortstop & 2nd base Eddie and Johnny are identical twins. They made a successful jump from the college campus to become the Pirates' regular keystone combination last year. Johnny had the third best Fielding Average among regular N.L. Second Basemen. He took part in 48 Double Plays and Eddie in 39, most of them together.

	MAJOR LEAGUE BATTING RECORD								FIELDING RECORD			
	Games	At Bat	Runs	Hits	Doubles	Triples	H.R.	R.B.I.	B. Avg.	P.O.	Assists	Errors	F. Avg.
*Edw.	89	261	21	62	5	3	0	14	.238	122	207	23	.935
John	89	279	28	69	13	2	2	22	.247	172	210	7	.982

*These are lifetime records.

INSIDE BASEBALL

The O'Briens are the 1st twins on the same Big League club!

They were All-America basketball stars at Seattle University!

They became a star double-play combination after Eddie was switched from the outfield to 2nd base!

©T.C.G. Printed in U.S.A.

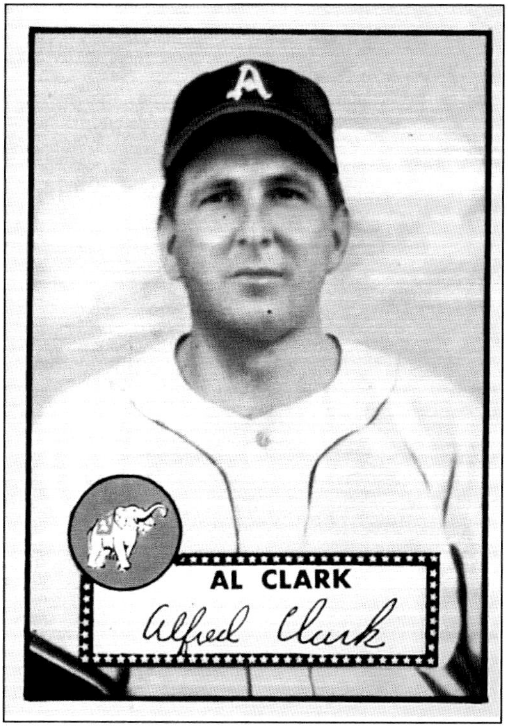

Probably the most well-known player, because he played for a local team, the New York Yankees, is Alfred "Allie" or "Alfie" Clark, who also played for the Cleveland Indians and Philadelphia Athletics.

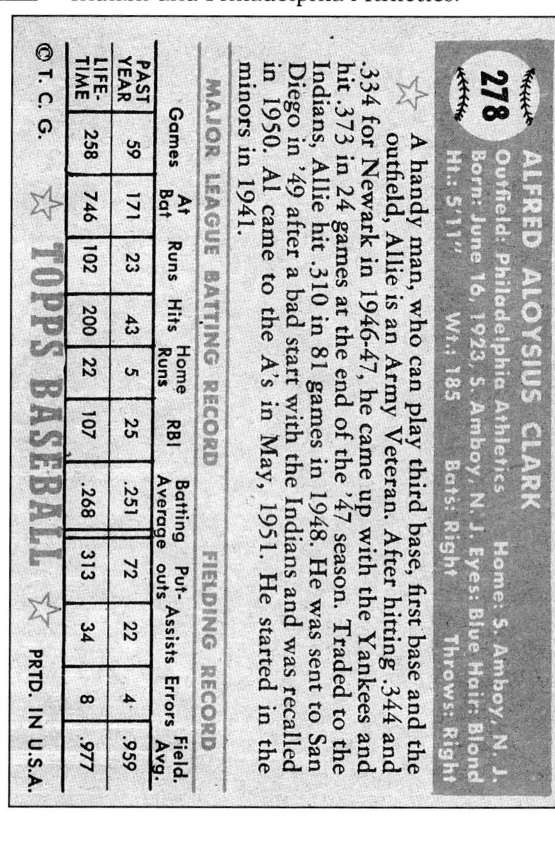

278

ALFRED ALOYSIUS CLARK

Outfield: Philadelphia Athletics Home: S. Amboy, N. J.
Born: June 16, 1923, S. Amboy, N. J. Eyes: Blue Hair: Blond
Ht.: 5'11" Wt.: 185 Bats: Right Throws: Right

A handy man, who can play third base, first base and the outfield, Allie is an Army Veteran. After hitting .344 and .334 for Newark in 1946-47, he came up with the Yankees and hit .373 in 24 games at the end of the '47 season. Traded to the Indians, Allie hit .310 in 81 games in 1948. He was sent to San Diego in '49 after a bad start with the Indians and was recalled in 1950. Al came to the A's in May, 1951. He started in the minors in 1941.

	MAJOR LEAGUE BATTING RECORD							FIELDING RECORD			
	Games	At Bat	Runs	Hits	Home Runs	RBI	Batting Average	Put-outs	Assists	Errors	Field. Avg.
PAST YEAR	59	171	23	43	5	25	.251	72	22	4	.959
LIFE-TIME	258	746	102	200	22	107	.268	313	34	8	.977

© T. C. G. TOPPS BASEBALL PRTD. IN U.S.A.

Allie is pictured here in his Yankee uniform. South Amboy's baseball and softball complex at the waterfront is named for him. "My greatest thrill was when I walked into Yankee Stadium for the first time," Clark said recently.

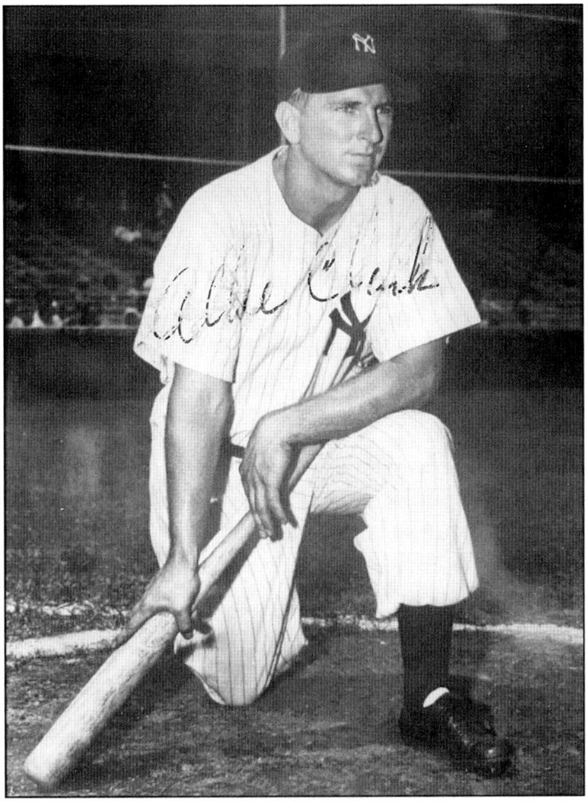

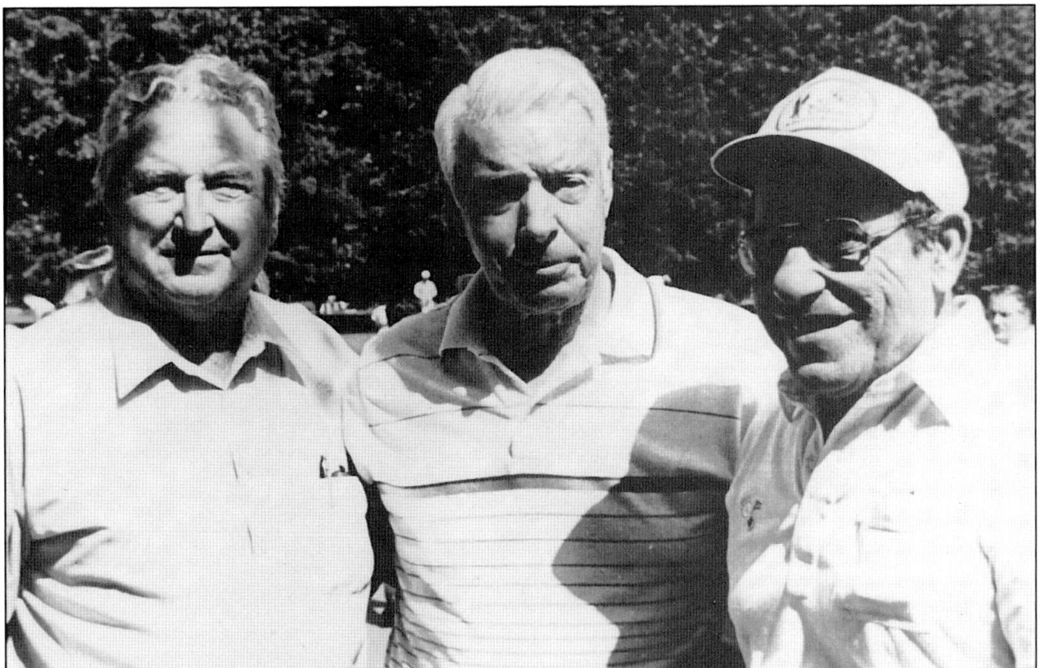

Allie is seen here with a couple of famous Yankees, Joe DiMaggio and Yogi Berra.

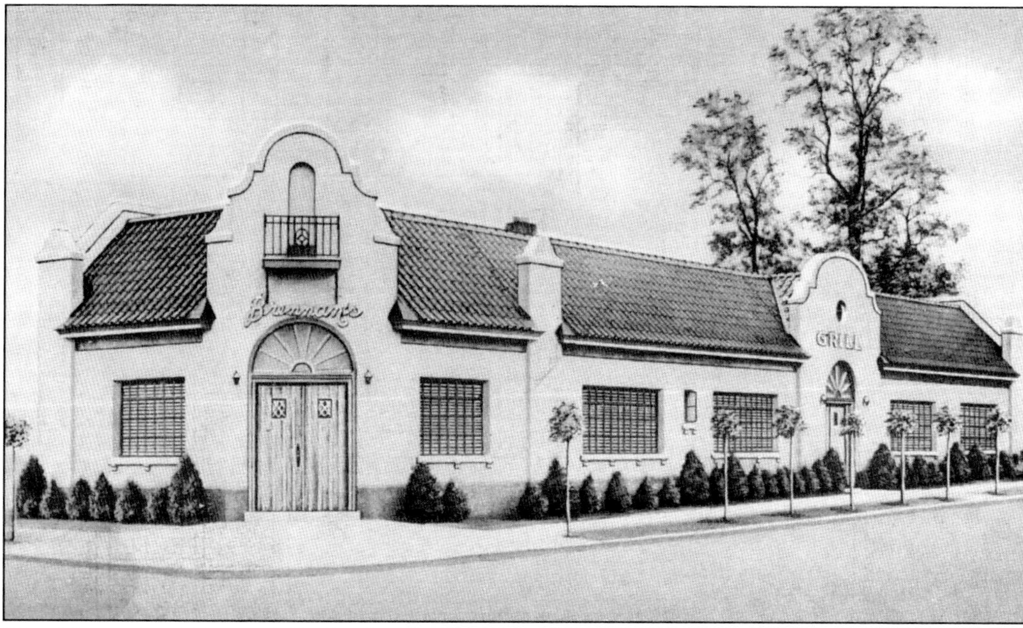

The Clover Leaf Bar and Grill, also known as Brennan's and, later, Fatso Fogarty's, is located at the corner of John Street and Broadway. In the late 1990s it is being rebuilt as a steak house.

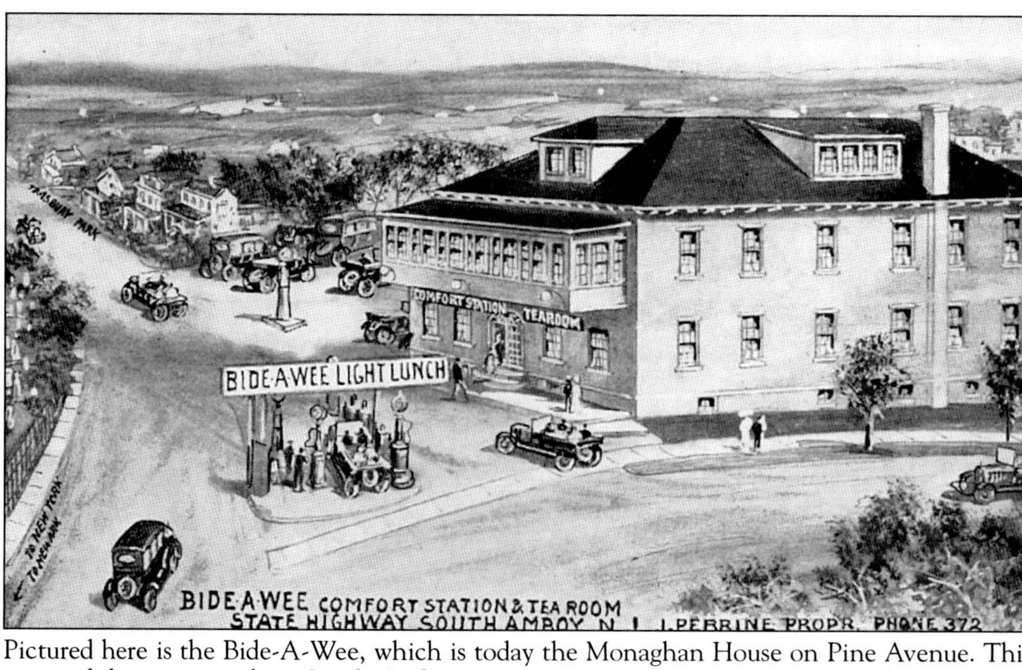

Pictured here is the Bide-A-Wee, which is today the Monaghan House on Pine Avenue. This postcard demonstrates how South Amboy was once a major stopping point on the way to the Jersey Shore, as Pine Avenue was once Route 35, before the highway was shifted to the west.

A parade is passing in front of Joe Jerome's, now Lagoda's Saloon, on Broadway.

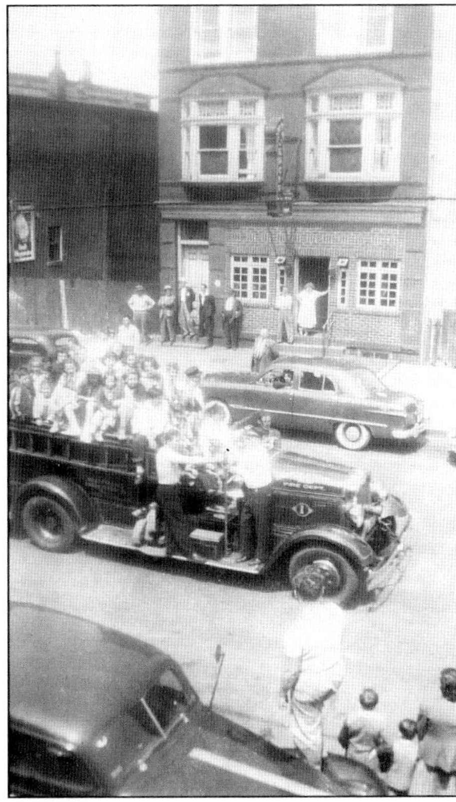

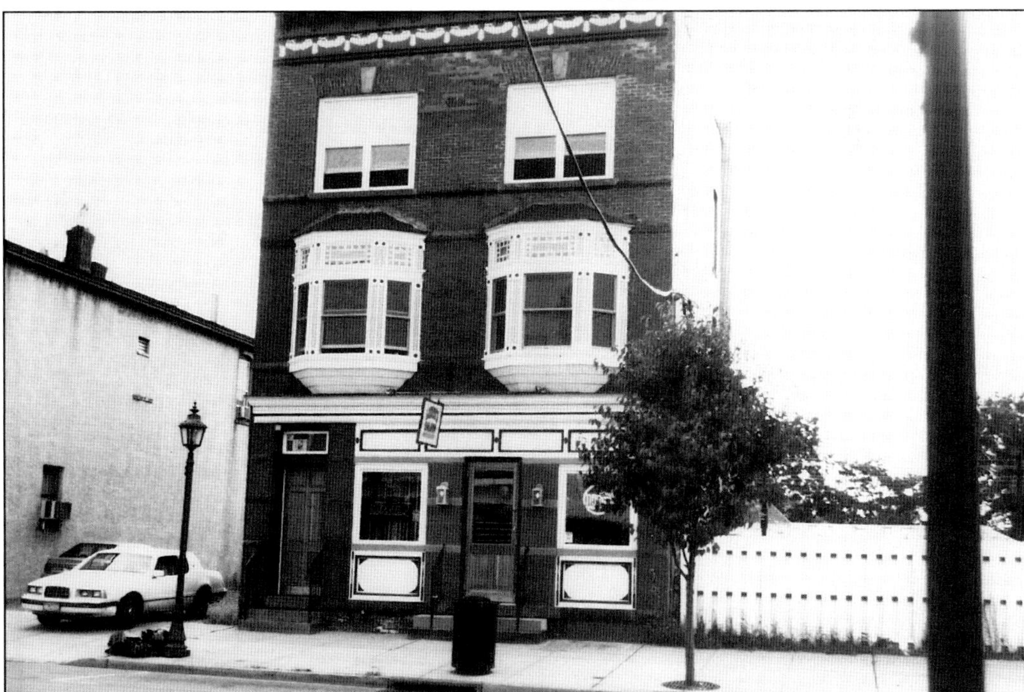

Here is Lagoda's as it looks today, in the late 1990s.

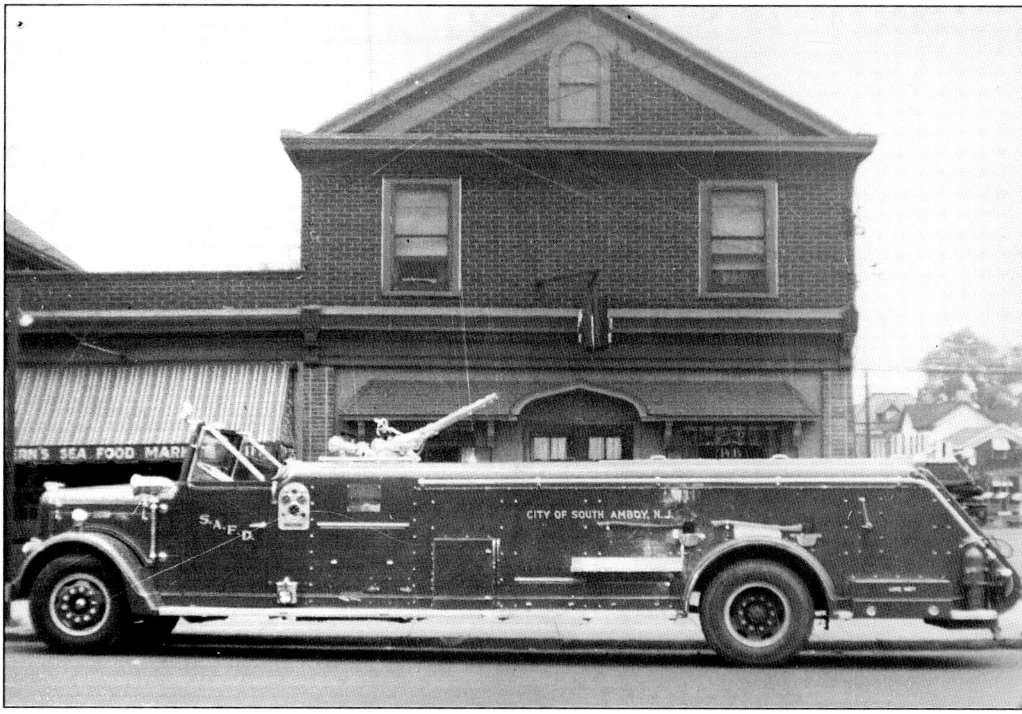

Today this building is the Landmark, one of the city's most popular gathering spots, operated by Robert Heiser.

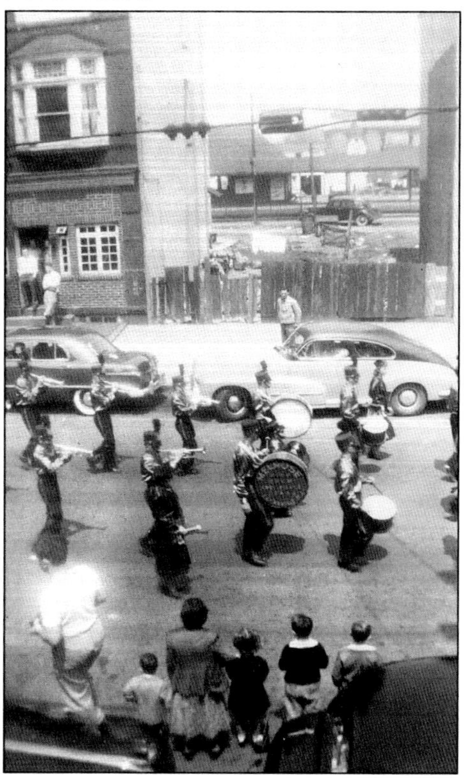

The Melrose Drum and Bugle Corps, a fixture at any of the city's parades, is seen here passing in front of Lagoda's. Although based in Melrose, a section of neighboring Sayreville, many of the band members come from South Amboy.

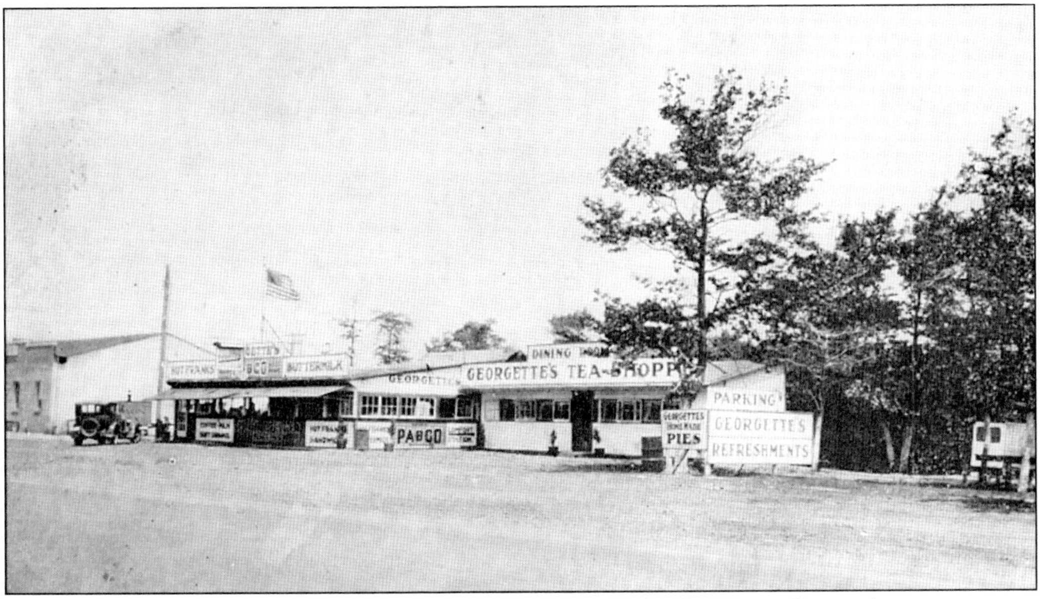

Georgette's restaurant was located on lower Main Street, also known as Route 4, a major route for travelers to the shore. It was next to the former Abe Korb junkyard, and was a popular stop for buses and travelers. Shown here in the 1920s, it was named for Georgette Harris Deegan.

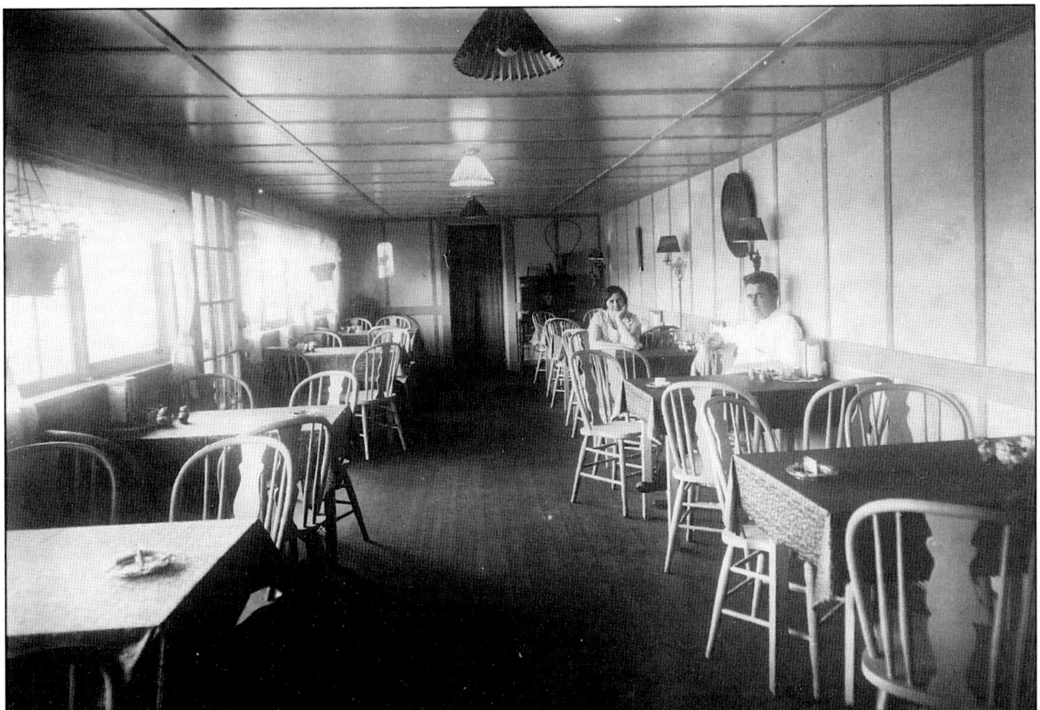

Here is the interior of Georgette's, with Georgette and John Deegan at one of their tables. The restaurant later moved to Route 35 at Raritan Street in Sayreville; since the 1980s, it has been the Costa Verde Restaurant.

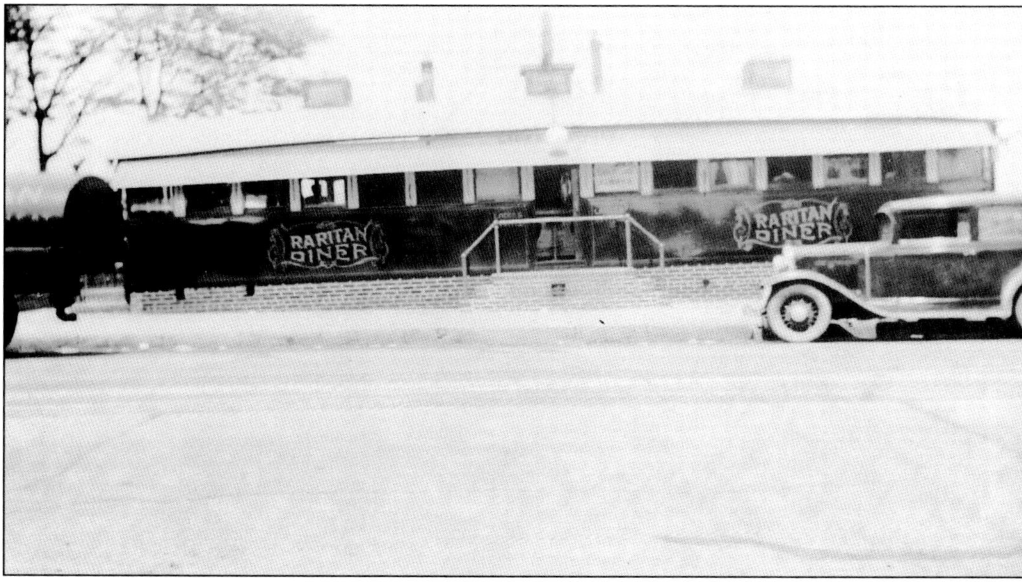

This is an early photo of the Raritan Diner, when it had a full awning. It was used in Woody Allen's 1985 movie *Purple Rose of Cairo*. South Amboy also turned up, in name only, in the movie *The Freshman*, with Matthew Broderick and Marlon Brando, when Brando mentions it as the home of a mafia family.

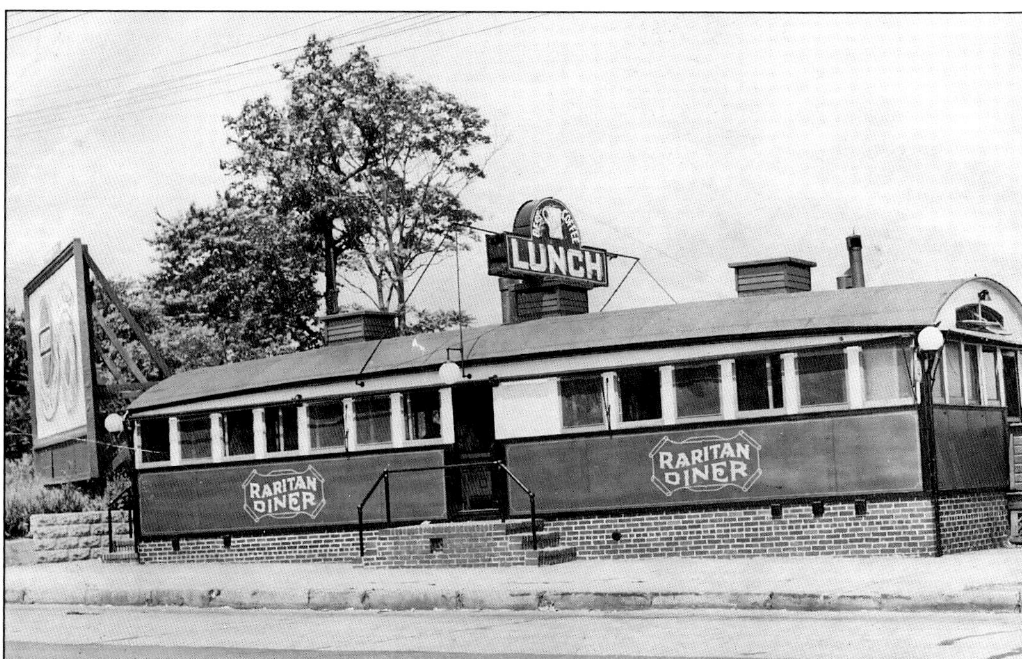

The Raritan Diner, on Bordentown Avenue, was the traditional train-car style of diner, and was owned by Tom Lenahan. It was later purchased by Ed Munn.

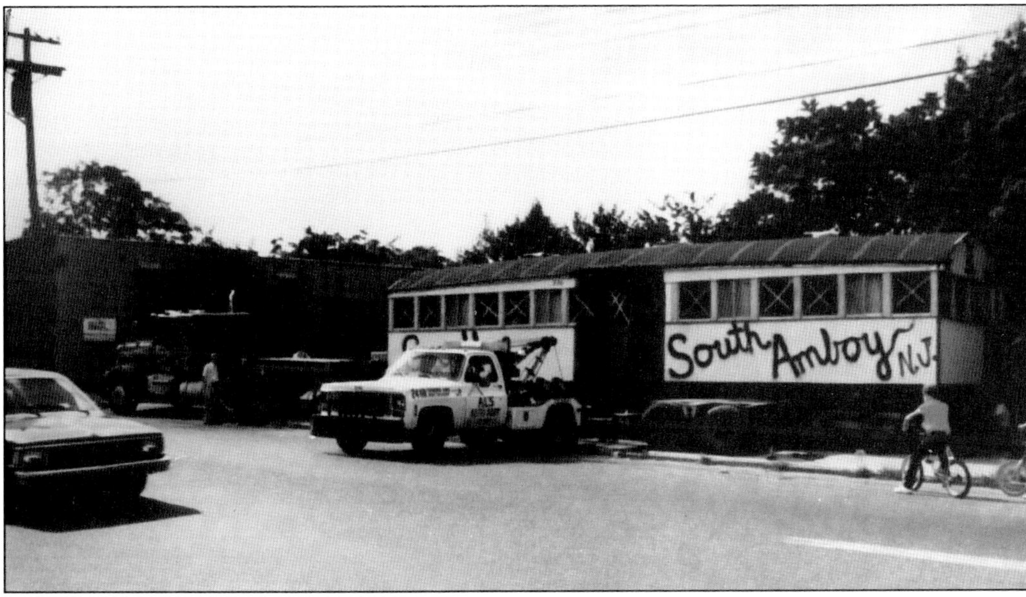

The Raritan Diner is shown here being towed away to Ithaca, New York, where it reportedly still sits on the property of another restaurant.

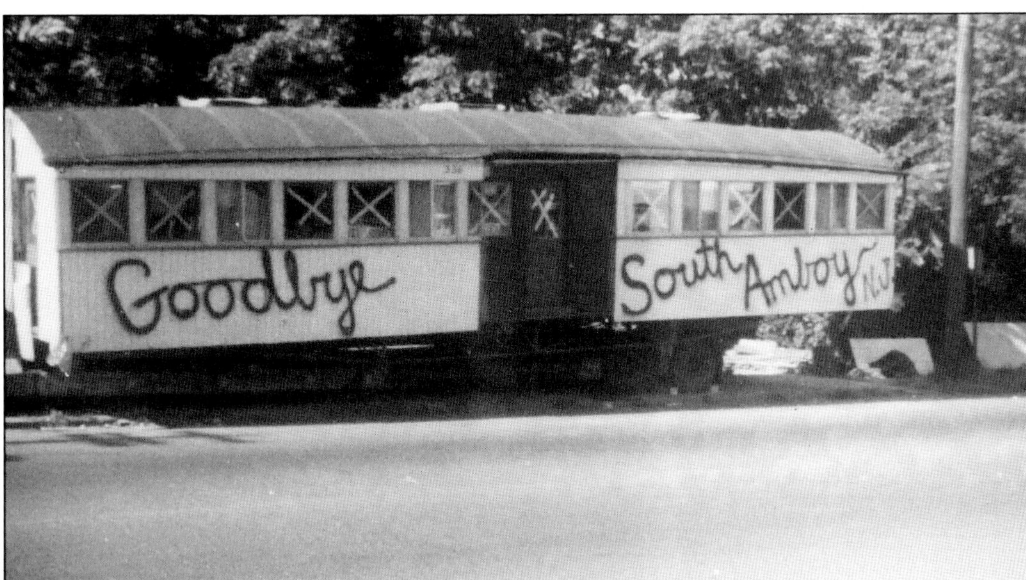

The Raritan Diner is loaded up and signing off.

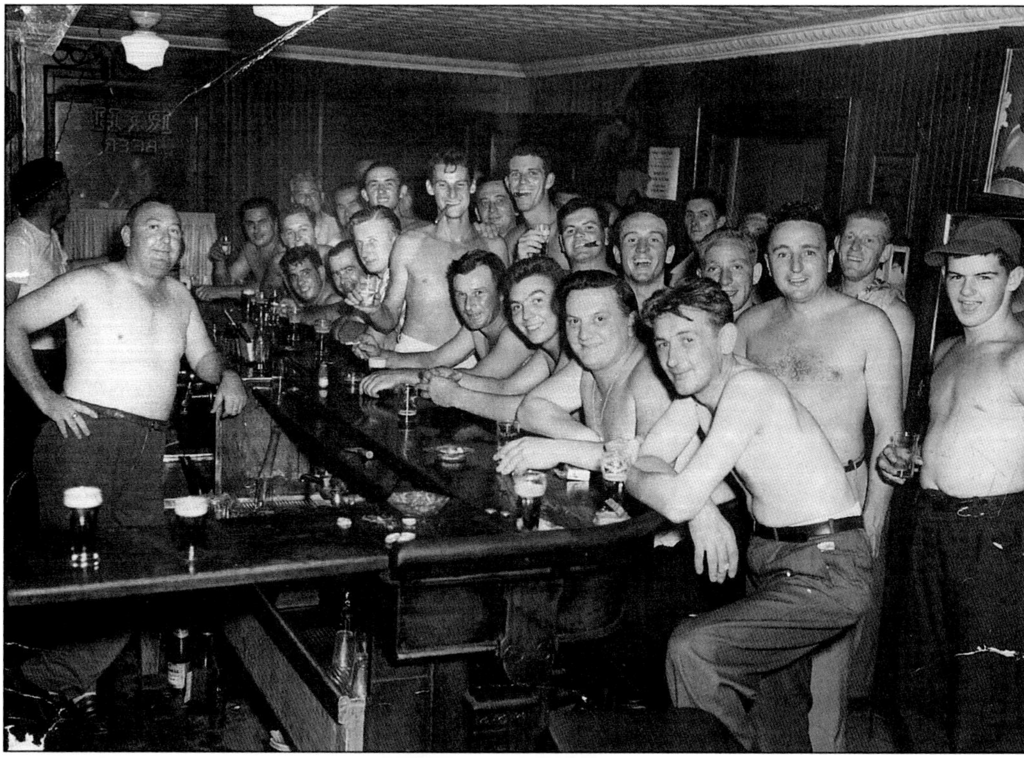

This is the interior of Tom and Box's bar on Feltus Street, which in the mid-1990s became the Munckee Bar.

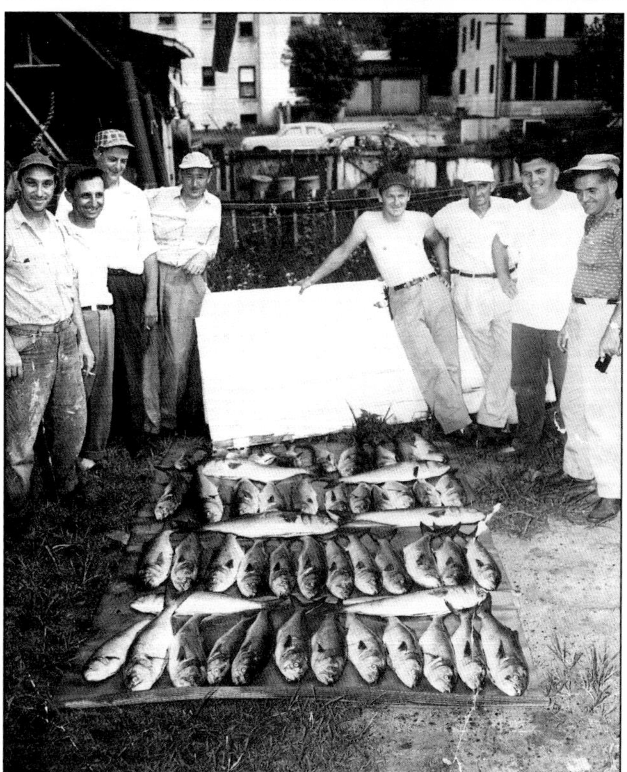

With a location on the bay, there is plenty of opportunity for fishing. This appears to have been a pretty good day, in the 1950s, for bluefish. Pictured from left to right are Joe Szraga, Mike Szraga, Jack Howley, Ray Parish, an unidentified man, Bob Hollowell, and John Kever.

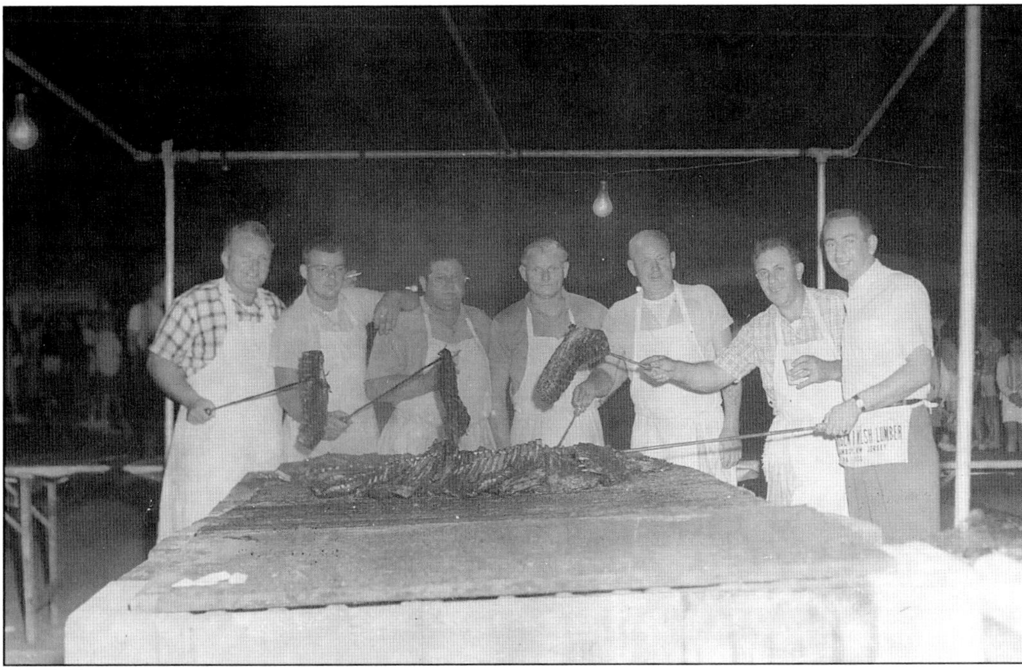

Another culinary tradition in South Amboy are Satski's Ribs, named for the Szatkowskis, a family of firefighters who keep the recipe a closely guarded secret. This appears to be one of the early rib barbecues, possibly at Sacred Heart Church. From left to right are Eugene Dobrynski, Thomas Ryan, Ed Szatkowski Sr., Larry McMahon, Louie "Firpo" Nemeth, Anthony Charmello, and Lawrence Olzak.

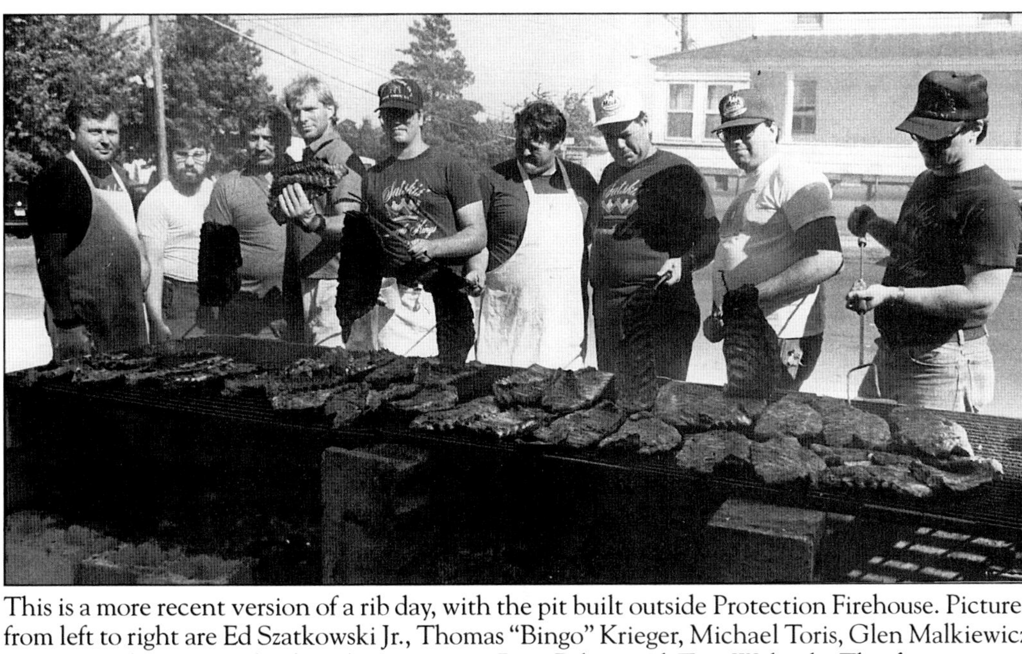

This is a more recent version of a rib day, with the pit built outside Protection Firehouse. Pictured from left to right are Ed Szatkowski Jr., Thomas "Bingo" Krieger, Michael Toris, Glen Malkiewicz, Jamie Norek, Ken Walczak, John McKeon, Don Riley, and Tim Walczak. The fire company makes the ribs for a fund-raiser about one Saturday a month in mild-weather months.

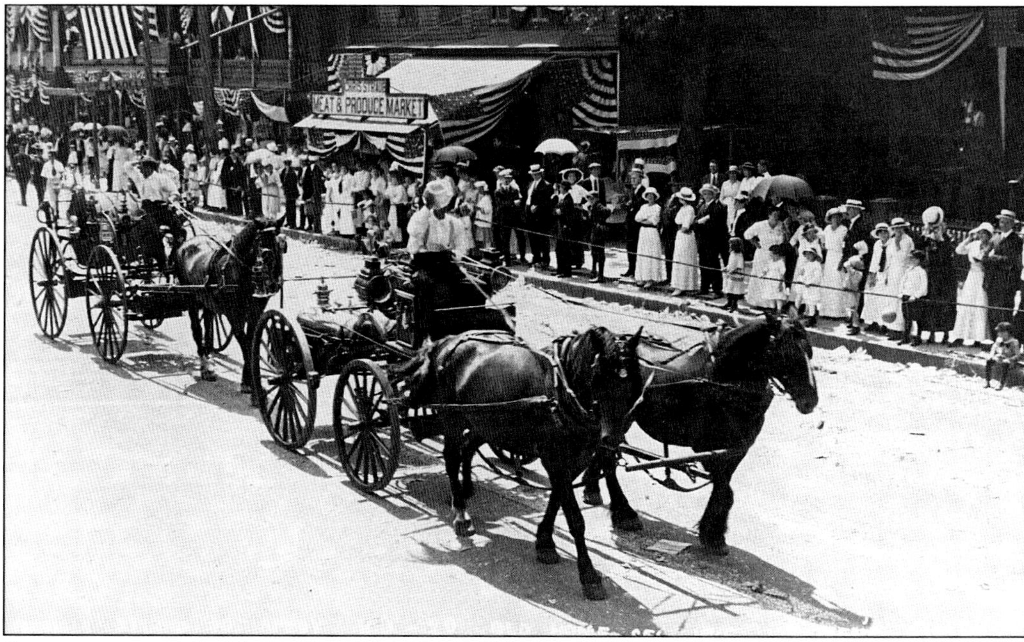

Firemen are parading here in 1915 for an "Old Home Celebration." With Straub's market as a landmark, this was Broadway, just north of Augusta Street.

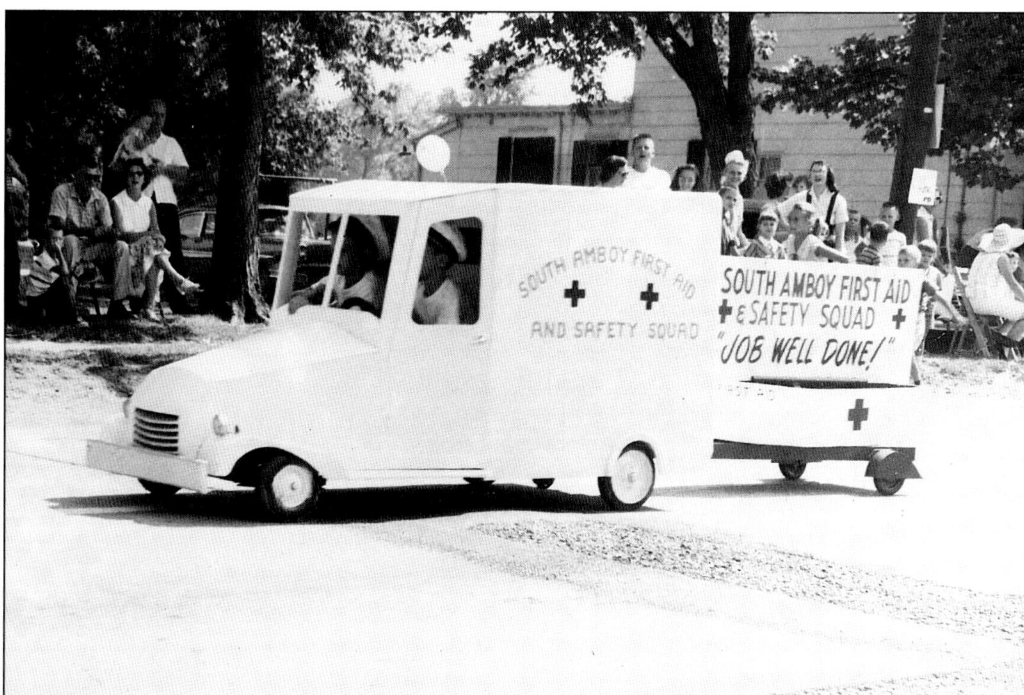

Pictured here is one of the parade floats of the South Amboy First Aid and Safety Squad in the 1950s.